Lecture Notes in Computer Science 9629

Commenced Publication in 1973
Founding and Former Series Editors:
Gerhard Goos, Juris Hartmanis, and Jan van Leeuwen

More information about this series at http://www.springer.com/series/7408

Anne Remke · Boudewijn R. Haverkort (Eds.)

Measurement, Modelling and Evaluation of Dependable Computer and Communication Systems

18th International GI/ITG Conference, MMB & DFT 2016
Münster, Germany, April 4–6, 2016
Proceedings

 Springer

Editors
Anne Remke
Universität Münster
Münster
Germany

Boudewijn R. Haverkort
University of Twente
Enschede
The Netherlands

ISSN 0302-9743   ISSN 1611-3349   (electronic)
Lecture Notes in Computer Science
ISBN 978-3-319-31558-4   ISBN 978-3-319-31559-1   (eBook)
DOI 10.1007/978-3-319-31559-1

Library of Congress Control Number: 2016933469

LNCS Sublibrary: SL2 – Programming and Software Engineering

Printed on acid-free paper

This Springer imprint is published by Springer Nature
The registered company is Springer International Publishing AG Switzerland

Preface

Welcome to the proceedings of MMB and DFT 2016! We are very pleased to present this LNCS volume with its contributions on performance and dependability evaluation techniques for distributed and embedded systems, computer and software architectures, and communication networks.

This volume contains the papers that were presented at the 18th International GI/ITG Conference on Measurement, Modelling and Evaluation of Computing Systems and Dependability and Fault Tolerance (MMB and DFT 2016) held during April 4–6, 2016, in Münster, Germany.

Following a thorough review procedure with at least three reviews per submission and a careful selection process, the Program Committee of MMB and DFT 2016 compiled an interesting scientific program comprising 12 regular papers and three tool presentations.

Since the start of the biennial MMB conference series in the early 1980's, we have seen substantial changes in the field of performance evaluation, dependability, and fault-tolerance of computer and communication systems. This is, for example, reflected in the relatively large number of submissions that deal with a very interesting and highly relevant field of research, namely, smart grids. We believe that for this community, it is very important to address new and exciting applications and investigate how the knowledge that is available in our community can be applied to these.

Besides the main program, the conference hosted three satellite workshops covering related research topics:

- The 8th International Workshop on Practical Applications of Stochastic Modelling (PASM)
- The Third Workshop on Network Calculus (WoNeCa)
- The Workshop on E-mobility and Smart Grids: Challenges and Opportunities (E-mobility)

By hosting these workshop, we hope to foster interaction between strongly related communities.

We were very fortunate to include two very interesting and relevant keynote presentation in the conference program:

- "DDoS 3.0: How Terrorists Bring Down the Internet" by Prof. Dr. Ir. Aiko Pras, University of Twente, The Netherlands
- "From Transient Analysis to Probabilistic Model Checking of Markov Regenerative Processes" by Prof. Dr. Enrico Vicario, University of Florence, Italy

To enable cross-fertilization between the conference and the satellite workshops, we included two additional invited talks that covered the research areas of the satellite workshops and that fit, from our perspective, very well in the scope of the main conference:

- "Critical Machine-to-Machine Communications: Performance Models vs. Reality in the 10^{-10} Regime," by Prof. Dr. James Gross, Royal Institute of Technology, Stockholm, Sweden
- "Open Analysis of Crowdsourced Car Sensor Data: The enviroCar Project," by Dr. Christoph Stasch, 52 North, Münster, Germany

As conference chairs, we express our gratitude to all members of the Program Committee and all external reviewers for their dedicated service, maintaining the quality objectives of the conference, and for the timely provision of their valuable reviews.

We thank all the authors for their submissions, all the speakers for their lively presentations, and all the participants for their contributions to interesting discussions. We acknowledge the support of the EasyChair conference system and express our gratitude to its management team for their commitment to serve the scientific community. Further, we thank Springer for unceasing support and excellent management of the LNCS publishing process.

Finally, it is our hope that readers will find these MMB and DFT 2016 proceedings informative and useful for their future research on measurement, modelling, analysis, and performance evaluation of advanced computer and communication systems.

February 2016   Anne Remke
                                                      Boudewijn R. Haverkort

Organization

Program Committee

Lothar Breuer	University of Kent, UK
Peter Buchholz	TU Dortmund, Germany
Hans Daduna	University of Hamburg, Germany
Hermann De Meer	University of Passau, Germany
Johannes Dr. Riedl	ITG MMB
Klaus Echtle	University of Duisburg-Essen, Germany
Markus Fidler	Leibniz Universität Hannover, Germany
Reinhard German	University of Erlangen, Germany
Gerhard Hasslinger	T-Systems ENPS Darmstadt, Germany
Boudewijn Haverkort	University of Twente, The Netherlands
Holger Hermanns	Saarland University, Germany
Joost-Pieter Katoen	RWTH Aachen University, Germany
Peter Kemper	College of William and Mary, USA
Udo Krieger	Otto Friedrich University, Germany
Kai Lampka	Uppsala University, Sweden
Wolfram Lautenschlaeger	Alcatel-Lucent Deutschland AG, Germany
Axel Lehmann	Universität der Bundeswehr München, Germany
Ralf Lehnert	Technical University of Dresden, Germany
Michael Menth	University of Tübingen, Germany
Peter Reichl	University of Vienna, Austria
Anne Remke	University of Twente, The Netherlands
Ramin Sadre	Université catholique de Louvain, Belgium
Francesca Saglietti	University of Erlangen-Nuremberg, Germany
Jens Schmitt	TU Kaiserslautern, Germany
Markus Siegle	Bundeswehr University Munich, Germany
Dietmar Tutsch	University of Wuppertal, Germany
Kurt Tutschku	Blekinge Institute of Technology (BTH), Sweden
Oliver Waldhorst	Daimler AG, Germany
Verena Wolf	Saarland University, Germany
Bernd Wolfinger	Universität Hamburg, Germany
Katinka Wolter	Freie Universität zu Berlin, Germany
Armin Zimmermann	Technische Universität Ilmenau, Germany

Additional Reviewers

Beck, Michael
Berger, Daniel
Heidtmann, Klaus
Heimgaertner, Florian
Jongerden, Marijn

Junges, Sebastian
Krcal, Jan
Krüger, Thilo
Lück, Alexander
Mandarawi, Waseem

Abstracts of Invited Talks

DDoS 3.0 - How Terrorists Bring Down the Internet

Aiko Pras, José Jair Santanna, Jessica Steinberger,
and Anna Sperotto

University of Twente
Enschede, The Netherlands
{a.pras,j.j.santanna,a.sperotto}@utwente.nl,
jessica.steinberger@h-da.de

Abstract. Dependable operation of the Internet is of crucial importance for our society. In recent years Distributed Denial of Service (DDoS) attacks have quickly become a major problem for the Internet. Most of these attacks are initiated by kids that target schools, ISPs, banks and web-shops; the Dutch NREN (SURFNet), for example, sees around 10 of such attacks per day. Performing attacks is extremely simple, since many websites offer "DDoS as a Service"; in fact it is easier to order a DDoS attack than to book a hotel! The websites that offer such DDoS attacks are called "Booters" or "Stressers", and are able to perform attacks with a strength of many Gbps. Although current attempts to mitigate attacks seem promising, analysis of recent attacks learns that it is quite easy to build next generation attack tools that are able to generate DDoS attacks with a strength thousand to one million times higher than the ones we see today. If such tools are used by nation-states or, more likely, terrorists, it should be possible to completely stop the Internet. This paper argues that we should prepare for such novel attacks.

Open Analysis of Crowdsourced Car Sensor Data - The enviroCar Project

Christoph Stasch, Albert Remke, Arne de Wall, and Matthes Rieke

52°North Open Source Software GmbH, Münster, Germany
{c.stasch, a.remke, a.dewall, m.rieke}@52north.org

Cars are equipped with various sensors used to monitor the engine and its environment. By using the so-called On-Board-Diagnostics II (OBD-II) interface, these sensors can be assessed by external devices. The enviroCar project[1] consists of an open infrastructure that utilizes this technology in order to enable drivers to collect, analyze, share and discuss car sensor data [1]. As shown in Fig. 1, the enviroCar infrastructure consists of an app, a server component, various analysis tools, and a community portal. The enviroCar app allows car drivers to connect their Android mobile phones to car sensors using an OBD bluetooth adapter. The app provides feedback while driving and allows uploading recorded tracks to the enviroCar server, where the data is publicly and anonymized accessible as open data. Thereby, the user still has full control on all of his tracks and can view them or delete them, in case he does not want a specific track to be shared. The enviroCar server is implemented as a RESTful Web Service with a MongoDB at the backend. It receives new tracks as JSON and provides several additional formats like CSV for download.

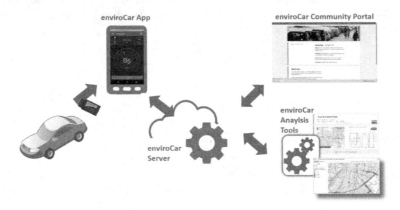

Fig. 1. Overview on the enviroCar infrastructure

The enviroCar community portal serves as the main entry point for enviroCar members. Members can explore and analyze their own tracks, compare their driving statistics to other members, and share tracks via social media platforms like Facebook

---

[1] General information about the project can be found at http://www.envirocar.org.

or Twitter. Several additional analysis tools using the open enviroCar data set (or subsets of it) are currently developed. These include, for instance, an R package[2] allowing to load enviroCar tracks into R and to apply further statistical analysis or interpolations. Based upon this, a fuzzy-based map matching algorithm following Quddus [2] has been implemented in R to match the track measurements to street segments in OSM[3]. In addition, several online maps that aggregate the tracks are available, e.g. for showing emission hotspots or aggregated speed measurements[4].

Current research of the enviroCar project focuses on improving and automating the map matching of tracks, on developing common interfaces and tools to collaborate on and exchange analysis functionality and discuss analysis results. Other topics include statistical analysis of trajectories. As fuel consumption and emissions are not directly measured, they need to be estimated from other parameters like mass air flow and lambda voltage sensors which measure the proportion of oxygen exhaust. Improving this estimation and accessing the uncertainty in the estimates is a further topic of current research.

Future potential applications of the enviroCar infrastructure are manifold: Urban and traffic planners can use the platform for discussing traffic measures and monitoring the measures' effects with the public. Scientists may utilize the data for developing and evaluating novel analysis methods and algorithms. As an example, first attempts for using the data for consumption-based routing have resulted in promising results. However, for this purpose the data base still needs to be enlarged and problems like, for example, selection bias need to be considered.

While the current data is gathered from fuel-powered cars, we also consider the enviroCar infrastructure as a basis for monitoring the future deployment of e-cars. The approach for consumption-based routing may also be applied to e-cars. Furthermore, information about power consumption of individual drivers may be used to derive individual ranges that drivers may reach without re-charging the battery.

References

1. Bröring, A., Remke, A., Stasch, C., Autermann, C., Rieke, M., Möllers, J.: enviroCar: a citizen science platform for analyzing and mapping crowd-sourced car sensor data. Trans. GIS **19**(3), 362–376 (2015)
2. Quddus, M.A.: High integrity map matching algorithms for advanced transport telematics applications. PhD thesis, Imperial College London, UK (2006)

---

[2] More information about the enviroCaR package can be found at https://github.com/enviroCar/enviroCaR.

[3] The package can be downloaded from https://cran.r-project.org/src/contrib/Archive/fuzzyMM/.

[4] See the Maps & Statistics section on http://envirocar.org for more information.

From Transient Analysis to Probabilistic Model Checking of Markov Regenerative Processes

Enrico Vicario

Department of Information Engineering, University of Florence, Florence, Italy
enrico.vicario@unifi.it

Keywords: non-Markovian models • Stochastic Petri nets • Numerical solution • Markov regenerative processes • Markov renewal theory • Probabilistic model checking

1 Talk Outline

In the engineering of systems exposed to the intertwined effects of concurrency and uncertainty, verification of quantitative properties of stochastic models enables early assessment of design choices and provides model driven guidance for implementation and integration stages. To this end, probabilistic model checking enables a systematic practice through which the same model can be verified against multiple probabilistic properties specified in some well defined language, able to analyze the impact on quality of different patterns of behavior, and open to automated regression verification when the model evolves.

Empirical evidence [3] shows that most quantitative requirements encountered in the construction of software intensive systems can be effectively expressed through a set of probabilistic specification patterns, where the most prominent role is played by the probabilistic until operator $\mathcal{P}_{\geq p}\{\phi_1 \ Unt^{[\alpha,\beta]}\phi_2\}$ which specifies that: with probability not lower than p, some property ϕ_2 will be eventually satisfied within the time bound $[\alpha, \beta]$ and property ϕ_1 is satisfied in all the states visited until that time.

A number of techniques and tools have been proposed, relying on statistical discrete event simulation or numerical solution. In particular, numerical solution approaches aim at computing results with high accuracy and confidence through exhaustive state-space analysis, often relying on some restriction on the class of models amenable to verification. In the most notable case, if all model durations are exponentially distributed (EXP), the model always satisfies the Markov condition, and an efficient numerical solution can be attained by composition of behaviors according to a renewal argument referred to the time point α [1, 2].

However, the construction of a valid model may require that some durations break the EXP memoryless property and be generally distributed (GEN), as occurring for instance in aging processes accumulating memory over time, or in real-time systems or network protocols where correctness depends on firm time bounds. In a more philosophical perspective, since the properties that are being verified capture a firm requirement on the time interval $[\alpha, \beta]$ in which ϕ_2 must be satisfied, it is much likely that the system under verification will rely on structural mechanisms enforcing firmly bounded response times.

Unfortunately, when the model includes GEN durations, the state of the system will depend on time elapsed between past events, and the Markov condition can be satisfied only at some special regeneration points. In this case, probabilistic model checking becomes much harder, combining together the complexities of non-Markovian analysis with the additional constraints posed by the model checking formulation. In a structural perspective, much of this depends on the overlapping memories contributed by durations in the model and by the time constraints in the property specification.

In this talk, we recall the salient traits of the method of stochastic state classes [4] implemented in the Oris tool (www.oris-tool.org) for transient analysis of models with multiple concurrent GEN durations. We specifically focus on the class of models that always encounter a regeneration within a bounded number of steps, and we report on recent results [5] that exploit stochastic state classes as a measure of probability over sets of runs and apply the principles of Markov regenerative analysis to enable efficient evaluation of a probabilistic until operator. The outlined solution, also provides the basis for a reflection about hurdles and structural limits that arise when Markov regenerative analysis is cast in the shape of probabilistic model checking.

References

1. Baier, C., Haverkort, B., Hermanns, H., Katoen, J.-P.: Model-checking algorithms for continuous-time Markov chains. IEEE Trans. Softw. Eng. **29**(6), 524–541 (2003)
2. Donatelli, S., Haddad, S., Sproston, J.: Model checking timed and stochastic properties with CSL^{TA}. IEEE Trans. Softw. Eng. **35**(2), 224–240, (2009)
3. Grunske, L.: Specification patterns for probabilistic quality properties. In: ICSE 2008, pp. 31–40. ACM, May 2008
4. Horváth, A., Paolieri, M., Ridi, M., Vicario, E.: Transient analysis of non-Markovian models using stochastic state classes. Perform. Eval. **69**(7–8), 315–335 (2012)
5. Paolieri, M., Horváth, A., Vicario, E.: Probabilistic model checking of regenerative concurrent systems. IEEE Trans. Softw. Eng. Accepted August 2015 (to appear)

Critical Machine-to-Machine Communications: Performance Models vs. Reality in the 10^{-10} Regime

James Gross

KTH, Stockholm, Sweden
james.gross@ee.kth.se, www.jamesgross.org

Abstract. Over the last few years, so called critical machine-to-machine communications has received more and more research attention. Spurred by flexibility and cost constraints in various industries, this area refers to wireless communication systems that can guarantee extremely high reliabilities at rather low latencies. Envisioned requirements reach down to maximum application layer packet error rates of 10^{-10} over latencies of a few milliseconds. While such systems potentially have a big relevance for safety-critical applications in industry, it is open how such systems should be designed.

In this talk, we will address selected design issues of such systems from a practical and theoretical perspective by employing communication-theoretic arguments, stochastic network calculus and probabilistic model checking. We will show that the area consists of a rich set of mostly open performance evaluation questions: Under which conditions is such communication possible at all? Which system components play a key role for the performance? Do model-based findings carry over to practical settings? Which methods can be employed to develop such systems in practise?

Contents

DDoS 3.0 - How Terrorists Bring Down the Internet

Aiko Pras[✉], José Jair Santanna, Jessica Steinberger, and Anna Sperotto

University of Twente, Enschede, The Netherlands
{a.pras,j.j.santanna,a.sperotto}@utwente.nl, jessica.steinberger@h-da.de

Abstract. Dependable operation of the Internet is of crucial importance for our society. In recent years Distributed Denial of Service (DDoS) attacks have quickly become a major problem for the Internet. Most of these attacks are initiated by kids that target schools, ISPs, banks and web-shops; the Dutch NREN (SURFNet), for example, sees around 10 of such attacks per day. Performing attacks is extremely simple, since many websites offer "DDoS as a Service"; in fact it is easier to order a DDoS attack than to book a hotel! The websites that offer such DDoS attacks are called "Booters" or "Stressers", and are able to perform attacks with a strength of many Gbps. Although current attempts to mitigate attacks seem promising, analysis of recent attacks learns that it is quite easy to build next generation attack tools that are able to generate DDoS attacks with a strength thousand to one million times higher than the ones we see today. If such tools are used by nation-states or, more likely, terrorists, it should be possible to completely stop the Internet. This paper argues that we should prepare for such novel attacks.

1 Current DDoS Attacks

Current DDoS attacks are often performed by youngsters via websites that offer "DDoS as a Service". Such websites, which are called "Booters" or Stressers", are able to generate attacks with strengths of many Gbps. A simple Google search shows that hundreds of such Booters are currently active; the costs to perform a series of attacks is typically a few dollars [1,2]. In general Booters do not attack their targets directly, but use one or two levels of intermediate systems to strengthen and anonymise the attacks. The first level is formed by botnets that start the attack once they receive specific commands from the Booter. The second level is used to amplify the attack and can, for example, involve a set of DNS or NTP servers that react upon the reception of relatively small requests by sending large response packets. The ratio between response and request message size is the amplification factor; in practice we find factors between ten and hundred. Particularly popular for amplification attacks are so-called open DNS resolvers, which are basically misconfigured DNS servers that answer DNS queries irrespective of their origin. To target a specific victim, the attacker does not put its own IP-address in the request, but the address of the target. Response packets will therefore be routed towards the victim, and the identity of the attacker remains unknown (IP spoofing).

© Springer International Publishing Switzerland 2016
A. Remke and B.R. Haverkort (Eds.): MMB & DFT 2016, LNCS 9629, pp. 1–4, 2016.
DOI: 10.1007/978-3-319-31559-1_1

2   Analysis of Current DDoS Attacks

To understand how Booters operate, we will discuss a series of attacks which we performed on our own infrastructure [2]. Nine Booters were used; two of which generated so-called CharGen attacks whereas the other seven performed DNS amplification attacks. An interesting observation was that only two of these Booters shared their attack infrastructure. In other words, if an attacker would not use a single Booter but instead all available Booters, the strength of the combined attack would be nearly the sum of all individual attacks.

The strongest CharGen attack we performed had a strength of 7.5 Gbps, whereas the DNS amplification attacks varied in strength between 0.4 and 1.6 Gbps (Fig. 1). Since CharGen attacks can easily be mitigated by filtering UDP port 19, in the remainder we will focus on DNS attacks, which are much harder to mitigate. Figure 2 shows the average DNS response message size for each Booter attack; for three of them the size remains below thousand bytes, whereas the three top Booters showed average sizes between 3000–4000 bytes. These differences can be explained from the fact that the various Booters queried different DNS host names. If the Booters that performed the weakest attacks would just change these host names, their attacks would become a factor three to four more powerful. Such changes can be implemented within a few seconds by just modifying a single line in the attack source code.

Finally we observed that each booter used between 3000 to 8000 DNS resolvers for amplifying the DNS attack. It should be clear that the strength of the attacks can easily be increased by using far more DNS resolvers.

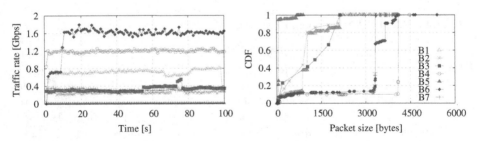

Fig. 1. DNS traffic rate   **Fig. 2.** DNS packet size distribution

We may conclude that DDoS attacks can easily be made stronger if (1) youngsters combine the forces of different Booters, (2) if Booter operators optimise their DNS queries and (3) more DNS resolvers are used.

3   How to Make DDoS Attacks More Powerful

The interesting question is how a group of skilled "professionals" would proceed to generate attacks far beyond anything we've seen yet. Such "professionals" could be nation states or, more likely, a group of terrorists that aim at disrupting our current society. Instead of relying on standard Booters that operate under the control of some unknown entity, such "professionals" would likely build their own attack tools and infrastructure.

As opposed to Booters that use a limited set of 3000 to 8000 open DNS resolvers, "professionals" might use the potential of all existing open DNS resolvers to amplify attacks. According to the Open Resolver Project, around 20 million of such systems exist [3]. Alternatively, amplification can also be achieved by using standard authoritative DNS servers; there are hundreds of millions of such servers that allow amplification with a factors between 6 and 12. Particularly interesting may be the 3.5 million DNSSEC servers, which include digital signatures in their responses and therefore allow much higher amplification factors; factors between 40 and 55 should be realistic [4]. In addition to DNS systems, attackers can also use open NTP (4 million), open SNMP (8 million) or other servers to amplify attacks [5,6].

An important component is the botnet that coordinates and distributes the attack; the bigger the botnet, the more powerful the attack. An interesting question therefore is "how easy would it be to create a botnet with thousands of systems". One answer to this question can be found by examining the Carna Botnet that was created as part of the "Internet Census 2012" [7]. The creators of that botnet targeted access routers and other embedded devices running OpenWRT. They found 1.2 Million unprotected devices, of which 420 thousand were used for their Carna botnet. It took the developer(s) six months to develop the software and setup the infrastructure; once deployment started it took only a single day to infect the first 100 thousand systems.

Instead of hacking OpenWRT routers, "professionals" could also exploit the emerging Internet of Things (IoT) for their attacks. Recent reports by Garner and HP predicted that by 2020 there will be 26 billion active IoT devices, of which 60 % will be insecure [8]. Even if only a fraction of them could be misused for DDoS attacks, it should be easy to generate attacks of hundreds of Tbps. If such attacks would target crucial systems, it is clear that the entire Internet would collapse with devastating consequences for our society.

4   Conclusions

In the previous section we argued that it is relatively easy to perform DDoS attacks with a strength thousand to one million times higher than the ones we see today. Such attacks can be launched by nation states or, more likely, terrorists. The question is not if massive DDoS attacks with a strength of hundreds of Tbps will take place, but when.

We should therefore prepare for such attacks, and create plans on how to react once such attacks take place. Like traditional terrorist attacks, governments need to play a crucial role in the coordination of mitigation strategies; it is not acceptable to leave such role at Internet Service Providers (ISPs) or security companies. Governments should force ISPs to develop tools and techniques to automatically quarantaine customers with hacked devices that participate in massive DDoS attacks. ISPs should join forces and create "Trusted Networks" to ensure that some limited form of communication remains possible once such attacks take place.

Acknowledgments. This research is funded by FLAMINGO, a Network of Excellence project (318488) supported by the European Commission under its Seventh Framework Programme.

References

1. Chromik, J.J., Santanna, J.J., Sperotto, A., Pras, A.: Booter websites characterization: towards a list of threats. In: Brazilian Symposium on Computer Networks and Distributed Systems (SBRC) (2015)
2. Santanna, J.J., van Rijswijk-Deij, R., Sperotto, A., Hofstede, R., Wierbosch, M., Granville, L.Z., Pras, A.: Booters - an analysis of DDoS-as-a-service attacks. In: IFIP/IEEE International Symposium on Integrated Network Management (IM) (2015)
3. Website: Open Resolver Project (2016). http://openresolverproject.org
4. van Rijswijk-Deij, R., Sperotto, A., Pras, A.: DNSSsec and its potential for DDoS attacks. In: Proceedings of the Fourteenth ACM Internet Measurement Conference, pp. 449–460 (2014)
5. Website: Open NTP Project (2016). http://openntpproject.org
6. Website: Open SNMP Project (2016). http://opensnmpproject.org
7. Website: Internet Census 2012 - the Carna Botnet (2012). http://internetcensus 2012.bitbucket.org
8. HP: Internet of things research study. Technical report, HP (2015)

SGsim: Co-simulation Framework for ICT-Enabled Power Distribution Grids

Abdalkarim Awad$^{(\boxtimes)}$, Peter Bazan, and Reinhard German

Computer Networks and Communication Systems, Department of Computer Science,
University of Erlangen, Erlangen, Germany
abdalkarim.awad@cs.fau.de

Abstract. Empowering power grids with ICT is fundamental for the future power grid. Simulation plays an essential role for evaluating emerging smart grid applications. The presented co-simulation framework SGsim is based on two main simulators, OMNeT++ and OpenDSS. With newly added components, smart grid applications in the electricity distribution network can now be investigated and evaluated. Conservation Voltage Reduction (CVR) is a mechanism to reduce the power demand which eventually will reduce the energy consumption. In a case study, the co-simulation framework is used to explore the potential energy saving by applying a closed-loop CVR inside a residential power grid.

Keywords: Smart grid · Co-simulation · Electricity distribution network · Communication system · Conservation voltage reduction

1 Introduction

Smart grid presents a set of practices and technologies to run the power grid in an efficient, secure, reliable, sustainable and economic way. Information and Communication Technology (ICT) can contribute most to optimizing the operation of the future power grid. Applications such as CVR or Volt/VAR optimization have the potential to reduce the power consumption especially during the peak hours. The rapidly increasing penetration of fluctuating renewable energy sources brings new challenges to the power grid, especially inside the distribution network. In addition to the loads and supplies, a distribution grid contains also components such as transformers, capacitor banks and energy storage elements. Connecting these components together through a data communication network is very crucial. It will make it possible to operate the power grid in an optimal way. Moreover, it will be possible to react very fast to emergency conditions. SGsim [1] is a co-simulation framework for the design and analysis of such systems. We are planning to provide the framework as open source for the education and research community.

2 Description of SGsim

The co-simulation framework SGsim is based on two main simulators: OpenDSS [3] and OMNeT++ [5]. In addition to a stand-alone executable program,

© Springer International Publishing Switzerland 2016
A. Remke and B.R. Haverkort (Eds.): MMB & DFT 2016, LNCS 9629, pp. 5–8, 2016.
DOI: 10.1007/978-3-319-31559-1_2

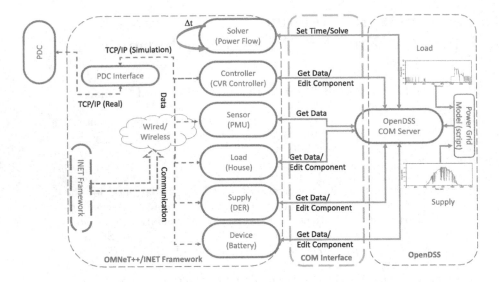

Fig. 1. Structure of the co-simulation framework with the connections between the different components

OpenDSS provides an in-process Component Object Model (COM) server DLL designed to be driven from an external program. OMNeT++ is mainly a data communication simulator. Additionally several frameworks, such as the INET framework, have been developed with well-tuned data communication components such as TCP/IP, 802.11 and Ethernet. In order to enable the use of the framework in the field of smart grid applications, we have integrated new components for the electricity distribution network. Figure 1 shows the different components of the simulator. Through the COM interface, it is possible to control the execution of the circuit and to change/add/remove different components. This is very helpful when simulating time-dependent scenarios. The main components of the simulator are:

- Power Grid Model: The OpenDSS is fed with the a script that describes the different components of the power grid and the interconnections. Furthermore, time-dependent loads and supplies can be provided as text files. For household demand and photovoltaic supply real data from Pecan Street [4] will be used. This database provides an 1-min resolution aggregated power usage signal as well as power consumption of individual devices. This can be very suitable in exploring applications such as Demand Response (DR).
- Solver: It controls the OpenDSS execution through the COM interface. It ensures time synchronization between the OpenDSS and OMNeT++.
- Load: It is the OMNeT++ component of the load in the power grid, e.g., a house. It can measure power grid parameters such as voltage, current and power at a specific time through the COM interface. It is also possible to change load parameters, e.g., running time for DR applications.

- Supply: It represents a power generation unit in OMNeT++, e.g., Distributed Energy Resources (DER). It is also possible to change supply parameters, e.g., regulate the output power (active and reactive power).
- Device: It represents power grid devices (e.g., Battery, Switch, Capacitor bank, ...). Through the COM interface, it is possible to change the parameters, e.g., power factor.
- Sensor: It can only read data on a specific component (e.g., Bus, Load, DER) and send it to other components. For instance Phasor Measurement Unit (PMU) is considered as a sensor and it sends data to Phasor Data Concentrator (PDC) interface using simulated TCP/IP packets. The data is formatted using a standard (IEEE c37.118) so that the real PDC can interpret the packets.
- Controller: It represents an intelligent unit within the system. It receives data from other components and then, based on specific algorithms, it can adapt system parameters. For instance a CVR controller can change the voltage settings of Load Tap Changer (LTC) in order to change the voltage of the transformer.
- PDC interface: It receives simulated packets inside the simulator. It converts it to real TCP/IP packets and forwards them to real software components such as OpenPDC. In this case, the simulation should be run in real-time mode.

3 Case Study: Conservation Voltage Reduction (CVR)

CVR is a method used by utilities to reduce the power demand by decreasing voltage levels. The main idea is that some devices will consume less power when the actual voltage is lower than the designed voltage. An important aspect here is to insure that the voltage at the costumer side is within the standardized limits (e.g., in Germany $230 \pm 10\%$). In this case study we apply a closed-loop CVR inside neighborhood with 10 houses connected to a transformer. The closed-loop CVR uses feedback information, i.e. voltage at houses, to adapt the output voltage at the transformer. A CVR controller is installed near the transformer. The loads at the houses are modeled as ZIP loads with the parameters ($Z_P = 0.85, I_P = -1.12, P_P = 1.27$) [2]. Equation 1 gives the current power as a function of current voltage (V). The constants P_0 and V_0 are the design power and voltage respectively.

$$P = P_0 \left[Z_p \left(\frac{V}{V_0} \right)^2 + I_p \left(\frac{V}{V_0} \right) + P_p \right] \tag{1}$$

The controller can change the voltage output of the transformer by sending an edit command through the COM interface. Edit commands are used to change the parameters of a specific component. Each house sends periodically data messages to the CVR controller. The messages contain the measured voltage at the load. Additionally, if the voltage exceeds specific limits, a warning

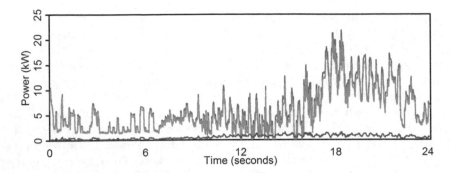

Fig. 2. Power consumed by the neighborhood with (green) and without (red) CVR and the difference (blue) (Color figure online).

message is sent to the controller which in turns reacts by changing the voltage at the transformer. Figure 2 shows the power flow through the transformer with and without applying CVR. The green and red curves show the power consumption with and without applying CVR, respectively. The blue curve, depicts the difference between the two curves. As it can be seen, the power reduction is higher when the load is high. The energy consumption without CVR is 145.7 kWh compared to 131.6 kWh when applying CVR. This represents a daily saving of about 14 kWh for the 10 houses. An important aim of CVR in addition to save energy is reducing the power demand, especially during the peak periods. In fact, CVR can provide Ancillary Services to the grid, i.e., provide regulation power to maintain balance of supply and demand and alleviate grid stress. This saves utility companies building addition power plants (i.e., additional spinning reserve). As can be seen in Fig. 2, at 6 PM, the power difference is about 2 kW. If we scale this value up to a city with thousands of houses, this would mean we can save building new several mega watts power plant.

References

1. Awad, A., Bazan, P., German, R.: SGsim: a simulation framework for smart grid applications. In: IEEE (ed.) Proceedings of the IEEE International Energy Conference, pp. 730–736 (2014)
2. Diaz-Aguilo, M., Sandraz, J., Macwan, R., de Leon, F., Czarkowski, D., Comack, C., Wang, D.: Field-validated load model for the analysis of CVR in distribution secondary networks: energy conservation. IEEE Trans. Power Deliv. **28**(4), 2428–2436 (2013)
3. EPRI Electrical Power Research Institute: Home page. http://sourceforge.net/projects/electricdss/
4. Pecan street database. http://www.pecanstreet.org
5. Varga, A.: The OMNeT++ discrete event simulation system. In: European Simulation Multiconference (ESM 2001), Prague, Czech Republic, June 2001

Improving Cross-Traffic Bounds in Feed-Forward Networks – There is a Job for Everyone

Steffen Bondorf[(✉)] and Jens Schmitt

Distributed Computer Systems (DISCO) Lab, University of Kaiserslautern,
Kaiserslautern, Germany
bondorf@cs.uni-kl.de

Abstract. Network calculus provides a mathematical framework for deterministically bounding backlog and delay in packet-switched networks. The analysis is compositional and proceeds in several steps. In the first step, a general feed-forward network is reduced to a tandem of servers lying on the path of the flow of interest. This requires to derive bounds on the cross-traffic for that flow. Tight bounds on cross-traffic are crucial for the overall analysis to obtain tight performance bounds. In this paper, we contribute an improvement on this first bounding step in a network calculus analysis. This improvement is based on the so-called total flow analysis (TFA), which so far saw little usage as it is known to be inferior to other methods for the overall delay analysis. Yet, in this work we show that TFA actually can bring significant benefits in bounding the burstiness of cross-traffic. We investigate analytically and numerically when these benefits actually occur and show that they can be considerable with several flows' delays being improved by more than 40 % compared to existing methods – thus giving TFA's existence a purpose finally.

1   Introduction

Network Calculus (NC) is a versatile methodology for queueing analysis of resource sharing systems. The high modeling power of NC has been transposed into several important applications for network engineering problems, traditionally in the Internet's Quality of Service proposals IntServ and DiffServ, and more recently in diverse environments such as wireless sensor networks [18], switched Ethernets [12], data centers [20], or System-on-Chip [15].

A network calculus analysis requires a feed-forward network in order to avoid cyclic dependencies between flows and thus be able to compute flow characteristics inside the network. In fact, the typical first step in a NC analysis, given a flow of interest (foi), is to reduce the feed-forward network to a tandem consisting of the servers on the foi's path. To that end, arrival constraints of the foi's cross-traffic burstiness and rate have to be computed. Accurate burstiness constraints are indeed crucial for the subsequent tandem analysis to achieve accurate end-to-end performance bounds. As we discuss in Sect. 2, much research has been invested in tightening the tandem analysis, silently assuming that the reduction

© Springer International Publishing Switzerland 2016
A. Remke and B.R. Haverkort (Eds.): MMB & DFT 2016, LNCS 9629, pp. 9–24, 2016.
DOI: 10.1007/978-3-319-31559-1_3

step from the feed-forward network to the tandem had already been performed. However, this step becomes very important for the quality of the bounds in larger feed-forward networks. Consequently, we deal with this reduction step in our work and present a method to tighten the bounds on the burstiness of cross-traffic. Somewhat surprisingly, we achieve this by applying the so-called total flow analysis (TFA) to compute bounds on the server backlog just before the analyzed flow's path. This is surprising because the TFA has a "bad reputation" as an overall analysis method. This is due to its inferior results when bounding a foi's end-to-end performance metrics since it cannot exploit the pay burst only once phenomenon (PBOO, see Sect. 3).

The beneficial effect of our burstiness bounding step is based on the following basic, intuitive insight: At the output of a server, any combination of flows can be at most as bursty as the maximum data backlog at this server. Based on this insight we formally prove how to characterize the output of a flow by its input arrival curve and the server backlog bound. The new burstiness bound can be exploited to potentially reduce cross-traffic arrival bounds that were computed conventionally with the (min,+)-deconvolution.

In fact, as we discuss below, this does not always lead to improved bounds, yet it works from certain utilizations onwards and can be considerable. The reasons why TFA can help here become clear in our detailed treatment below, but here is an intuition: TFA's aggregate (total) perspective avoids making too many assumptions on the relative priorities between flows. In contrast, the conventional method does so by separating cross-traffic flows from each other.

In short, we contribute a new method to compute arrival bounds for cross-traffic on a foi's path. It is based on backlog bounds from TFA. The rest of this paper is structured as follows: In Sect. 2 we discuss related work. Section 3 provides the necessary background and notation on feed-forward analysis with NC. The alternative way to calculate the output bound of a traffic flow is presented and proved in Sect. 4. Next, the rationale behind the new burstiness bounding procedure in feed-forward networks as well as a detailed discussion on the conditions when it can improve the existing methods is presented in Sect. 5. Results from numerical evaluation concerning larger feed-forward networks are reported in Sect. 6, before the paper is concluded in Sect. 7.

2   Related Work

As mentioned above, most work in network calculus focused on the second step in a feed-forward network analysis, where the problem has already been reduced to a tandem. There is a whole evolution from simple, but conservative methods to sophisticated, tight analyses which can be very involved computationally (see [6, 11] for recent overviews).

However, the first step of the feed-forward network analysis, bounding the cross-traffic burstiness, has so far been largely neglected. Most work starts directly with the tandem analysis or suggests to use straightforward techniques from basic NC results (more details are given in Sect. 3). An exception can be found in [10], where, for a single node under arbitrary multiplexing of several flows, tight output descriptions are derived for a single flow. However, when targeting a feed-forward network, we need to bound cross-flows that may have traversed several servers with potentially many other flows joining and leaving it. Hence, much more work is needed here.

In previous work of ours, we already addressed the cross-traffic arrival bounding. In [4], we focused on algorithmic efficiency and targeted a distributed execution of the analysis. In [5], we achieved more accurate bounds by improving the overall cross-traffic arrival bounding procedure. The results of this paper allow to further improve these bounds.

3   Network Calculus Background

Data Arrivals and Forwarding Service. Flows are characterized by functions cumulatively counting their data. They belong to the set $\mathcal{F}_0$ of non-negative, wide-sense increasing functions:

$$\mathcal{F}_0 = \{f : \mathbb{R} \to \mathbb{R}_\infty^+ \mid f(0) = 0,\ \forall s \leq t : f(s) \leq f(t)\},\ \mathbb{R}_\infty^+ := [0, +\infty) \cup \{+\infty\}.$$

We are particularly interested in the functions $A(t)$ and $A'(t)$ cumulatively counting a flow's data put into a server s and put out from s, both until time t. These functions allow for simple definitions of performance measures.

Definition 1 (Backlog and Delay). Assume a flow with input function A traverses a system $\mathcal{S}$ and results in the output function A'. The *backlog* of the flow at time t is defined as

$$B(t) = A(t) - A'(t).$$

The *(virtual) delay* for a data unit arriving at $\mathcal{S}$ at time t is defined as

$$D(t) = \inf\{\tau \geq 0 \mid A(t) \leq A'(t + \tau)\}.$$

Note, that the order of data within the flow needs to be retained for the (virtual) delay calculation [17].

NC operates in the interval time domain, i.e., its functions of $\mathcal{F}_0$ bound the maximum data arrivals of a flow during any duration of length d.

Definition 2 *(Arrival Curve).* Given a flow with input A, a function $\alpha \in \mathcal{F}_0$ is an arrival curve for A iff

$$\forall t\, \forall d,\ 0 \leq d \leq t\ :\ A(t) - A(t - d) \leq \alpha(d).$$

For example, sensors reporting measurement values may generate packets of size b that are periodically sent with a minimum inter-arrival time t_δ. Then, the data flow they generate has a maximum data arrival rate of $r = \frac{b}{t_\delta}$ in the fluid model of $\mathcal{F}_0$. The resulting shape of the arrival curve is commonly referred to as token bucket and belongs to the class $\mathcal{F}_{\text{TB}} \subset \mathcal{F}_0$:

$$\mathcal{F}_{\text{TB}} = \{\gamma_{r,b} \mid \gamma_{r,b}(0) = 0, \forall d > 0\ :\ \gamma_{r,b}(d) = b + r \cdot d\}.$$

Scheduling and buffering leading to the output function $A'(t)$ depend on a server's forwarding. It is lower bounded in interval time as well.

Definition 3 *(Service Curve).* If the service provided by a server s for a given input A results in an output A', then s offers a service curve $\beta \in \mathcal{F}_0$ iff

$$\forall t \ : \ A'(t) \ \geq \ \inf_{0 \leq d \leq t} \{A(t - d) + \beta(d)\}.$$

For example, TDMA channel access [13], duty cycling sensor nodes [2], as well as the service offered by Ethernet connections [12] can be modeled with so-called rate-latency service curves $\mathcal{F}_{\mathrm{RL}} \subset \mathcal{F}_0$:

$$\mathcal{F}_{\mathrm{RL}} = \{\beta_{R,T} \mid \beta_{R,T}(d) = \max\{0, R \cdot (d - T)\}.$$

A number of servers fulfill a stricter definition of service curves that guarantees a higher output during periods of queued data, the so-called backlogged periods of a server.

Definition 4 *(Strict Service Curve).* Let $\beta \in \mathcal{F}_0$. Server s offers a strict service curve β to a flow iff, during any backlogged period of duration d, the output of the flow is at least equal to $\beta(d)$.

The Network. In general, networks are modeled as graphs where a node represents a network device like a router or a switch. Devices can have multiple inputs and multiple outputs to connect to other devices. This network model does not fit well with NC' server model for queueing analysis. NC therefore analyzes so-called *server graphs*. Assuming that a network device's input buffer is served at line speed, queueing effects manifest at the output buffers. These are modeled by the graph's servers. For instance, in wireless sensor networks, nodes usually possess a single transmitter. Thus, one sensor node corresponds to one server and the transmission range defines the server graph's links [2,4].

(min,+)-Operations. Network calculus [8,9] was cast in a $(\min, +)$-algebraic framework in [7,14]. The following operations allow to manipulate arrival and service curves while retaining their worst-case semantic.

Definition 5 *((min, +)-Operations).* The $(\min, +)$ aggregation, convolution and deconvolution of two functions $f, g \in \mathcal{F}_0$ are defined as

$$\begin{aligned}
aggregation \ : \ (f + g)(t) \ &= \ f(t) + g(t), \\
convolution \ : \ (f \otimes g)(t) \ &= \ \inf_{0 \leq s \leq t} \{f(t - s) + g(s)\}, \\
deconvolution \ : \ (f \oslash g)(t) \ &= \ \sup_{u \geq 0} \{f(t + u) - g(u)\}.
\end{aligned}$$

The service curve definition then translates to $A' \geq A \otimes \beta$, the arrival curve definition to $A \otimes \alpha \geq A$, and performance characteristics can be bounded with the deconvolution $\alpha \oslash \beta$:

Theorem 1 (Performance Bounds). *Consider a server s that offers a service curve β. Assume a flow (aggregate) with arrival curve α traverses the server. Then we obtain the following performance bounds for the flow:*

delay: $\forall t \in \mathbb{R}^+ :\ D(t) \leq \inf\{d \geq 0 \,|\, (\alpha \oslash \beta)(-d) \leq 0\} =: h(\alpha, \beta),$

backlog: $\forall t \in \mathbb{R}^+ :\ B(t) \leq (\alpha \oslash \beta)(0) =: v(\alpha, \beta),$

output: $\forall d \in \mathbb{R}^+ :\ \alpha'(d) = (\alpha \oslash \beta)(d),$

where the delay and backlog bounds are abbreviated by D and B, respectively, as they hold independent of parameter t and α' is an arrival curve for A'.

The delay bound equals the horizontal deviation between α and β, $h(\alpha, \beta)$. In case the arrival curve belongs to a single flow, the order of data within this flow must be retained (FIFO per µFlow property [17]). In case α belongs to a flow aggregate, FIFO multiplexing between the aggregated flows is additionally required (cf. Definition 1). In contrast, for the backlog bound, i.e., the vertical deviation $v(\alpha, \beta)$, no FIFO assumptions are required.

Analyzing a flow in an end-to-end fashion while considering cross-traffic on its path is enabled by the following theorems. Table 1 provides the notation required to analyze such a path tandem of servers.

Table 1. Network calculus notation for flows, arrivals and service.

Quantifier	Definition
$\mathbb{F}$	Generic notation for a flow aggregate
$\{f_n, ..., f_m\}$	Flow aggregate containing flows $f_n, ..., f_m$
$\langle s_x, ..., s_y \rangle$	Tandem of consecutive servers s_x to s_y
$\alpha^f, \alpha^{\mathbb{F}}$	Arrival curve of flow f, set of flows $\mathbb{F}$
$\alpha_s^f, \alpha_s^{\mathbb{F}}$	Arrival bound at server s
β_s	Service curve of server s
$\beta^{\text{l.o.}f}, \beta^{\text{l.o.}\mathbb{F}}$	Left-over service curve

Theorem 2 (Concatenation of Servers). *Consider a flow (aggregate) $\mathbb{F}$ crossing a tandem of servers $\langle s_1, \ldots, s_n \rangle$ and assume that each s_i, $i \in \{1, \ldots, n\}$, offers a service curve β_{s_i}. The overall service curve offered to $\mathbb{F}$ is their concatenation*

$$\beta_{s_1} \otimes \ldots \otimes \beta_{s_n} = \bigotimes_{i=1}^{n} \beta_{s_i}.$$

Theorem 3 *(Left-Over Service Curve). Consider a server s that offers a strict service curve β_s. Let s be crossed by two flow aggregates $\mathbb{F}_0$ and $\mathbb{F}_1$ with aggregate arrival curves $\alpha^{\mathbb{F}_0}$ and $\alpha^{\mathbb{F}_1}$, respectively. Then $\mathbb{F}_1$'s worst-case residual* *resource share under arbitrary multiplexing at s, i.e., its left-over service curve at s, is*

$$\beta_s^{\mathrm{l.o.F_1}} = \beta_s \ominus \alpha^{\mathrm{F_0}}$$

with $(\beta \ominus \alpha)(d) := \sup\{0 \le u \le d \,|\, (\beta - \alpha)(u)\}$ denoting the non-decreasing upper closure of $(\beta - \alpha)(d)$.

Network Analysis. A network calculus analysis computes the end-to-end delay bound for a specific flow (flow of interest, foi). Conceptually, algebraic NC is compositional and its feed-forward analyses proceed in two steps [3,4]:

1. First, the analysis abstracts from the feed-forward network to the flow of interest's path (a tandem of servers). This step is enabled by recursively decomposing the server graph into tandems [5] and bounding the output arrivals of cross-traffic with Theorem 1, the output bound. After this step, a bound on the worst-case shape of cross-flows is known at the location of interference with the foi. Then, the following step need not consider the part of the network traversed by cross-flows nor the potentially complex interference patterns they are subject to.
2. The foi's end-to-end delay bound in the feed-forward network can now be calculated with a less complex *tandem analysis*. The foi's end-to-end left-over service curve is derived and the delay bound computed.

The second step of the feed-forward analysis (FFA) procedure has seen much treatment in the literature. Effort constantly focused on improving the ability to capture flow scheduling and cross-traffic multiplexing effects and thus provide more accurate delay bounds. One of the earliest improvements was made with the step from the total flow analysis to the separate flow analysis.

Total Flow Analysis (TFA) [9]: The Total Flow Analysis directly applies the basic results from Theorem 1. Given the arrival curve for the totality of flows (a flow aggregate) present at a server and the server's service curve, TFA allows to derive deterministic worst-case bounds on the delay a flow (aggregate) experiences when crossing the analyzed server as well as the server's buffer requirement for handling all traffic without suffering from overflows. The backlog bound coincides with the total buffer demand of a server. The TFA is a server-local analysis, i.e., all bounds it derives hold for a specific server and the totality of traffic crossing it, not for a single flow of interest because flows are not analyzed individually. When TFA is used as a tandem analysis in FFA-step 2 of the above scheme, the flow of interest's end-to-end delay bound is computed by summing up the server-local delay bounds on its path.

The Separate Flow Analysis (SFA) and the PBOO-Effect [14]: The TFA delay bound can be improved by separating the analysis' flow of interest from its cross-traffic. In this preparatory step, the so-called left-over service curve calculation, cross-traffic arrivals are subtracted from the service curves in the foi's path. The SFA is a straight-forward, hop-by-hop application of Theorems 2 and 3: First subtract cross-traffic arrivals such that βs become $\beta^{\mathrm{l.o.foi}}$s and then concatenate the left-over service curves. Deriving the delay bound with a single, end-to-end left-over service curve considers the flow of interest's burst term only once. This effect is therefore called Pay Bursts Only Once (PBOO).

Note, that TFA and SFA both define the procedure for FFA-step 2 only. In the first step of the feed-forward analysis procedure, only flows that eventually interfere with the flow of interest are considered – cross-traffic arrival bounding is therefore limited to these flows. They are separated from their own cross-traffic and bounded in an aggregate fashion. The former defines the difference to the TFA backlog bounding where all flows at a server are considered, regardless their subsequent hop [14]. The latter defines the *aggregate PBOO Arrival Bounding* (PBOO-AB) [5]. Thus, both approaches incorporate different degrees of flow aggregation. We exploit a combination of both, yet without explicitly tracing them throughout the entire arrival bounding [16] but with the TFA's additional benefits for bounding a server's output burstiness.

4   An Alternative Output Bound

In this section, we derive an alternative output bound. As presented in Sect. 5 and numerically evaluated in Sect. 6, this alternative output bound enables an improved arrival bounding step (FFA-step 1).

Let A, A' be input and output to/from a system. We assume to have an arrival curve α for the arrivals A and a service curve β offered by the system. Let us further assume that the arrival curve α is such that for $d > 0$ it can be written as

$$\alpha(d) = \tilde{\alpha}(d) + \alpha(0^+),$$

with $\tilde{\alpha}$ being a concave function (defined for $d > 0$ by the above equation and with $\tilde{\alpha}(0) = 0$), and $\alpha(0^+) = \lim_{d \to 0^+} \alpha(d)$. Clearly, this means that α is also a concave function. Further note that, for instance, any concave piecewise-linear arrival curve meets this condition, hence it is not restrictive in practice (e.g., the Disco Deterministic Network Calculator, DiscoDNC, uses such functions as arrival curves [3]). As $\tilde{\alpha} \in \mathcal{F}_0$ and is concave, it is also sub-additive, which is crucial as we see below.

Noting that we can bound the backlog for any given arrival process A by

$$B(t) = A(t) - A'(t) \leq A(t) - (A \otimes \beta)(t) = \sup_{0 \leq u \leq t} \{A(t) - A(u) - \beta(t - u)\},$$

we provide the alternative output bound in the following theorem.

Theorem 4. *Under the above assumptions and notations, an output bound on the departure flow (aggregate) A' can be calculated as*

$$\alpha'(d) = \alpha(d) + (v(\alpha, \beta) - \alpha(0^+)) \cdot 1_{\{d > 0\}}.$$

Proof. Let $s < t$:

$$A'(t) - A'(s) = A(t) - A(s) + B(s) - B(t)$$

$$\leq A(t) - A(s) + B(s)$$

$$\leq A(t) - A(s) + \sup_{0 \leq u \leq s} \{A(s) - A(u) - \beta(s - u)\}$$

$$= \sup_{0 \leq u \leq s} \{A(t) - A(u) - \beta(s - u)\}$$

$$\leq \sup_{0 \leq u \leq s} \{\alpha(t - u) - \beta(s - u)\}$$

$$= \sup_{0 \leq u \leq s} \{\tilde{\alpha}(t - u) + \alpha(0^+) - \beta(s - u)\}$$

$$\leq \sup_{0 \leq u \leq s} \{\tilde{\alpha}(t - s) + \tilde{\alpha}(s - u) + \alpha(0^+) - \beta(s - u)\}$$

$$= \tilde{\alpha}(t - s) + \sup_{0 \leq u \leq s} \{\alpha(s - u) - \beta(s - u)\}$$

$$\leq \tilde{\alpha}(t - s) + v(\alpha, \beta)$$

$$= \alpha(t - s) + v(\alpha, \beta) - \alpha(0^+) = \alpha'(t - s).$$

For $s = t$: $A'(t) - A'(s) = 0 = \alpha'(t - s)$.   □

Note that this result resembles a known basic result that can be found in Chang's textbook in Lemma 1.4.2 [7]. This lemma states that for a server with a bound on the queue $\bar{q}$ and a $\gamma_{r,b}$-constrained input, an output bound can be given as $\gamma_{r,b+\bar{q}}$. Besides generalizing this lemma, we point out that we actually improve it, as we basically get rid of the burst term and would obtain $\gamma_{r,\bar{q}}$ as an output bound under Chang's assumptions.

5   TFA-Assisted PBOO Arrival Bounding

In this section, we demonstrate how to exploit the basic insight about the alternative output characterization from the previous section. It gives us the choice between the existing PBOO arrival bounding (PBOO-AB), which applies the conventional output bound, and an approach where we use a backlog bound for the cross-traffic and apply Theorem 4. This backlog bound is obtained from TFA, i.e., it actually considers flows that demultiplex from cross-traffic and do not interfere with the foi. In the following we discuss why and when this can actually lead to an improvement.

Consider the network configuration of Fig. 1 where f is the flow of interest, xf is its cross-flow and xxf is the cross-traffic of xf. Although the network is

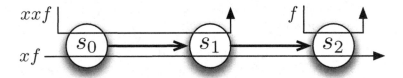

Fig. 1. Sample network.

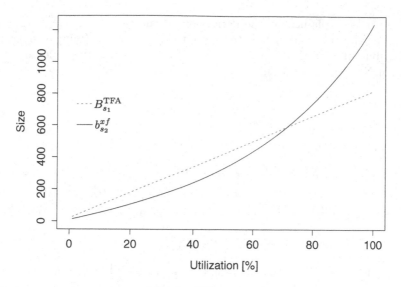

Fig. 2. Different scaling behaviors of $B_{s_1}^{\text{TFA}}$ and $b_{s_2}^{xf}$ with respect to the network utilization.

depicted as a tandem, we cannot apply a simple tandem analysis because the flow of interest f does not cross all servers, i.e., cross-traffic arrival bounding is necessary in this network: Deriving f's performance bounds with the SFA requires bounding xf's arrival at s_2, $\alpha_{s_2}^{xf}$, (FFA-step 1) with PBOO-AB first. It's result is used to separate f by computing f's left-over service curve at s_2 that is then used to derive f's delay bound (FFA-step 2).

PBOO-AB retains the worst-case when arbitrarily multiplexing of flows, i.e., in contrast to FIFO multiplexing, data of xf may always be served after xxf's data – independent of their relative arrival times. Thus, burstiness of $\alpha_{s_2}^{xf}$, denoted by $b_{s_2}^{xf} := \alpha_{s_2}^{xf}(0^+)$, increases when more data of xxf arrives in shorter intervals, i.e., its arrival curve α^{xxf} increases. In our illustrative numerical evaluation of this section, service curves are chosen to be rate latency functions $\beta_{R,T} = \beta_{20,20}$ and arrival curves to be token buckets $\alpha = \gamma_{r,10}$ where the rate r is variable. In this parameterized homogeneous setting, α^{xxf} increases with parameter r that we use to show xf's worst-case burstiness increase with a growing network utilization.

Figure 2 shows the utilization's impact on the PBOO-AB burstiness of f's cross-traffic, $b_{s_2}^{xf}$, and on the TFA backlog bound at server s_1, $B_{s_1}^{\text{TFA}}$. TFA considers all flows at s_1 and derives the backlog bound based on their aggregate arrival curve. Being the backlog of all incoming traffic at the server, i.e., a superset of f's cross-traffic xf, $B_{s_1}^{\text{TFA}}$ is also a backlog bound for xf. In Fig. 2, $B_{s_1}^{\text{TFA}}$ scales linearly whereas $b_{s_2}^{xf}$ scales super-linearly with the utilization. Consequently, both curves intersect and $b_{s_2}^{xf}$ exceeds $B_{s_1}^{\text{TFA}}$, such that using the TFA backlog bound and Theorem 4 indeed achieves an improvement over PBOO-AB.

This can be explained by the derivation of the two values, $B_{s_1}^{\mathrm{TFA}}$ and $b_{s_2}^{xf}$. For detailed information on how to compute the result of $(\min, +)$-operations for token-bucket arrival curves and rate-latency service curves, please refer to the DiscoDNC documentation [1].

$$
\begin{aligned}
b_{s_2}^{xf} &= \left(\alpha^{xf} \oslash \beta_{\langle s_0, s_1\rangle}^{\mathrm{l.o.}xf}\right)(0) \\
&= \left(\alpha^{xf} \oslash \left(\beta_{s_0}^{\mathrm{l.o.}xf} \otimes \beta_{s_1}^{\mathrm{l.o.}xf}\right)\right)(0) \\
&= \left(\alpha^{xf} \oslash \left(\left(\beta_{s_0} \ominus \alpha_{s_0}^{xxf}\right) \otimes \left(\beta_{s_1} \ominus \alpha_{s_1}^{xxf}\right)\right)\right)(0) \\
&= \left(\alpha^{xf} \oslash \left(\left(\beta_{s_0} \ominus \alpha^{xxf}\right) \otimes \left(\beta_{s_1} \ominus \left(\alpha_{s_0}^{xxf} \oslash \beta_{s_0}^{\mathrm{l.o.}xxf}\right)\right)\right)\right)(0) \\
&= \left(\alpha^{xf} \oslash \left(\left(\beta_{s_0} \ominus \alpha^{xxf}\right) \otimes \left(\beta_{s_1} \ominus \left(\alpha^{xxf} \oslash \left(\beta_{s_0} \ominus \alpha_{s_0}^{xf}\right)\right)\right)\right)\right)(0) \\
&= \left(\gamma_{r,10} \oslash \left(\left(\beta_{20,20} \ominus \gamma_{r,10}\right) \otimes \left(\beta_{20,20} \ominus \left(\gamma_{r,10} \oslash \left(\beta_{20,20} \ominus \gamma_{r,10}\right)\right)\right)\right)\right)(0) \\
&\stackrel{(1)}{=} \left(\gamma_{r,10} \oslash \left(\beta_{20-r,\frac{410}{20-r}} \otimes \left(\beta_{20,20} \ominus \left(\gamma_{r,10} \oslash \beta_{20-r,\frac{410}{20-r}}\right)\right)\right)\right)(0) \\
&\stackrel{(2)}{=} \left(\gamma_{r,10} \oslash \left(\beta_{20-r,\frac{410}{20-r}} \otimes \left(\beta_{20,20} \ominus \gamma_{r,\frac{410r}{20-r}+10}\right)\right)\right)(0) \\
&\stackrel{(3)}{=} \left(\gamma_{r,10} \oslash \left(\beta_{20-r,\frac{410}{20-r}} \otimes \left(\beta_{20,20} \ominus \gamma_{r,\frac{400r+200}{20-r}}\right)\right)\right)(0) \\
&\stackrel{(4)}{=} \left(\gamma_{r,10} \oslash \left(\beta_{20-r,\frac{410}{20-r}} \otimes \beta_{20-r,\frac{8200}{(20-r)^2}}\right)\right)(0) \\
&= \left(\gamma_{r,10} \oslash \beta_{20-r,\frac{410}{20-r}+\frac{8200}{(20-r)^2}}\right)(0) \\
&\stackrel{(5)}{=} \left(\gamma_{r,10} \oslash \beta_{20-r,\frac{16400-410r}{(20-r)^2}}\right)(0) \\
&\stackrel{(6)}{=} \frac{4000 + 16000r - 400r^2}{400 - 40r + r^2}
\end{aligned}
$$

We can see that $b_{s_2}^{xf}$ monotonically increases because the numerator is larger as well as faster growing than the denominator and the stability condition $r \le 10$ leads to an always positive denominator.

Next, let us see how the polynomial expression's degree builds up during the above derivation. Multiplication by the arrival rate is required to compute the burstiness of an output arrival curve, i.e., every time we deconvolve – see steps from (1) to (2) and from (5) to (6). Subsequent left-over service curve operations, e.g., from (3) to (4), retain the rate in the latency term's denominator, as does the convolution of service curves in the step from (4) to (5). Deconvolution is required for output bounding and thus occurs at every level of the recursive arrival bounding procedure. In this example, xf is bounded in the first recursion level and it requires bounding xxf in a second level; hence, we obtain a rational function of degree 2 (with a pole at $r = 20$).

The TFA backlog bound derivation for server s_1 proceeds as follows:

$$
\begin{aligned}
B_{s_1}^{\mathrm{TFA}} &\stackrel{(1)}{=} v\left(\{\alpha_{s_1}^{xf}, \alpha_{s_1}^{xxf}\}, \beta_{s_1}\right) \\
&= v\left(\{\alpha_{s_0}^{xf}, \alpha_{s_0}^{xxf}\} \oslash \beta_{s_0}^{\mathrm{l.o.}\{\alpha_{s_1}^{xf}, \alpha_{s_1}^{xxf}\}}, \beta_{s_1}\right)
\end{aligned}
$$

$$\overset{(2)}{=} v\left(\{\alpha_{s_0}^{xf}, \alpha_{s_0}^{xxf}\} \oslash \beta_{s_0}, \beta_{s_1}\right)$$

$$\overset{(3)}{=} v\left((\gamma_{r,10} + \gamma_{r,10}) \oslash \beta_{20,20}, \beta_{20,20}\right)$$

$$\overset{(4)}{=} v\left(\gamma_{2r,20} \oslash \beta_{20,20}, \beta_{20,20}\right)$$

$$\overset{(5)}{=} v\left(\gamma_{2r,20+2r\cdot20}, \beta_{20,20}\right)$$

$$= 80r + 20$$

The derivation takes advantage of aggregation in (1) and (3), which prevents recursive cross-traffic arrival bounding in our example. xxf is not considered cross-traffic of xf as both belong to the same flow aggregate and therefore no action has to be taken to derive the left-over service curve at s_0 in (2). The only relevant deconvolution in $B_{s_1}^{\text{TFA}}$'s derivation is found in the computation of the aggregate's output bound after crossing s_0. The deconvolution in the backlog bounding operation $v\left(\{\alpha_{s_1}^{xf}, \alpha_{s_1}^{xxf}\}, \beta_{s_1}\right)$ executed in the step from (4) to (5) is, in contrast to the $b_{s_2}^{xf}$-derivation not affecting the polynomial expression's degree because its latency is not depending on r. Thus, the entire term grows linearly with the flow arrival rate.

Remark 1. It is not possible to improve xf's output bound by using the backlog bound for flow xf at server s_1, i.e., $B_{s_1}^{xf}$, because $B_{s_1}^{xf}$ and $b_{s_2}^{xf}$ are equal due to [14], Theorem 3.1.12, Rule 12:

$$B_{s_1}^{xf} = \left((\alpha^{xf} \oslash \beta_{s_0}^{\text{l.o.}xf}) \oslash \beta_{s_1}^{\text{l.o.}xf}\right)(0)$$
$$= \left(\alpha^{xf} \oslash (\beta_{s_0}^{\text{l.o.}xf} \otimes \beta_{s_1}^{\text{l.o.}xf})\right)(0) = b_{s_2}^{xf}$$

From this reformulated derivation of $b_{s_2}^{xf}$ we obtain another explanation for its function being of degree 1 in the above example: There is only one deconvolution.

Remark 2. Theorem 1.4.5 in Le Boudec and Thiran's text book [14] presents conditions for tight output arrival bounds. These are satisfied in both our derivations above, yet, we improve xf's output bound by incorporating $B_{s_1}^{\text{TFA}}$. At first glance, this may seem like a contradiction, however, we gain tightness from additional considerations of a feed-forward analysis that are not addressed in [14], Theorem 1.4.5. It remains valid, yet only with respect to the given service curves that, in turn, might be tightness-compromising left-overs like in Remark 1.

In a more complex feed-forward network, we often have multi-level recursions for cross-traffic of cross-traffic in the arrival bounding phase of the derivations [5] – also for the backlog bound at a server – and therefore polynomial expressions of higher degrees occur in both alternative bounds on the output burstiness. For the ease of presentation, we continue to illustrate the impact of the differing scaling behaviors as well as the service curve latency and the initial burstiness of flows in the simple network from Fig. 1. In Sect. 6, we extend our evaluation to more involved feed-forward networks.

Above, we discussed that left-over service curve computations retain the arrival rate in their results' latency term. For instance, the left-over latency

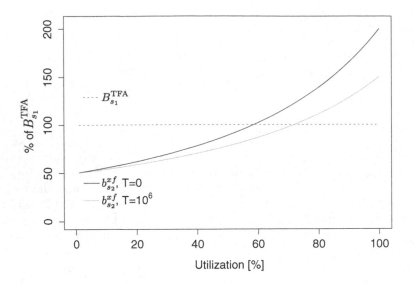

Fig. 3. Relative difference: Influence of β's latency T.

at server s_0 is $\frac{T_{s_0} \cdot R_{s_0} + b^{xxf}}{R_{s_0} - r^{xxf}} = T_{s_0} + \frac{r^{xxf} \cdot T_{s_0} + b^{xxf}}{R_{s_0} - r^{xxf}}$, i.e., it consists of a fixed and a variable part. The fixed part is defined by the service curves' initial latency $T_{s_0} = T_{s_1} = T_{s_2} =: T$ (equal for all servers in out homogeneous sample network) whose influence on the total burstiness we evaluate – increasing T naturally decreases the impact of the variable part containing the crucial factor r. We check $T = 0$, i.e., the natural lower limit of the latency, and $T = 10^6$, a value several orders of magnitude larger than the service rate $R = 20$ and thus safe to be assumed as a realistic upper bound on T. The resulting range of T's impact is depicted by the relative difference between $B_{s_1}^{\mathrm{TFA}}$ and $b_{s_2}^{xf}$ in Fig. 3. Most notably, the network utilization required for the TFA backlog bound to outperform the separated flow's output burstiness is between 59 % to 72 % – that is, it always exists and resides at utilizations considerably lower than the network's capacity limit. Moreover, $b_{s_2}^{xf}$'s relative benefit of 50 % over $B_{s_1}^{\mathrm{TFA}}$ for low utilizations is in fact small in absolute values (cf. Fig. 2) whereas its disadvantage (right of the intersection) grows fast to become large in absolute numbers.

Last, we evaluate the impact of the remaining variable parameter besides utilization and the service curve latency: The initial burstiness of flows b in the homogeneous network. We reduced the service curve latency's influence by assigning $\beta = \beta_{20,0.1}$. Arrival curves are $\alpha = \gamma_{r,b}$ where r is defined by the network utilization (i.e., relative to the service rate R) and b is slowly increased from 0 to the previously used value of 10. Figure 4 depicts the relative difference between $B_{s_1}^{\mathrm{TFA}}$ and $b_{s_2}^{xf}$ for three levels of network utilization: 59 % and 72 % (the intersections of both values in the latency evaluation of Fig. 3) as well as 100 %. We can see that the TFA backlog bound at server s_1 is in fact always within the output burstiness of the same utilizations found for the latency – for 59 %, $B_{s_1}^{\mathrm{TFA}}$

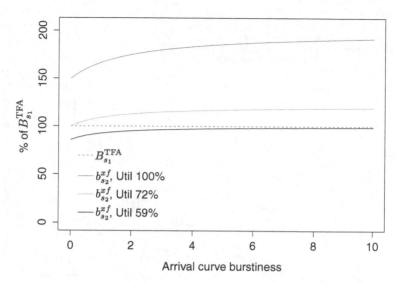

Fig. 4. Relative difference: Influence of the arrival burstiness on the backlog bound at s_1 and xf's worst-case burstiness assumed at s_2.

is an asymptote when increasing b, and for 72 % the $b_{s_2}^{xf}$-value starts at the server backlog bound. The impact of initial burstiness of flows is similar to the latency's impact. For the maximum network utilization, $b_{s_2}^{xf}$ always exceeds $B_{s_1}^{\mathrm{TFA}}$ by at least 50 % in our sample network, i.e., utilization remains most impactful.

Based on these observations, we propose to improve the arrival bound of a flow (aggregate) with the TFA backlog bound and Theorem 4 applied at the last hop of this flow (aggregate) – of course, only if it actually improves the bound. We call this new method: *TFA-assisted PBOO Arrival Bound.*

6   Feed-Forward Network Evaluation

The potential improvement of cross-traffic bounds can be quite considerable in the small scenario of Sect. 5. Now we turn to the investigation of the impact on the end-to-end delay bound of flows traversing larger feed-forward networks. That is, we evaluate the improvements gained by reduced cross-traffic interference that ultimately tightens delay bounds. We have extended the Disco Deterministic Network Calculator (DiscoDNC) [3] with the TFA-assisted PBOO Arrival Bounding in order to benchmark the resulting new variant against the existing one without this improvement (plain PBOO-AB).

The exemplary network we generated for evaluation consists of 150 homogeneous servers with service curves $\beta_{R,T} = \beta_{200,0.1}$. 600 flows with random paths and arrival curve $\alpha = \gamma_{2,0.1}$ were added to the network. They are supposed to randomly generate hotspots of considerable, yet, uncontrolled utilization for the evaluation. These hotspots see the highest numbers of flows such that the

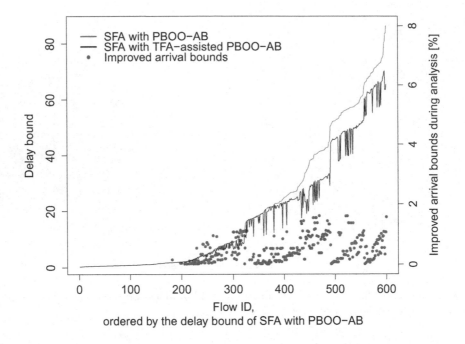

Fig. 5. Delay analysis of a feed-forward network.

impact of separation vs. aggregation can be observed – similar to heterogeneous networks where some flows outweigh others. We chose a small initial burstiness to additionally check the above claim that unavoidable burstiness increases are sufficient to cause impact of the TFA's assistance to the delay analysis.

The TFA-assisted PBOO-AB improved 369 out of 600 flow delay bounds over those derived with plain PBOO-AB (see Fig. 5). In total, 61.5 % of flows cross a hotspot that: (1) enables the TFA to aggregate flows such that its backlog bounding requires less recursion levels, making it grow slower with the utilization, and (2) has a utilization large enough to allow for its backlog bound to fall below the output bound burstiness. For the 33 % of flows with largest delay bound (using plain PBOO-AB), we achieved an average improvement of 17.93 %, with a maximum improvement of 44.41 %.

The distribution of brown dots for these rightmost 200 flows in Fig. 5 shows that this improvement was achieved without ever capping more than 2 % of the arrival bounds derived during the entire feed-forward analysis (right y-axis). Moreover, it is clearly visible that an increased share of burstiness improvements causes a larger delay bound reduction. For the rightmost 200 flows in Fig. 5, the dots form a pattern of three "peaks" whose beginning and end both demarcate a step in the improved delay bounds depicted above them.

Another interesting observation is that these distinguishable peaks in improved worst-case burstiness cause a non-uniform decrease of delay bounds. The global network delay bound – the maximum delay bound of all flows in the network – is not defined by the same flow anymore. Applying our new analysis, 11 flows that had a smaller delay bound than this flow now have a larger one. This reordering indicates that even when delay bounds are just used as a relative figure of merit, such as in design space explorations [19], an accurate network delay analysis is important and the first step of the FFA procedure is crucial.

7   Conclusion

In network calculus, the Total Flow Analysis (TFA) had been abandoned since it is inferior to other methods for overall network delay analysis. In this paper, we demonstrate that the TFA can actually be very useful to improve the bounding of cross-traffic arrivals in a feed-forward network. The trick is to use TFA's backlog bound as an upper bound on the burstiness at the servers where cross-traffic joins the analyzed flow of interest. We showed that the improvement can be quite significant, with some delay bounds reduced by more than 40 %. So, we see: There is a job for everyone!

References

1. The Disco Deterministic Network Calculator. http://disco.cs.uni-kl.de/index.php/projects/disco-dnc
2. Bondorf, S., Schmitt, J.: Statistical response time bounds in randomly deployed wireless sensor networks. In: Proceedings of IEEE LCN (2010)
3. Bondorf, S., Schmitt, J.: The DiscoDNC v2 - A comprehensive tool for deterministic network calculus. In: Proceedings of ValueTools (2014)
4. Bondorf, S., Schmitt, J.: Boosting sensor network calculus by thoroughly bounding cross-traffic. In: Proceedings of IEEE INFOCOM (2015)
5. Bondorf, S., Schmitt, J.: Calculating accurate end-to-end delay bounds - you better know your cross-traffic. In: Proceedings of ValueTools (2015)
6. Bouillard, A.: Algorithms and efficiency of Network calculus. Habilitation thesis, École Normale Supérieure (2014)
7. Chang, C.-S.: Performance Guarantees in Communication Networks. Springer, London (2000)
8. Cruz, R.L.: A calculus for network delay, Part I: network elements in isolation. IEEE Trans. Inf. Theor. **37**, 114–131 (1991)
9. Cruz, R.L.: A calculus for network delay, Part II: network analysis. IEEE Trans. Inf. Theor. **37**, 132–141 (1991)
10. Echagüe, J., Cholvi, V.: Tight arrival curve at the output of a work-conserving blind multiplexing server. Informatica **21**, 31–40 (2010)
11. Fidler, M.: Survey of deterministic and stochastic service curve models in the network calculus. Commun. Surv. Tutorials **12**, 59–86 (2010)
12. Frances, F., Fraboul, C., Grieu, J.: Using network calculus to optimize AFDX network. In: Proceedings of ERTS (2006)
13. Gollan, N., Schmitt, J.: Energy-efficient TDMA design under real-time constraints in wireless sensor networks. In: Proceedings of IEEE/ACM MASCOTS (2007)
14. Le Boudec, J.-Y., Thiran, P.: Network Calculus: A Theory of Deterministic Queuing Systems for the Internet. Springer, Heidelberg (2001)

15. Maxiaguine, A., Kunzli, S., Chakraborty, S., Thiele, L.: Rate analysis for streaming applications with on-chip buffer constraints. In: Proceedings of ASP-DAC (2004)
16. Perathoner, S., Rein, T., Thiele, L., Lampka, K., Rox, J.: Modeling structured event streams in system level performance analysis. In: Proceedings of ACM LCTES (2010)
17. Schmitt, J., Gollan, N., Bondorf, S., Martinovic, I.: Pay bursts only once holds for (some) non-FIFO systems. In Proceedings of IEEE INFOCOM, April 2011
18. Schmitt, J., Zdarsky, F., Thiele, L.: A comprehensive worst-case calculus for wireless sensor networks with in-network processing. In: Proceedings of IEEE RTSS (2007)
19. Thiele, L., Chakraborty, S., Gries, M., Künzli, S.: Design space exploration of network processor architectures. In: Network Processor Design: Issues and Practices. Morgan Kaufmann Publishers (2002)
20. Zhu, T., Tumanov, A., Kozuch, M., Harchol-Balter, M., Ganger, G.: PriorityMeister: tail latency QoS for shared networked storage. In: Proceedings of ACM SOCC (2014)

Stochastic Analysis of Energy Consumption in Pool Depletion Systems

Davide Cerotti$^{(\boxtimes)}$, Marco Gribaudo, Riccardo Pinciroli,
and Giuseppe Serazzi

Dip. di Elettronica, Informazione e Bioingengeria, Politecnico di Milano,
via Ponzio 34/5, 20133 Milano, Italy
{davide.cerotti,marco.gribaudo,riccardo.pinciroli,
giuseppe.serazzi}@polimi.it

Abstract. The evolutions of digital technologies and software applications have introduced a new computational paradigm that involves initially the creation of a large pool of jobs followed by a phase in which all the jobs are executed in systems with limited capacity. For example, a number of libraries have started digitizing their old books, or video content providers, such as YouTube or Netflix, need to transcode their contents to improve playback performances. Such applications are characterized by a huge number of jobs with different requests of computational resources, like CPU and GPU. Due to the very long computation time required by the execution of all the jobs, strategies to reduce the total energy consumption are very important.

In this work we present an analytical study of such systems, referred to as *pool depletion systems*, aimed at showing that very simple configuration parameters may have a non-trivial impact on the performance and especially on the energy consumption. We apply results from queueing theory coupled with the absorption time analysis for the depletion phase. We show that different optimal settings can be found depending on the considered metric.

Keywords: Stochastic models · Energy efficiency · Performance evaluation

1 Introduction

In this paper we focus on systems in which there is a fixed and huge number of jobs, referred to as a *pool*, waiting to be admitted for execution in a set of service centers with limited capacity. Many current real life problems require models with this structure. For example, video content providers, such as YouTube or NetFlix, often need to transcode a huge pool of videos [6] to multiple formats suitable to be sent and playback by several different devices (e.g. smart-phone, smart-TV, tablet, . . .). Similarly, several big data applications generate during the map phase a huge pool of data that can subsequently be split and executed in parallel on different systems with limited capacity for performance reasons.

© Springer International Publishing Switzerland 2016
A. Remke and B.R. Haverkort (Eds.): MMB & DFT 2016, LNCS 9629, pp. 25–39, 2016.
DOI: 10.1007/978-3-319-31559-1_4

The behavior of this system can be regarded as divided into two phases. An initial phase, in which the system is loaded with the maximum number of jobs allowed, and every job completed is immediately replaced by another one admitted from the pool. Then, when the pool empties a new phase starts, referred to as *depletion* phase, and the number of jobs in execution continues to decrease until all jobs are completed.

Since the jobs may have very different resource demands, in our analysis we consider *multi-class* workloads. To study the behavior of this type of systems, that are not at the equilibrium, we applied the stochastic analysis implementing the CTMC of the different cases.

The problem approached is: given a workload, i.e., pool size and characteristics of the classes of jobs (service demands and fractions in execution), and a system with finite capacity study a scheduling admission policy so that the global amount of time to execute the complete pool of jobs, i.e., the duration of the full capacity phase plus the depletion phase, is minimized.

To reach this objective, the load admission policy that schedule the sequence of executions must be able to fully exploit the capacity of *all* the resources of the system. In other words, the saturation of the resources must be reduced as much as possible controlling the bottlenecks. Let us remark that minimizing the time required from the execution of the complete workload is equivalent to minimize the energy required for this task. Thus, we may say that our ultimate objective is to minimize the energy needed to execute a workload through a suitable admission policy based on the bottleneck control.

We adopt known results of queuing networks for the full capacity phase, and the absorption time analysis for the depletion phase. By queuing theory, it is known that the performance of systems with multi-class workloads depends on the fraction of the classes of jobs in execution (referred to as *population mix*). More precisely, given the service demands of the classes, it is possible to identify a set of population mixes that saturate more than one resource concurrently. Moreover, one of these population mixes allow resources to be equiutilized regardless the population sizes. This operational condition is optimal since it maximizes the utilization of all the resources and thus the system throughput [16].

The main objectives are to study the impact of both the size of the job pool and the maximum processing capacity, in term of maximum number of jobs in execution, to the depletion time. Moreover, in multi-class workload, we want to examine the effect of the population mix to optimize depletion time, energy consumption, and response time in order to identify an optimal trade-off between them.

The remainder of the paper is structured as follows. In Sect. 2 we review some metrics used for energy consumption measurement. Section 3 presents in detail the pool depletion models both with single and multi-class workload and the Markov Chains utilized. In Sect. 4 we investigate the behavior of the model and show that the energy consumption is minimized when the system works with an optimal population mix. Section 5 concludes the paper and presents some future directions of work.

2   Energy Consumption

Several works, e.g. [7,15], show the existence of a linear relationship between the power consumption of a server and the utilization of its CPU. For such reason, a widespread used approximation of the power consumption $P(U)$ of a server is given by:

$$P(U) = P_{idle} + U\,(P_{max} - P_{idle}) \qquad (1)$$

where P_{idle} is the power consumed when no user applications are running, P_{max} is the power drawn by the fully utilized server and U is the CPU utilization. Many improvements of this model have been proposed to take into account other devices likes memory [12] or disks [5], and consider non-linearity measured in some real applications.

Since the global energy consumed by a task of duration T can be computed as $E = P \cdot T$, there is a trade-off between two factors. On one hand, Eq. 1 suggests to reduce the utilization to decrease the power consumption; on the other, a low utilization yields a low server productivity, increasing the time T required to complete the given task and thus also the energy consumed. In addition, there is a related trade-off between the energy consumed and the performance provided by the system. Energy-Response time Product (ERP), also known as Energy-Delay Product (EDP), and Energy-Response time Weighted Sum (ERWS) are two metrics widely used to evaluate the performance-energy trade-off of a system. Both of depend on the total energy consumption (E) and the response time (R). The index ERP [8,9,11,13] is defined as their product:

$$ERP = E\,R, \qquad (2)$$

whereas ERWS [1–3,10] is defined as their weighted sum:

$$ERWS = w_1\,R + w_2\,E, \quad w_1, w_2 \geq 0. \qquad (3)$$

The *average energy consumed per job* EJ is a further metric to compute such trade-off [4]. It is defined as:

$$EJ = \frac{E}{C} = \frac{P \cdot T}{C} = \frac{P}{X}, \qquad (4)$$

where C is number of jobs completed during a time interval of length T and X is the *system throughput*. Equation 4 holds for a resource processing a single-class workload, but it is not fair with a workload composed by jobs of different classes, especially when the time required to complete a job varies significantly according to its class. To overcome such problem, exploiting *the utilization law* a multi-class extension of Eq. 4 has been proposed as:

$$EJ = D\,\frac{P}{U}, \qquad (5)$$

where D is the aggregate demand (i.e. the total service demand of all the classes) and U is the resource utilization. The details of the Eq. 5 derivation and its extension to take into account systems composed of several resources can be found in [4].

3   Model Description

Let us consider the depletion model of a system composed by two resources r_1 and r_2 as shown in Fig. 1. Resources can represent important parts of a computing architecture: in the following we will use one resource to model a single-core CPU, and the other to model a GPU. The system executes two classes of jobs A and B. Each class requires an exponentially random distributed amount of execution time at each resource, and it is characterized by its average D_{rc}, with $r \in \{1,2\}$ and $c \in \{A,B\}$. The two resources satisfy the classical BCMP assumptions: they either work in processor sharing, or in first-come-first-served with all the requests of identical size, but possibly with different visit ratio. The total number of jobs that must be executed in the two classes are respectively N_A and N_B. However, only $K = k_A + k_B$ jobs are executed in parallel, with k_A jobs of class A and k_B jobs of class B. We call this constraint as *Finite Capacity Region* (FCR). Whenever a class A job completes and leaves the system, another class A jobs is started. If all the class A jobs are finished, but there are still class B jobs to be executed, class B jobs enter the system in place of class A jobs, to maintain its workload to K jobs. If there are no more jobs waiting to be executed, as soon as a job finishes, it is not replaced by other activity until all the $N_A + N_B$ jobs have been completed. Class B jobs behaves in the symmetrical way.

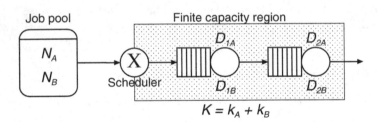

Fig. 1. A pool depletion model with two class and two resources.

Figure 2 shows the temporal evolution of the system. First jobs are loaded from the pool into the first resource, until the size of the FCR is reached (*Phase 0*). To simplify the presentation, we will consider the duration of this phase to be negligible, and we consider the system starting from a state in which there are k_A class A jobs and k_B class B jobs in execution in the first resource r_1. During normal execution, as soon as one job finishes, another one of the same class immediately starts (*Phase I*): this is the time in which the system works at regime, and it is also the moment in which optimization can take place. As soon as the jobs of one class in the pool finishes, the system moves to *Phase II*, where the scheduler cannot really perform a decision since it can only start jobs of the remaining class to fill the number of tasks in concurrent execution. Finally, when there are no more new jobs that can be started, the *depletion* phase begins (*Phase III*). In this case the number of jobs in execution

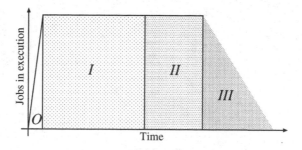

Fig. 2. Temporal evolution of the system.

reduces progressively until all the tasks have been completed. Note that both in *Phase II* and *Phase III*, one class of jobs might finish much earlier than the other, reducing the system to a single class behavior.

For each model we construct the corresponding underlying CTMC. Even if the proposed model seems to be very simple, the underlying Markov process is characterized by lot of asymmetries that makes its description a bit involved. To simplify the presentation, we start by presenting a simple single-class example with fixed parameters, and then we extend it to the two-classes general case.

3.1   Single-Class Model

Let us consider a single-class model with $N_A = 5$ jobs to be completed, in which $K = k_A = 2$ jobs at a time are executed in parallel by the system. The corresponding CTMC is shown in Fig. 3, and its state is identified by a tuple: (n_{OA}, n_{1A}, n_{2A}), where n_{OA} is the number of jobs that are still waiting to be started, n_{1A} is the number of jobs in resource r_1 and n_{2A} is the number of jobs in resource r_2.

Since we ignore the loading phase, all jobs that can be immediately executed starts in resource r_1. For this reason the initial state of the CTMC is $(n_{OA} - n_{1A}, n_{1A}, 0) = (3, 2, 0)$. Let us call $\mu_1 = 1/D_{1A}$ the rate at which jobs leaves resource r_1, and $\mu_2 = 1/D_{2A}$ the rates at which jobs complete their execution. Jobs always leave from r_1 to r_2 at rate μ_1, producing a transition from state (n_{OA}, n_{1A}, n_{2A}) to state $(n_{OA}, n_{1A} - 1, n_{2A} + 1)$. The effect of the end of service at resource r_2 is different depending on whether there are jobs waiting to start $(n_{OA} > 0$ - *Phase II* in Fig. 2). If this is the case, the system performs a transition from state (n_{OA}, n_{1A}, n_{2A}) to state $(n_{OA} - 1, n_{1A} + 1, n_{2A} - 1)$ at rate μ_2 corresponding to the fact that whenever a job exits the system from resource r_2, one of the waiting job is immediately started at r_1. If instead the jobs waiting to be started are finished $(n_{OA} = 0$ - *Phase III* in Fig. 2), the system starts working on one less job performing a transition from state $(0, n_{1A}, n_{2A})$ to state $(0, n_{1A}, n_{2A} - 1)$, always at rate μ_2. When the last job ends, the system jumps in the absorbing state $(0, 0, 0)$.

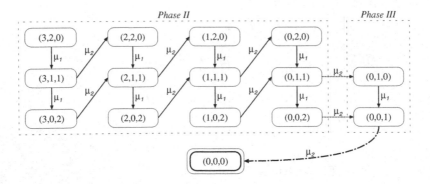

Fig. 3. The CTMC corresponding to a single class system with $N_A = 5$ and $k_A = 2$.

3.2 Multi-class Model

Figure 4 shows the basic transition structure of the CTMC underlying a two-class model. To simplify the presentation, only outgoing arcs are shown. In the two class case, the state is characterized by a six components tuple:

$$(n_{OA}, n_{OB}, n_{1A}, n_{1B}, n_{2A}, n_{2B})$$

which contains the count of jobs waiting outside, being executed at r_1 or at r_2 for both classes. If $n_{1A} + n_{1B} > 0$, jobs can complete their service at resource r_1. In this case we can have a transition either to state $(n_{OA}, n_{OB}, n_{1A} - 1, n_{1B}, n_{2A} + 1, n_{2B})$ or to state $(n_{OA}, n_{OB}, n_{1A}, n_{1B} - 1, n_{2A}, n_{2B} + 1)$ at rate μ_{1c} (with $c \in \{A, B\}$):

$$\mu_{1c} = \frac{n_{1c}}{n_{1A} + n_{1B}} \frac{1}{D_{1c}}. \tag{6}$$

The first part of the equation represents the processor sharing policy used by the resource. The end of service of a job at resource r_2 can instead trigger four different types of behaviors, each leading to a different pattern for the next state. Let us focus on a class A job: the case for class B will be symmetrical.

If the there are still class A jobs waiting to be started ($n_{OA} > 0$ - *Phase I* in Fig. 2), the system will allow a new class A job to start its execution. This leads the system to state $(n_{OA} - 1, n_{OB}, n_{1A} + 1, n_{1B}, n_{2A} - 1, n_{2B})$ and it is represented in the figure by arrows drawn with a continuous line.

If there are no more class A jobs waiting to be started ($n_{OA} = 0$) but still class B jobs ($n_{OB} > 0$ - *Phase II* in Fig. 2), then the end of a class A job triggers the start of a class B job to exploit the maximum parallel running capacity K of the system. This is represented in Fig. 4 as a dashed arrow, and leads the system to state $(0, n_{OB} - 1, n_{1A}, n_{1B} + 1, n_{2A} - 1, n_{2B})$.

If there are no more jobs to be started of either classes ($n_{OA} = 0$ and $n_{OB} = 0$ - *Phase III* in Fig. 2), then the system starts working with less than K jobs in parallel, by jumping to state $(0, 0, n_{1A}, n_{1B}, n_{2A} - 1, n_{2B})$. This is the depletion phase, which is represented in the figure by a dotted line.

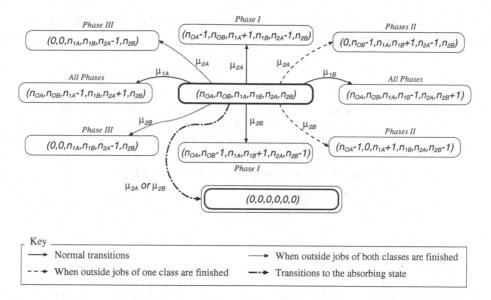

Fig. 4. Portion of the CTMC corresponding to a two class system.

Finally, when the last job ends the system jumps to the absorbing state $(0, 0, 0, 0, 0, 0)$. This is represented with a dash-dotted line in the figure. Again, due to the processor sharing nature of the system, ending of jobs at resource r_2 occurs at rate μ_{2c} (with $c \in \{A, B\}$):

$$\mu_{2c} = \frac{n_{2c}}{n_{2A} + n_{2B}} \frac{1}{D_{2c}}. \tag{7}$$

3.3 Model Analysis

In order to compute the depletion time, we apply the well-known technique for the evaluation of the upto-absorption time. Let us consider the CTMC of the general model with absorbing state $(0,0,0,0,0,0)$ and infinitesimal generator matrix $\mathbf{Q} = [q_{ij}]$ and let us call B the set of non-absorbing states. We define the mean time spent by the CTMC in state i until absorption as $z_i = \int_0^\infty \pi_i(\tau)d\tau$, where $\pi_i(\tau)$ is the unconditional probability of the CTMC being in state i at time τ. The row vector $\mathbf{z} = [z_i]$ satisfies the following equation:

$$\mathbf{z}\, \mathbf{Q}_B = -\pi_B(0), \tag{8}$$

where π_B and $\mathbf{Q}_B$ are the transient probability vector and the infinitesimal generator matrix restricted to the non-absorbing states only. Following [14], the mean time to absorption T of the CTMC can be computed from the solution of Eq. 8:

$$T = \sum_{i \in B} z_i.$$

If we call P_i the average power consumed in state i, then the average total energy consumed by the system is:

$$E = \sum_{i \in B} z_i \cdot P_i .$$

In a similar way, if we call u_{ri} an indicator function that tells us if a resource r is used in state i, $\phi_i(X)$ an indicator function that tells us if state i belongs to phase $X \in \{I, II, III\}$, and m_i the number of jobs in the FCR in state i, then we can compute the average utilization U_r of resource r, the average time $\Phi(X)$ spent in phase X, and the average number of jobs in the FCR as:

$$U_r = \frac{1}{T} \sum_{i \in B} z_i \cdot u_{ri} \qquad \Phi(X) = \sum_{i \in B} z_i \cdot \phi_i(X) \qquad M = \frac{1}{T} \sum_{i \in B} z_i \cdot m_i . \qquad (9)$$

4   Results

We have implemented the model described in Sect. 3 and run several analytical experiments both with single-class and multi-class workloads. Models are analyzed by generating their underlying CTMC and solving it according to Sect. 3.3 using a linear algebra library implemented in C language. Performance indices can be computed in few minutes on a standard Linux laptop even for the cases with the largest state space. In particular, the size of the state space can vary from 201 states when we work with a single-class model and $K = 1$, to 470 771 states when we are considering the multi-class model with $K = 40$.

4.1   Single-Class Model

In the first set of experiments, we analyze the pool depletion system working with single-class workloads. In particular, we want to characterize the behavior of the model as a function of the number of jobs simultaneously admitted into the FCR.

The total number of jobs in the system is $N_A + N_B = 100$, and the service demands D_r used in the experiments for the two resources are given in Table 1. The number of jobs that can enter the FCR at the same time varies from $K = 1$ to $K = 100$. In case of $K = 1$, only one job can be processed at once. When $K = 100$, all the jobs that are in the system can enter the FCR and they are concurrently serviced with a processor sharing policy.

Table 1. Service demands used for the single-class model.

	Conf. 1	Conf. 2	Conf. 3	Conf. 4
D_1	0.75	0.64	1.95	1.2
D_2	0.48	1.25	0.6	1.6

Figure 5 shows the performance indexes of the pool depletion systems with single-class workloads as a function of the FCR size K. In order to emphasize the results for small values of K, a base-10 log scale is used on the x-axis.

The energy consumption is computed setting the idle power consumption of system $P_{idle} = 70\,\mathrm{W}$, the maximum power of the system when only resource r_1 is used $P_{busy1} = 160\,\mathrm{W}$, the maximum power when only resource r_2 is used $P_{busy2} = 130\,\mathrm{W}$ and the maximum power of the system when both resources are used $P_{busy} = 210\,\mathrm{W}$. As shown in Fig. 5a, larger values of K reduce the energy consumption, since they reduce the total completion time.

Figure 5b shows the average response time to complete a job: the average time a job is running. This index does not account for the time spent outside the FCR, and it is computed using Little's law as:

$$R = \frac{M}{X} = \frac{M}{(N_A + N_B)/T}$$

where M is the average number of jobs in the FCR defined in Eq. 9. As it can be seen, R increases with K since resources are shared by a larger number of jobs. ERP and ERWS are plotted in Fig. 5c and d, respectively. For ERWS, we define w_1 and w_2 in order to normalize the values of response time and energy consumption. Thus, for each configuration, w_1 is set to $1/max(R_k)$ $\forall k$ and w_2 is set to $1/max(E_k)$ $\forall k$, where k is the number of considered jobs into the FCR.

ERP identifies Conf. 1 as the best configuration and the optimal point is when only a job is in the FCR. Instead, for ERWS the best configuration is Conf. 4 and the minimum coincides with four jobs concurrently executed by the system[1].

4.2   Multi-class Model

Next, we consider a multi-class model where the total number of jobs in the system is $N_A + N_B = 80$ and the number of jobs admitted in the FCR $K = 20$. We consider the following service demands:

$$D_{1A} = 0.26 \quad D_{1B} = 0.01$$
$$D_{2A} = 0.08 \quad D_{2B} = 0.19.$$

In Fig. 6, we plot the main performance indexes as a function of the inner population mix k_A and k_B. Each curve corresponds to a different outer population mix N_A and N_B. The dashed line is the outer population mix for which the system can provide the best result. Note that, the optimal outer population mix can slightly change based on the considered index. We now consider two more indexes (i.e. depletion time T and the energy per job EJ) since, with multi-class workloads, they behave differently from the energy consumption E. In particular, we evaluate EJ using Eq. 5:

---

[1] Providing evidence about which is the best metric between ERP and ERWS is out of the purposes of this paper.

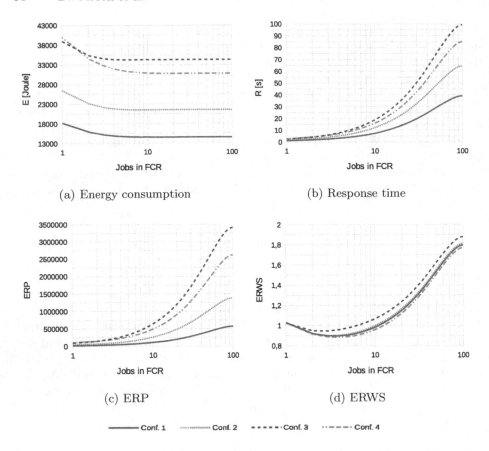

(a) Energy consumption

(b) Response time

(c) ERP

(d) ERWS

——— Conf. 1   ·············· Conf. 2   ----·Conf. 3   ··——·Conf. 4

Fig. 5. Performance indexes for the single-class system.

$$EJ = D\frac{P}{U} = \left(\sum_{r,c} D_{rc}\right) \frac{\frac{E}{T}}{U_1 + U_2},$$

where U_r is computed according to Eq. 9 and the average power consumption P is computed dividing the average energy E by the average total time T.

We plot energy consumption in Fig. 6a. We used the same values of power as for the single-class case. With multi-class workloads, it is possible to identify a set of inner population mixes k_A and k_B where the energy consumption is lower. Moreover, the lower is the number of class A jobs, the lower is the energy consumption of the system. This is due to the power consumption values that we used and to the time the jobs of class A spend into the system.

Depletion time can reach the minimum value when $N_A = 37$ and $N_B = 43$ (i.e. the dashed line). Nonetheless, configuration with $N_A = 30$ and $N_B = 50$ can provide better results when the inner population mix is highly unbalanced.

The main difference between depletion time in Fig. 6b and average response time in Fig. 6c is between configurations 20–60 and 50–30. In particular, the system has always a lower depletion time with $N_A = 20$ and $N_B = 60$. Instead, the average response time of that configuration is slightly greater than the one computed with $N_A = 50$ and $N_B = 30$.

ERP, ERWS and EJ are plotted in Figs. 6d, e and f respectively. All the three metrics indicate a different configuration as the best one. More generally, ERWS and EJ agree on the good performance of the 40-40 configuration, whereas ERP shows an improvement with $N_A = 30$ and $N_B = 50$.

Focusing in the 40-40 configuration (that seems to provide good results for most of the considered cases) we also analyze how a different size of the FCR K can affect the performance indexes. Results for ERP, ERWS and EJ are shown in Fig. 7. Each curve corresponds to a different value of K (i.e. $K = \{10, 20, 30, 40\}$) and they are plotted as a function of the inner population mix.

The ERP metric shown in Fig. 7a indicates that the smaller is the FCR size, the better will be the energy-response time trade-off of the system. In Fig. 7b, ERWS seems to depends on both the FCR size and the considered inner population mix. For example, when the workload is composed for the 60 % by class A jobs, it is better to work with $K = 10$. Instead, when there are only jobs of class B the system should run with $K = 30$. EJ is shown in Fig. 7c. As opposed to the ERP metric, the larger is the FCR size, the better are the performance of the system. It is true especially when the system is strongly unbalanced.

Figure 7d compares the minimum value that the previous analyzed metrics (i.e. ERP, ERWS and EJ) can achieve for different FCR sizes K. In order to provide a fair comparison of the considered metrics, all values are normalized in the $[0, 1]$ range according to the following rules. First we compute:

$$\tau(K) = min_\beta(V_\beta(K)), \tag{10}$$

where β represents the inner population mix (i.e. $k_A = \beta \cdot K$ and $k_B = K - k_A$), and $V_\beta(K)$ is the value of the metric computed for specific β and K. From Eq. 10, we compute the normalized value of each metric with the following formula:

$$\alpha(K) = \frac{\tau(K) - min_K(\tau(K))}{max_K(\tau(K)) - min_K(\tau(K))}. \tag{11}$$

To that purpose, ERP has been defined as a function of both R (i.e. $ERP(R) = \mathbb{E}[R] \cdot \mathbb{E}[E]$) and T (i.e. $ERP(T) = \mathbb{E}[T] \cdot \mathbb{E}[E]$). It is interesting to see that the four metrics have different trends. Since ERP(R) is defined on R and ERP(T) on T, the two metrics have different behaviors with respect to the number of jobs in the FCR: the former is increasing and the latter is decreasing. Also EJ depends on T (see Eq. 4), thus it is decreasing too. Instead, ERWS has a parabolic shape.

Finally, in Fig. 8, we plot the length of the phases $\Phi(I)$, $\Phi(II)$, $\Phi(III)$ described in Eq. 9. The considered configuration is the 40-40, with 20 jobs admitted at the same time in the FCR. We divide *Phase II* and *Phase III* in three sub-phases in order to distinguish among all the available possibilities (i.e. both class A and class B jobs, only class A jobs or only class B jobs are in execution). Note that, the sum of the duration of all the phases is equal to the depletion

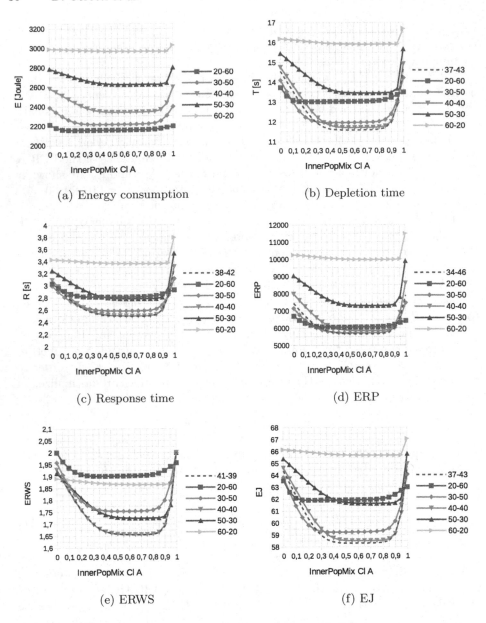

(a) Energy consumption

(b) Depletion time

(c) Response time

(d) ERP

(e) ERWS

(f) EJ

Fig. 6. Performance indexes for the multi-class system with different outer population mixes. X-Y means $N_A = X$ and $N_B = Y$.

time for that specific configuration. In general, it would be arguable that the longer is the *Phase I*, the shorter is the depletion time of the system, since the scheduler can only work in that phase. In Fig. 8, this can be seen when there are 12 jobs of class A and 8 jobs of class B in the FCR. Unfortunately, this is not

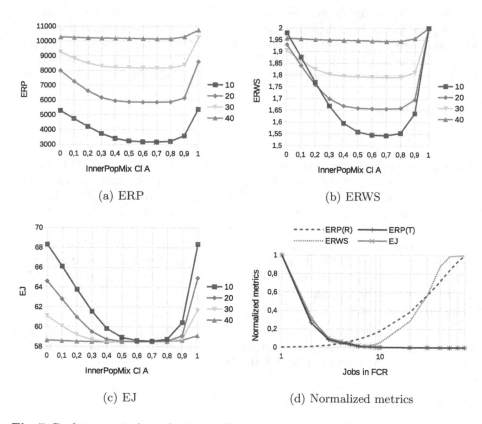

(a) ERP

(b) ERWS

(c) EJ

(d) Normalized metrics

Fig. 7. Performance indexes for the multi-class system with different size of the FCR.

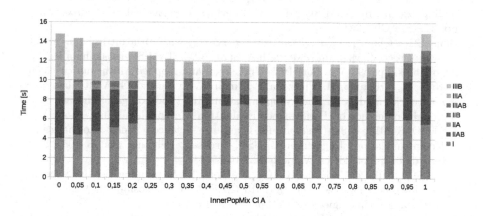

Fig. 8. Length of each phase for the execution of a two-class workload with $n_A = 40$, $n_A = 40$ and with $K = 20$ jobs in the FCR.

true for all the configurations; for example, when there are 50 jobs of class A and 30 jobs of class B in the whole system, the longest *Phase I* and the shortest depletion time do not meet the same inner population mix. In that case, the system has the longest *Phase I* when 95 % of jobs in the FCR belong to class A, whereas the shortest depletion time is reached when only the 70 % of jobs in the FCR are of class A.

5 Conclusion

In this paper we investigated the performance of models of a computational paradigm consisting of a given pool of jobs of known size that must be executed by a system having a limited capacity. The objective is to optimize the performance so that the energy consumption required to execute a complete workload is minimized. To this aim, with a multi-class workload we have considered a scheduling policy that try to optimize the mix of jobs of the different classes in concurrent execution. Future works will investigate different policies and will focus on the analytical computation of the optimal point for a given metric. We are also implementing specific benchmarks to validate our theoretical approach against measurements.

Acknowledgment. This work was partially funded by the European Commission under the grant ANTAREX H2020 FET-HPC-671623.

References

1. Albers, S., Fujiwara, H.: Energy-efficient algorithms for flow time minimization. ACM Trans. Algorithms (TALG) **3**(4), 49 (2007)
2. Andrew, L.L., Lin, M., Wierman, A.: Optimality, fairness, and robustness in speed scaling designs. In: ACM SIGMETRICS Performance Evaluation Review, vol. 38, pp. 37–48. ACM (2010)
3. Bansal, N., Chan, H.L., Pruhs, K.: Speed scaling with an arbitrary power function. In: Proceedings of the Twentieth Annual ACM-SIAM Symposium on Discrete Algorithms, pp. 693–701. Society for Industrial and Applied Mathematics (2009)
4. Cerotti, D., Gribaudo, M., Piazzolla, P., Pinciroli, R., Serazzi, G.: Multi-class queuing networks models for energy optimization. In: Proceedings of the 8th International Conference on Performance Evaluation Methodologies and Tools, VALUETOOLS 2014, ICST (Institute for Computer Sciences, Social-Informatics and Telecommunications Engineering), ICST, Brussels, Belgium, pp. 98–105 (2014). http://dx.org/10.4108/icst.Valuetools.2014.258214
5. Chen, D., Goldberg, G., Kahn, R., Kat, R., Meth, K.: Leveraging disk drive acoustic modes for power management. In: 2010 IEEE 26th Symposium on Mass Storage Systems and Technologies (MSST), pp. 1–9, May 2010
6. Diaz-Sanchez, D., Marin-Lopez, A., Almenarez, F., Sanchez-Guerrero, R., Arias, P.: A distributed transcoding system for mobile video delivery. In: Wireless and Mobile Networking Conference (WMNC), 2012 5th Joint IFIP, pp. 10–16, September 2012

7. Fan, X., Weber, W.D., Barroso, L.A.: Power provisioning for a warehouse-sized computer. In: Proceedings of the 34th Annual International Symposium on Computer Architecture, ISCA 2007, pp. 13–23. ACM, New York (2007). http://doi.acm.org/10.1145/1250662.1250665
8. Gandhi, A., Gupta, V., Harchol-Balter, M., Kozuch, M.A.: Optimality analysis of energy-performance trade-off for server farm management. Perform. Eval. **67**(11), 1155–1171 (2010)
9. Gonzalez, R., Horowitz, M.: Energy dissipation in general purpose microprocessors. IEEE J. Solid-State Circuits **31**(9), 1277–1284 (1996)
10. Hyytiä, E., Righter, R., Aalto, S.: Task assignment in a heterogeneous server farm with switching delays and general energy-aware cost structure. Perform. Eval. **75**, 17–35 (2014)
11. Kang, C.W., Abbaspour, S., Pedram, M.: Buffer sizing for minimum energy-delay product by using an approximating polynomial. In: Proceedings of the 13th ACM Great Lakes Symposium on VLSI, pp. 112–115. ACM (2003)
12. Kant, K.: A control scheme for batching dram requests to improve power efficiency. In: Proceedings of the ACM SIGMETRICS Joint International Conference on Measurement and Modeling of Computer Systems, SIGMETRICS 2011, pp. 139–140. ACM (2011)
13. Kaxiras, S., Martonosi, M.: Computer architecture techniques for power-efficiency. Synth. Lect. Comput. Archit. **3**(1), 1–207 (2008)
14. Muppala, J., Malhotra, M., Trivedi, K.: Markov dependability models of complex systems: analysis techniques. In: Ozekici, S. (ed.) Reliability and Maintenance of Complex Systems, vol. 154, pp. 442–486. Springer, Heidelberg (1996). http://dx.doi.org/10.1007/978-3-662-03274-9_24
15. Rivoire, S., Ranganathan, P., Kozyrakis, C.: A comparison of high-level full-system power models. HotPower **8**, 3 (2008)
16. Rosti, E., Schiavoni, F., Serazzi, G.: Queueing network models with two classes of customers. In: Proceedings of the Fifth International Symposium on Modeling, Analysis, and Simulation of Computer and Telecommunication Systems, MASCOTS 1997, pp. 229–234. IEEE (1997)

Moving Queue on a Network

Hans Daduna[✉]

Department of Mathematics, Hamburg University, 20146 Hamburg, Germany
daduna@math.uni-hamburg.de

Abstract. We describe a queueing network model for mobile servers on a network's graph. The principle behind resembles the procedure to consider a "referenced node" in a static network or a network of mobile nodes. We investigate an integrated model where a "referenced mobile node" is described jointly with all other mobile nodes. The distinguished feature is that we operate on distinct levels of detail, microlevel for the "referenced mobile node", macrolevel for all other moving nodes. The main achievement is the explicit stationary distribution which is of product form and indicates separability of the system in equilibrium.

Keywords: Jackson networks · Mobile nodes · Sensor nodes · Random waypoint models · Product form equilibrium · Separability

1 Introduction

Analytically solvable models of sensor networks often exploit Jackson networks and their generalizations, e.g. BCMP and Kelly networks. This seems to be natural whenever the sensor nodes are deployed in a predefined area and remain on their position as static sensors. For an in-depth study of an advanced setting see [MAG06], a more recent study is [WYH12] which elaborates on a simpler network but incorporates refined details. In these settings each node of the Jackson network represents a sensor: Its message queue is modeled by an exponential queueing system which constitutes the internal structure of the node.

It seems to be less obvious that Jackson networks can serve as models for networks of mobile sensor nodes but there is now a bulk of studies available where this methodology was successfully applied, a survey is [WDW07]. In general the authors proceed as follows: In a first step a single "referenced node" is investigated in detail collecting the other nodes and more (external) information into the node's environment. Thereafter, the nodes are combined by some approximating procedure to enforce closed form steady state solutions of the steady state equations, typical examples are [Li11, LTL05, ZL11, QFX+11].

Although in all these papers the authors propose that their two-step modeling procedure yields results which are in good agreement with simulation results, there still remains the weak point that formally the models do not fall into the class of product form networks of the Jacksonian type, where the exact solution of the global balance equations is at hand and yields a simple equilibrium distribution.

© Springer International Publishing Switzerland 2016
A. Remke and B.R. Haverkort (Eds.): MMB & DFT 2016, LNCS 9629, pp. 40–54, 2016.
DOI: 10.1007/978-3-319-31559-1_5

It is the aim of the present paper to go one first step on the path to such a theory: To start with a network model for a high dimensional system, to construct a Markov process for the evolution of the system over time, to write down the global balance equations, and to solve this equations explicitly without any intermediate decomposition-aggregation steps, and eventually to come up with a product form solution. In the language of product form calculus we end up with a proof that the system's coordinate processes are separable.

These coordinates are not only queue length processes, similarly e.g. to networks in a random environment, where some of the coordinates represent the external environment of a standard Jackson network. Examples for such mixed coordinate processes are described in the survey [Dad15]. Our model similarly will not fit into the class of Jackson or BCMP networks.

We emphasize that our model is a very stylized picture of the motivating real world systems, and we make simplifying assumptions as it is well established in the Jackson or BCMP setting. We will discuss this in detail below.

A special feature of our work is a two-scale modeling: We start with a network of moving servers (mobile nodes) and describe one distinguished server in full detail (on the microlevel), while the other servers are described on a macrolevel providing only rough information, which in our case is the overall number of "other" servers present at each vertex of the network.

A natural continuation of the project is to consider more moving servers on the microlevel. This is part of ongoing research.

Related Work: Besides the work mentioned in the second paragraph of this introduction it will come out that our model has close connections to sensor networks with static nodes where to enhance connectivity additional mobil nodes are moving in the network's area, for an investigation concentrating on end-to-end delay see [AK08] and the references there.

We owe a special feature of our model to Gannon, Pechersky, Suhov, and Yambartsev [GPE+14] who investigated models from statistical physics in an environment which has the structure of a Jackson network. Of special interest to our setting is their simplest model: A random walker on the nodes of a standard Jackson network. The interaction of the Jacksonian queues and the random walker is of the form that the random walker acts as an attractor or a repeller for standard customers to the node where the random walker resides.

The random walker model of Gannon, Pechersky, Suhov, and Yambartsev is not covered by the BCMP or Kelly networks framework [BCMP75, Kel79] but closely related.

The Paper's Structure: In Sect. 2 we describe typical scenarios of mobile sensor networks and extract general principles. We emphasize underlying mobility schemes, e.g. random waypoint regimes. In Sect. 3 we shortly present standard Jackson networks, and in Sect. 4 we describe how the distinguished moving server is added to the Jackson network and prove our main result on separability of this network under stationarity conditions. In Sect. 5 we summarize our findings and indicate directions of further research.

Notation and Conventions:

- $\mathbb{R}_0^+ = [0, \infty)$, $\mathbb{N} = 1, 2, 3, \ldots$, $\mathbb{N}_0 = \{0\} \cup \mathbb{N}$.
- Node set of our graphs (networks) is $\overline{J} := \{1, \ldots, J\}$. The "extended node set" is $\overline{J}_0 := \{0, 1, \ldots, J\}$, where "0" refers to the source and sink of the network.
- $\mathbf{e}_j$ is the standard j-th base vector in $\mathbb{N}_0^{\overline{J}}$ if $1 \leq j \leq J$.
- $\mathbf{n} = (n_j : j \in \overline{J})$ is the joint queue length vector of the Jackson network.
- Indicator function $1_A = 1$ if A is true, $1_A = 0$ otherwise.
- Kronecker-Delta $\delta_{xy} := 1_{[x=y]}$.
- Distances are denoted by d; if necessary, details will be given in the text.

2   Network Scenarios

The scenarios we have in mind encompass moving interdependent entities which are distributed in space. These entities usually carry a complex internal structure. Because we will end with a generalized queueing network model we will refer to the various entities, unless otherwise specified, as moving "customers" in a network, details will be introduced below.

Example 2.1. *[WWDL07] Given an area which is cell-partitioned into disjoint (non-overlapping) cells (subareas), collected in the cell set $\overline{J} = \{1, \ldots, J\}$, the customers are "delay/fault-tolerant mobile sensors", initially distributed randomly over the cells, and each sensor is associated with a home cell. The probability $r(m; i, j)$ that a sensor with home cell m, staying in cell i moves to cell j is inverse-proportional to the distance between cells m and j, $r(m; i, j) \simeq d(m, j)^{-1}$. Each sensor has a data queue (that contains maximum K messages) which receives and sends messages. Therefore the sensor's internal structure is that of a single server queue. A sensor with home cell m generates data and inserts data messages into its queue with rate λ_m. Moreover, it obtains data messages from other sensors to forward these in direction to a sink of the network. The message queue decreases with a rate which depends on the queue length and in general on the status of the nodes in the neighbourhood. In [WDW07][Sect. 3.4] this model of a cell-partitioned area is used to analyse movements in the ZebraNet.*

Example 2.2. *In [BH06][Sect. 5.1] a mobility model with geographic constraints is described: Customers' movements are restricted "to the pathways in the map". Customers in this example are non-stationary sensor nodes. The resulting model for the structure of the feasible movements is a random graph. The vertices of the graph usually represent buildings and/or street intersections of a city and the edges model streets and freeways of the city between these buildings, resp. intersections. Initially the customers are distributed randomly over the edges of the graph. Thereafter for each customer a destination vertex is chosen randomly and the customers move on a shortest path on the edges to their destination, staying there for a random time, and selects a new destination vertex for the next movement, and so on.*

Example 2.3. *Another mobility model in [BH06][Sect. 5.2] with geographic constraints is an "obstacle mobility model". The obstacles are buildings in the area under consideration and the pathways are found by construction of the Voronoi diagram with edges between the vertices defined by the buildings. The mobile nodes (customers) are allowed to move between the buildings on the Voronoi pathways only: Whenever a node leaves a vertex (after staying a random time there) it selects its next building randomly and moves towards this vertex on a shortest path over the edges.*

Summarizing the scenarios: In any case a finite set of vertices is connected by a structured set of edges. While in the second and third scenario the buildings and street intersections naturally can be modeled as vertices (points), in the first scenario we generate a vertex by contracting the cell to a point, which is in line with the analytical investigation in [WWDL07]. On this graph the customers (nodes) move according to some randomized regime. The number of customers may be fixed or varying, possibly without bound.

We will concentrate on the case of an unlimited number of customers which arrive from the exterior of the graph and depart eventually. The set of vertices is $\overline{J} = \{1, \ldots, J\}$, the edges will be determined by the transition graph of the mobility regime. We will assume that the routing decisions according to the mobility scheme of the customers are determined as follows: Whenever a customer leaves vertex i he selects his subsequent vertex j with probability $r(i,j) \geq 0$, given i independent of anything else. This procedure transforms Examples 2.2 and 2.3 into a (generalized) Jackson network, to be defined in Sect. 3.

This simple Jackson network like outcome for Examples 2.2 and 2.3 is possible because the themes in the survey [BH06] are mobility regimes, e.g. random waypoint models and their generalizations. The center of the present paper is to extend the Jackson network model to incorporate Example 2.1.

At present, analytical results for this extension seem to be out of reach. We therefore present a simplified network model which distinguishes different levels of detail. Our procedure is guided by the standard approach to investigate a "referenced node" in a network of mobile nodes: In a complex network of customers, pathways, and vertices only one customer is modeled in detail (="referenced node"), the influence of the rest of the network is incorporated into a simplified environment of this customer (="Jackson network"). The referenced node is **not** a node of this underlying Jackson network, but will be a moving $M/M/1/\infty$ queue itself, for more details, see e.g. [WDW07][Sect. 3.5], or [KD14].

To be more specific: We take one customer (traveling sensor node = Moving Queue = MQ) with explicit internal message queue. MQ cycles as a test customer forever in the network, while all the other customers around him on the graph's vertices are only counted as pure Jackson-type customers without internal structure. The challenging part of the model is the interaction of the test customer MQ and the other parts of the system.

From an abstract point of view this approach is a two-scale model where the test customer is investigated on the microlevel very detailed, while all the other parts of the system are described only on a macrolevel, determined similar to a mean-field approximation.

Remark: Neglecting the internal queue of the test customer and some further features (which will be introduced later on), this model resembles the structure of so-called mixed BCMP networks [BCMP75]: The mean-field customers are "external", coming from and going to an exterior world, while the test customer is "internal" for the network, cycling inside the network forever.

3   Standard Jackson Networks

We consider a Jackson network [Jac57] with node set $\overline{J} := \{1, \ldots, J\}$. Customers arrive in independent external Poisson streams, at node j with intensity $\lambda_j \geq 0$, we set $\lambda = \lambda_1 + \ldots + \lambda_J > 0$. Customers are indistinguishable, follow the same rules, and request for exponentially(1)-distributed service at all nodes. All these requests constitute an independent family of variables which are independent of the arrival streams. Nodes are exponential single servers with state dependent service rates and infinite waiting room under first-come-first-served (FCFS) regime. If at node i are $n_i > 0$ customers, either in service or waiting, service is provided there with intensity $\mu_i(n_i) > 0$. Routing is Markovian, a customer departing from node i immediately proceeds to node j with probability $r(i,j) \geq 0$, and departs from the network with probability $r(j,0)$. Taking $r(0,j) = \lambda_j/\lambda$, $r(0,0) = 0$, we assume that the extended routing matrix $r = (r(i,j) : i,j \in \overline{J}_0)$ is irreducible. Then the traffic equations

$$\eta_j = \lambda_j + \sum_{i=1}^{J} \eta_i r(i,j), \qquad j \in \overline{J}, \tag{3.1}$$

have a unique solution which we denote by $\eta = (\eta_j : j \in \overline{J})$. We extend the traffic Eq. (3.1) to a steady state equation for a routing Markov chain by

$$\eta_j = \sum_{i=0}^{J} \eta_i r(i,j), \qquad j = 0, 1, \ldots, J, \tag{3.2}$$

which is solved by $\eta = (\eta_j : j = 0, 1, \ldots, J)$, where $\eta_0 := \lambda$, the other η_j are from (3.1). We use η in both meanings and emphasize the later one by *extended traffic solution* η. η is in both cases usually not a stochastic vector.

Let $\mathbf{X} = (X(t) : t \geq 0)$ denote the vector process recording the queue lengths in the network. $X(t) = (X_1(t), \ldots, X_J(t))$ reads: at time t there are $X_j(t)$ customers present at node j, either in service or waiting. The assumptions put on the system imply that $\mathbf{X}$ is a Markov process on state space $\mathbb{N}_0^{\overline{J}}$. For an ergodic network process $\mathbf{X}$ Jackson's theorem [Jac57] states that the unique steady state and limiting distribution ξ on $\mathbb{N}_0^{\overline{J}}$ is with normalization constants $C(j)$ for the marginal (over nodes) distributions

$$\xi(\mathbf{n}) = \xi(n_1, \ldots, n_J) = \prod_{j=1}^{J} \prod_{m=1}^{n_j} \frac{\eta_j}{\mu_j(m)} C(j)^{-1}, \qquad \mathbf{n} \in \mathbb{N}_0^{\overline{J}}. \tag{3.3}$$

Assumption 3.1. Throughout we set the following assumption in force:

The extended routing matrix $r = (r(i,j) : i,j \in \overline{J}_0)$ *is reversible with respect to the measure* $\eta = (\eta_j : j \in \overline{J}_0)$, *i.e. it holds*

$$\eta_j r(j,i) = \eta_i r(i,j), \qquad \forall i,j = 0,1,\ldots,J. \tag{3.4}$$

4   Injecting a Moving Queue into the Jackson Network

We take the Jackson network from Sect. 3 and enlarge this network by adding a "distinguished customer" called MQ (= Moving Queue = mobile sensor node) who cycles on the nodes of the network forever, governed by an irreducible stochastic matrix $p = (p(i,j) : i,j \in \overline{J})$. In the language of BCMP models MQ is an "internal customer" while the other customers are "external" which arrive from the source and eventually depart to the sink. MQ is characterized by its position $k \in \overline{J}$ on the network and its queue length $\ell \in \mathbb{N}_0$. The internal service rates (death rates) $\delta(\ell) > 0$ and arrival rates (birth rates) $\beta(\ell) > 0$ for MQ's internal queue are strictly positive and in general queue length dependent.

It will come out that a Markov process description of the system is possible with state space $\mathbb{E} := \mathbb{N}_0^J \times \overline{J} \times \mathbb{N}_0$. The process of interest is denoted by

$$\mathbf{Z} = (\mathbf{X}, \mathbf{V}, \mathbf{Y}) = ((X(t), V(t), Y(t)) : t \geq 0)$$
$$= ((X_1(t), \ldots, X_J(t), V(t), Y(t)) : t \geq 0),$$

where $((X_1(t), \ldots, X_J(t), V(t), Y(t))$ indicates that at time t there are $X_j(t)$ external customers at node $j \in \overline{J}$, and that MQ is located at node $V(t) \in \overline{J}$ and has a queue length of $Y(t) \in \mathbb{N}_0$. A typical state of the system will be denoted by $(n_1, \ldots, n_J, k, \ell)$.

The dynamics of the MQ is influenced by the joint queue length process $\mathbf{X}$ only locally. If MQ resides at time t at node $V(t) = k$, additional capacity is provided there to "serve" MQ in parallel to the n_k other customers present which are served in a FCFS regime. The additional capacity to serve MQ results in a departure intensity

$$\nu^{(k)}(n_k, \ell) = e^{-\varphi n_k} \tag{4.1}$$

for MQ with a fixed constant $\varphi \in (-\infty, 0]$. Being served at k, MQ immediately jumps to node $k' \in \overline{J}$ with probability $p(k, k')$. p is not required to be reversible.

We further define for any $k \in \overline{J}$ an influence vector

$$\boldsymbol{\gamma}(k) = (\gamma_j(k) : j \in \overline{J}_0) \in (0,1]^{\overline{J}_0}, \qquad \text{with } \gamma_0(k) := 1, \tag{4.2}$$

which is in force whenever MQ resides in node k. These influence vectors describe in a compact way the consequences for the other Jackson customers, originating from MQ's actual position in the network.

Assume that at time t MQ stays at node $V(t) = k \in \overline{J}$ and the queue length at j is $X_j(t) = n_j \geq 1, j \in \overline{J}$. Then the customer at the head of the line of node j (if any) is served with intensity $\mu_j(n_j, k) := \mu_j(n_j) \cdot \gamma_j(k)$. When this customer's service expires, he departs immediately directed by the adjusted routing probability vector $r^{(k)} = (r^{(k)}(j,i) : j,i \in \bar{J}_0)$, which is defined for the non-diagonal transition probabilities $(i \neq j)$

$$
r^{(k)}(j,i) := \begin{cases}
\text{for } j = 0: \\
r(0,i) \cdot \gamma_i(k), & \text{if } i \neq k, \\
r(0,k) \cdot \gamma_k(k) \cdot e^\varphi, & \text{if } i = k, \\
\text{for } j \neq 0, j \neq k: \\
r(j,i) \cdot \gamma_i(k), & \text{if } i \in \bar{J}_0 \setminus \{j,k\}, \\
r(j,k) \cdot \gamma_k(k) \cdot e^\varphi, & \text{if } i = k, \\
\text{for } j = k: \\
r(k,i) \cdot \gamma_i(k), & \text{if } i \in \bar{J}_0 \setminus \{k\}.
\end{cases}
$$

The diagonal transition probabilities $(j = i)$ are

$$
r^{(k)}(j,j) := \begin{cases}
\text{for } j \in \bar{J}_0 \setminus \{k\}: \\
r(j,j) + \sum_{h \neq j,k} r(j,h) \cdot (1 - \gamma_h(k)) + r(j,k) \cdot (1 - \gamma_k(k) \cdot e^\varphi), \\
\text{for } j = k: \\
r(k,k) + \sum_{h \neq k} r(k,h) \cdot (1 - \gamma_h(k)).
\end{cases}
$$

This definition implies for the effective external arrival rates $\lambda_i(k) = \lambda \cdot r^{(k)}(0,i)$

$$
= \begin{cases}
\lambda r(0,i) \cdot \gamma_i(k), & \text{if } i \neq k; \\
\lambda r(0,k) \cdot \gamma_k(k) \cdot e^\varphi, & \text{if } i = k; \\
\lambda \left(\sum_{h \neq k} r(0,h) \cdot (1 - \gamma_h(k)) + r(0,k) \cdot (1 - \gamma_k(k) \cdot e^\varphi) \right), & \text{if } i = 0.
\end{cases} \quad (4.3)
$$

If MQ resides at k, then for $i = 0$ in (4.3) $\lambda - \lambda_0(k)$ is the effective arrival rate at the network, due to MQ's influence on the network when staying in k.

Remarks: (i) Consider the case $\varphi = 0$. If MQ stays at vertex k, setting the influence vector $\gamma(k)$ in force, the rerouting probabilities for the other customers can be considered as randomized reflection, defined in [KDO14][Sect. 2.2]: A customer departing from i who selects (with probability $r(i,j)$) to enter j is allowed to settle down at j with probability $\gamma_j(k)$; with probability $1 - \gamma_j(k)$ he is reflected at j and stays on at i to obtain another service. (ii) This is a random generalization of the well-known blocking resolution scheme *blocking-after-service* (BAS) in connection with *repeated service* and *random destination* (rs-rd) which is applied in transmission networks with finite buffers to protect against buffer overflow, see [Onv90][p. 502]. (iii) Randomized reflection has been used successfully to redirect routing of customers in Jackson networks in a random environment. Rerouting is interpreted there as a reaction of a network's (local) controllers when environment condition changes and therefore capacities in the network are changed, see [KDO16]. (iv) The factor e^φ can be replaced here and in (4.11) below by any number in $a \in (0,1]$. Setting a to e^φ gives notational credit to the paper [GPE+14], where it seemingly occurred first in this form.

Because of $\varphi \leq 0$, MQ acts as a repeller for the other Jackson customers who want to enter the vertex where MQ resides. On the other side, the form of

$\nu^{(k)}(n_k, \ell)$ enforces MQ to leave a cell or building where already many customers are present. The more involved case of MQ as an attractor, i.e. $\varphi \geq 0$ is part of our ongoing research.

Example 4.1. *For simplicity of presentation we have fixed FCFS regime for the Jackson network customers with state dependent service rates. This framework covers the seemingly most important special service rates to enclose the Example 2.1 in our setting. Recall that in this scenario the vertex $j \in \overline{J}$ is a representative for a cell where n_j mobile sensors are present. It is tempting to assume that the sensors move (almost) independently of one another. This can be modeled by taking $\mu_j(n_j) = \mu_j \cdot n_j$ for some (regional) cell specific constant μ_j, i.e. the vertex j acts as an $M/M/\infty$ node as long as $j \neq k$.*

If $j = k$, i.e. MQ resides in cell j, a similar conclusion via classical BCMP or Kelly framework of queueing networks seems to be not possible, but nevertheless it is tempting again to visualize the cell as an infinite server with the special property that the internal customer MQ is served with an additional locally state dependent capacity which is controlled by the function $e^{-\varphi n_k}$, similar to Kelly's $\phi_k(n_k + 1)$ [Kel79][p. 58].

Example 4.2. *For the Examples 2.2 and 2.3 a reference to infinite server systems is even more natural if we recall that in both scenarios the vertices are buildings or lane intersections, where customers stay for a random amount of time, while the edges are lanes between these vertices. The joint movement of entities on a lane is naturally modeled in transportation networks by being served at an infinite server. The "service" at the vertices might be modeled by more specific service disciplines, e.g. FCFS at a road intersection.*

Example 4.3. *The influence vectors $\gamma(k) = (\gamma_j(k) : j \in \overline{J}_0)$ are versatile devices to determine the influence of MQ. Denote by $d : \overline{J} \times \overline{J} \to \mathbb{N}_0$ the distance between vertices of the network, i.e. $d(i, j)$ is the minimal number of hops to reach vertex j from i, where $d(i, i) = 0$. If $\gamma(k)$ fulfils $\gamma_j(k) = 1$ unless $d(k, j) \leq 1$ the influence of MQ on the network is restricted to the 1-hop neighbourhood. If $\gamma(k)$ fulfils $\gamma_j(k) = 1$ unless $d(k, j) \leq 2$ its influence is restricted to the 2-hop range.*

The strictly positive transition rates of $\mathbf{Z}$ are

$$q(\mathbf{n}, k, \ell; \mathbf{n} + \mathbf{e}_i, k, \ell) = \lambda_i(k), \tag{4.4}$$

$$q(\mathbf{n}, k, \ell; \mathbf{n} - \mathbf{e}_j, k, \ell) = 1_{(n_j > 0)} \mu_j(n_j.k) r^{(k)}(j, 0), \tag{4.5}$$

$$q(\mathbf{n}, k, \ell; \mathbf{n} - \mathbf{e}_j + \mathbf{e}_i, k, \ell) = 1_{(n_j > 0)} \mu_j(n_j.k) r^{(k)}(j, i), \tag{4.6}$$

$$q(\mathbf{n}, k, \ell; \mathbf{n}, k', \ell) = \nu^{(k)}(n_k, \ell) p(k, k'), \tag{4.7}$$

$$q(\mathbf{n}, k, \ell; \mathbf{n}, k, \ell + 1) = \beta(\ell), \tag{4.8}$$

$$q(\mathbf{n}, k, \ell; \mathbf{n}, k, \ell - 1) = 1_{(\ell > 0)} \delta(\ell). \tag{4.9}$$

The proof of the next theorem is omitted. It is along the same lines as that of the following one.

Theorem 4.4. *Assume* **Z** *to be ergodic. Then its unique stationary and limiting distribution is with normalization constant* C

$$\pi(\mathbf{n}, k, \ell) = C^{-1} \prod_{g=1}^{J} \prod_{m=1}^{n_g} \frac{\eta_g}{\mu_g(m)} e^{\varphi n_k} \psi_k \prod_{s=0}^{\ell-1} \frac{\beta(s)}{\delta(s+1)}, \quad (\mathbf{n}, k, \ell) \in \mathbb{E}. \quad (4.10)$$

Here $(\eta_g : g \in \overline{J})$ is taken from (3.1) and $(\psi_k : k \in \overline{J})$ is the unique stationary distribution of MQ's routing matrix $p = (p(k, k') : k, k' \in \overline{J})$.

We now allow that the internal birth and death rates of MQ are not only queue length dependent, but also location dependent. So, if MQ resides at k, service rates are $\delta^{(k)}(\ell) > 0$ and arrival rates are $\beta^{(k)}(\ell) > 0$. Furthermore MQ's travel transition rates are now

$$\nu^{(k)}(n_k, \ell) = e^{-\varphi n_k} \cdot \prod_{s=0}^{\ell-1} \frac{\delta^{(k)}(s+1)}{\beta^{(k)}(s)}. \quad (4.11)$$

The strictly positive transition rates of the system are again (4.4)–(4.6) (invariant) and with adapted rates

$$q(\mathbf{n}, k, \ell; \mathbf{n}, k', \ell) = \nu^{(k)}(n_k, \ell) p(k, k'), \quad (4.12)$$

$$q(\mathbf{n}, k, \ell; \mathbf{n}, k, \ell + 1) = \beta^{(k)}(\ell), \quad (4.13)$$

$$q(\mathbf{n}, k, \ell; \mathbf{n}, k, \ell - 1) = 1_{(\ell>0)} \delta^{(k)}(\ell). \quad (4.14)$$

The global balance equations for **Z** are for $(\mathbf{n}, k, \ell) \in \mathbb{E}$

$$x(\mathbf{n}, k, \ell) \Big[\sum_{i \in \overline{J}} \lambda_i(k) + \sum_{i \in \overline{J}} 1_{(n_i > 0)} \mu_i(n_i, k)(1 - r^{(k)}(i, i))$$

$$+ \beta^{(k)}(\ell) + 1_{(\ell>0)} \delta^{(k)}(\ell) + \nu^{(k)}(n_k, \ell)(1 - p(k, k)) \Big]$$

$$= \sum_{i \in \overline{J}} 1_{(n_i > 0)} x(\mathbf{n} - \mathbf{e}_i, k, \ell) \lambda_i(k) + \sum_{j \in \overline{J}} x(\mathbf{n} + \mathbf{e}_j, k, \ell) \mu_j(n_j + 1, k) r^{(k)}(j, 0)$$

$$+ \sum_{i \in \overline{J}} 1_{(n_i > 0)} \sum_{j \in \overline{J} \setminus \{i\}} x(\mathbf{n} - \mathbf{e}_i + \mathbf{e}_j, k, \ell) \mu_j(n_j + 1, k) r^{(k)}(j, i)$$

$$+ 1_{(\ell>0)} x(\mathbf{n}, k, \ell - 1) \beta^{(k)}(\ell - 1) + x(\mathbf{n}, k, \ell + 1) \delta^{(k)}(\ell + 1)$$

$$+ \sum_{k' \in \overline{J} \setminus \{k\}} x(\mathbf{n}, k', \ell) \nu^{(k')}(n'_k, \ell) p(k', k).$$

Theorem 4.5. *Assume* **Z** *to be ergodic. Then its unique stationary and limiting distribution is with normalization constant* C

$$\pi(\mathbf{n}, k, \ell) = C^{-1} \prod_{g=1}^{J} \prod_{m=1}^{n_g} \frac{\eta_g}{\mu_g(m)} e^{\varphi n_k} \psi_k \prod_{s=0}^{\ell-1} \frac{\beta^{(k)}(s)}{\delta^{(k)}(s+1)}, \quad (\mathbf{n}, k, \ell) \in \mathbb{E}. \quad (4.15)$$

$(\eta_g : g \in \overline{J})$ is from (3.1) and $(\psi_k : k \in \overline{J})$ is the unique stationary distribution of MQ's stochastic routing matrix $p = (p(k, k') : k, k' \in \overline{J})$.

Proof. We exploit some detailed balance equations which underly the structure of the global balance equation. We first consider the terms concerning the queue length process **Y** of MQ and equate

$$x(\mathbf{n}, k, \ell)\Big[\beta^{(k)}(\ell) + 1_{(\ell>0)}\delta^{(k)}(\ell)\Big]$$
$$= 1_{(\ell>0)}x(\mathbf{n}, k, \ell-1)\beta^{(k)}(\ell-1) + x(\mathbf{n}, k, \ell+1)\delta^{(k)}(\ell+1),$$

which after inserting π and canceling $C^{-1}\prod_{g=1}^{J}\prod_{m=1}^{n_g}\frac{\eta_g}{\mu_g(m)}e^{\varphi n_k}\psi_k$ yields global balance equations for an ergodic birth-death process with parameters $\beta^{(k)}(\ell)$ and $\delta^{(k)}(\ell)$, respectively, which are parametrized by $(\mathbf{n}, k)$. Next, we equate

$$x(\mathbf{n}, k, \ell)\Big[\nu^{(k)}(n_k, \ell)(1 - p(k, k))\Big] = \sum_{k'\in\bar{J}\setminus\{k\}} x(\mathbf{n}, k', \ell)\nu^{(k')}(n'_k, \ell)p(k', k),$$

which after inserting π and canceling $C^{-1}\prod_{g=1}^{J}\prod_{m=1}^{n_g}\frac{\eta_g}{\mu_g(m)}$ yields

$$e^{\varphi n_k}\psi_k \prod_{s=0}^{\ell-1}\frac{\beta^{(k)}(s)}{\delta^{(k)}(s+1)}\Big[\prod_{s=0}^{\ell-1}\frac{\delta^{(k)}(s+1)}{\beta^{(k)}(s)}e^{-\varphi n_k}(1 - p(k, k))\Big]$$
$$= \sum_{k'\in\bar{J}\setminus\{k\}} e^{\varphi n'_k}\psi_{k'} \prod_{s=0}^{\ell-1}\frac{\beta^{(k')}(s)}{\delta^{(k')}(s+1)}\Big[\prod_{s=0}^{\ell-1}\frac{\delta^{(k')}(s+1)}{\beta^{(k')}(s)}e^{-\varphi n'_k}p(k', k)\Big].$$

This boils down to the balance equation of MQ's routing matrix $p = (p(k, k') : k, k' \in \bar{J})$ which by definition is solved by $(\psi_k : k \in \bar{J})$. The remaining terms are

$$x(\mathbf{n}, k, \ell)\Big[\sum_{i\in\bar{J}}\lambda_i(k) + \sum_{i\in\bar{J}}1_{(n_i>0)}\mu_i(n_i, k)(1 - r^{(k)}(i, i))\Big]$$
$$= \sum_{i\in\bar{J}}1_{(n_i>0)}x(\mathbf{n}-\mathbf{e}_i, k, \ell)\lambda_i(k) + \sum_{j\in\bar{J}}x(\mathbf{n}+\mathbf{e}_j, k, \ell)\mu_j(n_j+1, k)r^{(k)}(j, 0)$$
$$+ \sum_{i\in\bar{J}}1_{(n_i>0)}\sum_{j\in\bar{J}\setminus\{i\}}x(\mathbf{n}-\mathbf{e}_i+\mathbf{e}_j, k, \ell)\mu_j(n_j+1, k)r^{(k)}(j, i).$$

Note that constantly occurs (k, ℓ). Canceling $C^{-1}\psi_k\prod_{s=0}^{\ell-1}\frac{\beta^{(k)}(s)}{\delta^{(k)}(s+1)}$ and multiplying with $\Big(\prod_{g=1}^{J}\prod_{m=1}^{n_g}\frac{\eta_g}{\mu_g(m)}\Big)^{-1}$ we obtain the equation

$$e^{\varphi n_k}\Big[\sum_{i\in\overline{J}\setminus\{k\}} \lambda r(0,i)\cdot\gamma_i(k) + \lambda r(0,k)\cdot\gamma_k(k)\cdot e^{\varphi}$$

$$+ \sum_{i\in\overline{J}\setminus\{k\}} 1_{(n_i>0)}\mu_i(n_i)\gamma_i(k)\big(1-r(i,i)$$

$$- \sum_{h\in\overline{J}\setminus\{i,k\}} r(i,h)(1-\gamma_h(k)) - r(i,k)(1-\gamma_k(k)\cdot e^{\varphi}))$$

$$+ 1_{(n_k>0)}\mu_k(n_k)\cdot\gamma_k(k)\Big(1-r(k,k)-\sum_{h\in\overline{J}\setminus\{k\}} r(k,h)(1-\gamma_h(k))\Big)\Big]$$

$$= e^{\varphi n_k}\sum_{i\in\overline{J}\setminus\{k\}} 1_{(n_i>0)}\frac{\mu_i(n_i)}{\eta_i}\lambda r(0,i)\cdot\gamma_i(k)$$

$$+ e^{\varphi(n_k-1)}1_{(n_k>0)}\frac{\mu_k(n_k)}{\eta_k}\lambda r(0,k)\cdot\gamma_k(k)e^{\varphi}$$

$$+ e^{\varphi n_k}\sum_{j\in\overline{J}\setminus\{k\}} \frac{\eta_j}{\mu_j(n_j+1)}\mu_j(n_j+1)\gamma_j(k)r(j,0)$$

$$+ e^{\varphi(n_k+1)}\frac{\eta_k}{\mu_k(n_k+1)}\mu_k(n_k+1)\gamma_k(k)r(k,0)$$

$$+ e^{\varphi n_k}\sum_{i\in\overline{J}\setminus\{k\}} 1_{(n_i>0)}\sum_{j\in\overline{J}\setminus\{k,i\}} \frac{\mu_i(n_i)}{\eta_i}\frac{\eta_j}{\mu_j(n_j+1)}\mu_j(n_j+1)\gamma_j(k)r(j,i)\gamma_i(k)$$

$$+ e^{\varphi(n_k-1)}1_{(n_k>0)}\sum_{j\in\overline{J}\setminus\{k\}} \frac{\mu_k(n_k)}{\eta_k}\frac{\eta_j}{\mu_j(n_j+1)}\mu_j(n_j+1)\gamma_j(k)e^{\varphi}r(j,k)\gamma_k(k)$$

$$+ e^{\varphi(n_k+1)}\sum_{i\in\overline{J}\setminus\{k\}} 1_{(n_i>0)}\frac{\mu_i(n_i)}{\eta_i}\frac{\eta_k}{\mu_k(n_k+1)}\mu_k(n_k+1)\gamma_k(k)r(k,i)\gamma_i(k).$$

By canceling $e^{\varphi n_k}$ we obtain after some algebraic manipulations

$$\Big[\sum_{i\in\overline{J}\setminus\{k\}} \overbrace{\lambda r(0,i)\cdot\gamma_i(k)}^{(2)} + \overbrace{\lambda r(0,k)\cdot\gamma_k(k)\cdot e^{\varphi}}^{(1)}$$

$$+ \sum_{i\in\overline{J}\setminus\{k\}} 1_{(n_i>0)}\mu_i(n_i)\gamma_i(k)\Big(\sum_{h\in\overline{J}\setminus\{i,k\}} \overbrace{r(i,h)\gamma_h(k)}^{(6)} + \overbrace{r(i,k)\gamma_k(k)\cdot e^{\varphi}}^{(5)} + \overbrace{r(i,0)}^{(3)} \Big)$$

$$+ 1_{(n_k>0)}\mu_k(n_k)\cdot\gamma_k(k)\Big(\sum_{h\in\overline{J}\setminus\{k\}} \overbrace{r(k,h)\gamma_h(k)}^{(7)} + \overbrace{r(k,0)}^{(4)} \Big)\Big]$$

$$= \sum_{i\in\overline{J}\setminus\{k\}} \overbrace{1_{(n_i>0)}\frac{\mu_i(n_i)}{\eta_i}\lambda r(0,i)\cdot\gamma_i(k))}^{(3)} + \overbrace{1_{(n_k>0)}\frac{\mu_k(n_k)}{\eta_k}\lambda r(0,k)\cdot\gamma_k(k))}^{(4)}$$

$$+ \sum_{j \in \overline{J} \setminus \{k\}} \overbrace{\eta_j \gamma_j(k) r(j,0))}^{(2)} + \overbrace{e^{\varphi} \eta_k \gamma_k(k) r(k,0))}^{(1)}$$

$$+ \sum_{i \in \overline{J} \setminus \{k\}} 1_{(n_i > 0)} \sum_{j \in \overline{J} \setminus \{k,i\}} \overbrace{\frac{\mu_i(n_i)}{\eta_i} \eta_j \gamma_j(k) r(j,i) \gamma_i(k))}^{(6)}$$

$$+ 1_{(n_k > 0)} \sum_{j \in \overline{J} \setminus \{k\}} \overbrace{\frac{\mu_k(n_k)}{\eta_k} \eta_j \gamma_j(k) r(j,k) \gamma_k(k)}^{(7)}$$

$$+ \sum_{i \in \overline{J} \setminus \{k\}} e^{\varphi} 1_{(n_i > 0)} \overbrace{\frac{\mu_i(n_i)}{\eta_i} \eta_k \gamma_k(k) r(k,i) \gamma_i(k)}^{(5)}.$$

We are now enforced to recur to Assumption 3.1 and equate pairwise terms with the help of reversibility of r. We equate the indicated partial sums and obtain after premultiplication with associated factors from outside of brackets the following valid expressions.

Because of $\lambda = \eta_0$ the next four lines follow:

$$\lambda r(0,k) \cdot \gamma_k(k) \cdot e^{\varphi} \stackrel{(1)}{=} e^{\varphi} \eta_k \gamma_k(k) r(k,0),$$

$$\forall i \in \overline{J} \setminus \{k\}: \quad \lambda r(0,i) \cdot \gamma_i(k) \stackrel{(2)}{=} \eta_i \gamma_i(k) r(i,0),$$

$$\forall i \in \overline{J} \setminus \{k\}: \quad \eta_i 1_{(n_i > 0)} \mu_i(n_i) \cdot \gamma_i(k) r(i,0) \stackrel{(3)}{=} 1_{(n_i > 0)} \mu_i(n_i) \lambda r(0,i) \cdot \gamma_i(k),$$

$$\eta_k 1_{(n_k > 0)} \mu_k(n_k) \cdot \gamma_k(k) r(k,0) \stackrel{(4)}{=} 1_{(n_k > 0)} \mu_k(n_k) \lambda r(0,k) \cdot \gamma_k(k),$$

and the next lines are obvious from reversibility:

$$\forall i \in \overline{J} \setminus \{k\}: \quad \eta_i 1_{(n_i > 0)} \mu_i(n_i) \gamma_i(k) r(i,k) \gamma_k(k) e^{\varphi}$$
$$\stackrel{(5)}{=} e^{\varphi} 1_{(n_i > 0)} \mu_i(n_i) \eta_k \gamma_k(k) r(k,i) \gamma_i(k),$$

$$\forall i,j \in \overline{J} \setminus \{k\}: \eta_i 1_{(n_i > 0)} \mu_i(n_i) \gamma_i(k) r(i,j) \gamma_j(k)$$
$$\stackrel{(6)}{=} 1_{(n_i > 0)} \mu_i(n_i) \eta_j \gamma_j(k) r(j,i) \gamma_i(k),$$

$$\forall j \in \overline{J} \setminus \{k\}: \eta_k 1_{(n_k > 0)} \mu_k(n_k) \gamma_k(k) r(k,j) \gamma_j(k)$$
$$\stackrel{(7)}{=} 1_{(n_k > 0)} \mu_k(n_k) \eta_j \gamma_j(k) r(j,k) \gamma_k(k).$$

This validates π as the global balance equations of $\mathbf{Z}$.

Example 4.6 *We proved the theorems with service rates* $\mu_j(n_j, k) = \mu_j(n_j) \gamma_j(k)$ *when* n_j *Jackson network customers stay at vertex* j *and MQ resides at* k. *In Examples 4.1 and 4.2 we demonstrated that this covers especially the natural infinite server setting for the Jackson customers. This leads to the observation that by* $\gamma_j(k)$ *the service intensity of the individual customers is reduced:* $\mu_j(n_j, k) = (\mu_j \gamma_j(k)) n_j$.

Discussion of the Modeling Assumptions: (i) The process $\mathbf{Z}$ is not reversible although the pure Jackson network process without the MQ is reversible with respect to the stationary distribution $\xi(\mathbf{n})$ from (3.3) by Assumption 3.1. Reversibility of the underlying pure Jackson network process seems at the present stage of development indispensable. This clearly restricts applicability of the result of Theorem 4.5. For example it excludes one-way lanes for the traveling nodes. On the other side, starting with this case is worth for laying the ground for eventually more general settings. (ii) Introducing influence vectors $\gamma(k) = (\gamma_j(k) : j \in \overline{J}_0) \in (0,1]^{\overline{J}_0}$ which are in force whenever MQ resides in node k, and MQ's repeller function, goes back to ideas in [GPE+14,KDO14]. There this controls interactions between different components of a multidimensional system. Application of this scheme in the context of this paper is still restricted due to $0 < \gamma_j(k) \leq 1$, which means that for the influenced service rates holds $\mu(n_j, k) \leq \mu(n_j)$ for all n_j. The power of this scheme will come out when $0 \leq \gamma_j(k) < \infty$ is included as is demonstrated in [KDO16]. With $\varphi > 0$, in context of the models considered here (e.g. in Example 2.1) this means that whenever MQ is present at k, the rate of incoming other customers into cell k is increased. In the framework of [AK08] this would increase the connectivity of the network. This is part of our future research. (iii) The most critical point is in our opinion the choice of the portion of the vertices' capacity dedicated to MQ. For the situation of Theorem 4.4 we have taken $\nu^{(k)}(n_k, \ell) =: \widetilde{\nu}^{(k)}(n_k) = e^{-\varphi n_k}$ from [GPE+14]. Studying the balance equations there (and in our more complicated framework as well) reveals that this choice is essential to obtain the product form steady state via reversibility. We mention that in [GPE+14] there is no "moving queue" but only a "random walker" with reversible routing, but without any internal structure. MQ's routing matrix p is not required to be reversible. Moreover, in the framework of Theorem 4.4 we do not need additional special assumptions. These come into the play if the development of MQ's internal message queue is location dependent (i.e. $\beta^{(k)}(\cdot), \delta^{(k)}(\cdot)$) which is desirable in our opinion. We pay with requiring the complicated service rates $\nu^{(k)}(n_k, \ell)$ in (4.11).

Example 4.7. *Consider the scenario from [WWDL07] in Example 2.1 and take a distinguished moving node in the cell-partitioned area. If we want to reduce the other nodes to customers in a network, we are faced with the problem, that the routing of these customers is dependent on the position of their home-cell, i.e. we need customer types which carry this information.*

Our present oversimplified model does not offer this feature.

With our formalism it is possible to take the distinguished node's routing as the matrix p and then construct an averaged routing matrix r for the other customers, where averaging is done according to weights representing the population sizes of the home-cells. A similar averaging is necessary for the mean sojourn times for these other customers in the different cells they visit. To obtain these averaged values needs iterative procedures because we admit arrivals from and departures to the exterior for the other customers.

5   Conclusion and Further Research

We have developed a two-scale model for a network of mobile nodes, guided by scenarios from the literature on mobile sensor networks. The main outcome is the stationary distribution of the system which exhibits its separability in equilibrium.

Further research will be on including into the theory the case of the mobile customer being an attractor for the other customers, the possibility to have different classes of external customers with individual class dependent service time distributions, and to investigate on the microlevel two or more internal moving queues injected into the Jackson network and their interaction.

A seemingly hard problem will be to remove the assumption of reversibility of the underlying Jackson network.

Acknowledgement. I thank Sonja Otten and Ruslan Krenzler for helpful discussions on the subject of the paper. I am thankful for three reviewers' helpful comments on the first version of this paper.

References

[AK08] Almasaeid, H.M., Kamal, A.E.: Modeling mobility-assisted data collection in wireless sensor networks. In: Global Telecommunications Conference, IEEE GLOBECOM 2008, pp. 1–5 (2008)

[BCMP75] Baskett, F., Chandy, M., Muntz, R., Palacios, F.G.: Open, closed and mixed networks of queues with different classes of customers. J. Assoc. Comput. Mach. **22**, 248–260 (1975)

[BH06] Bai, F., Helmy, A.: A survey of mobility models in wireless adhoc networks. In: Wireless Ad-Hoc Networks, Chap. 1, pp. 1–30. Kluwer Academic Publisher, Dordrecht (2006)

[Dad15] Daduna, H.: Networks of queues in a random environment: survey of product form results. In: Proceedings MMBnet, Berichte des Fachbereichs Informatik der Universität Hamburg 302, pp. 7–23 (2015)

[GPE+14] Gannon, M., Pechersky, E., Suhov, Y., Yambartsev, V.: Random walks in a queueing network environment. Technical report arXiv: 1410.1460 (2014). Version 3: arxiv:1410.1460v3 (2015). To appear: J. Appl. Probab

[Jac57] Jackson, J.R.: Networks of waiting lines. Oper. Res. **5**, 518–521 (1957)

[KD14] Krenzler, R., Daduna, H.: Modeling and performance analysis of a node in fault tolerant wireless sensor networks. In: Fischbach, K., Krieger, U.R. (eds.) Measurement, Modelling, and Evaluation of Computing Systems and Dependability and Fault-Tolerance, pp. 73–78. Springer, Heidelberg (2014). GI/ITG

[KDO14] Krenzler, R., Daduna, H., Otten, S.: Randomization for Markov chains with applications to networks in a random environment. Preprint, Center of Mathematical Statistics und Stochastic Processes, University of Hamburg, No. 2014–02 (2014)

[KDO16] Krenzler, R., Daduna, H., Otten, S.: Jackson networks in non-autonomous random environments. Advances in Applied Probability (2016)

[Kel79] Kelly, F.P.: Reversibility and Stochastic Networks. Wiley, Chichester (1979)

[Li11] Li, W.W.: Several characteristics of active/sleep model in wireless sensor networks. In: New Technologies, Mobility and Security (NTMS), pp. 1–5 (2011)

[LTL05] Liu, J., Tong Lee, T.: A framework for performance modeling of wireless sensor networks. In: 2005 IEEE International Conference on Communications, ICC 2005, vol. 2, pp. 1075–1081 (2005)

[MAG06] Mehmet Ali, M.K., Gu, H.: Performance analysis of a wireless sensor network. In: Wireless Communications and Networking Conference, IEEE, vol. 2, pp. 1166–1171 (2006)

[Onv90] Onvural, R.O.: Closed queueing networks with blocking. In: Takagi, H. (ed.) Stochastic Analysis of Computer and Communication Systems, pp. 499–528. Amsterdam, North-Holland (1990)

[QFX+11] Qiu, T., Feng, L., Xia, F., Wu, G., Zhou, Y.: A packet buffer evaluation method exploiting queueing theory for wireless sensor networks. Comput. Sci. Inf. Syst. $8(4)$, 1027–1049 (2011)

[WDW07] Wang, Y., Dang, H., Wu, H.H.: A survey on analytic studies of delay-tolerant mobile sensor networks. Wirel. Commun. Mob. Comput. 7, 1197–1208 (2007)

[WWDL07] Wu, H., Wang, Y., Dang, H., Lin, F.: Analytic, simulation, and empirical evaluation of delay/fault-tolerant mobile sensor networks. IEEE Trans. Wireless Commun. $6(9)$, 3287–3296 (2007)

[WYH12] Wang, Z., Yang, K., Hunter, D.K.: Modelling and analysis of multi-sink wireless sensor networks using queuing theory. In: Proceedings of the 4th Computer Science and Electronic Engineering Conference (CEEC), University of Essex, pp. 169–174. IEEE, UK (2012)

[ZL11] Zhang, Y., Li, W.: An energy-based stochastic model for wireless sensor networks. Wirel. Sens. Netw. $3(9)$, 322–328 (2011)

A Multi-commodity Simulation Tool Based on TRIANA

Maryam Hajighasemi[✉], Gerard J.M. Smit, and Johann L. Hurink

Faculty EEMCS, University of Twente, Enschede, The Netherlands
{m.hajighasemi,g.j.m.smit,j.l.hurink}@utwente.nl

Abstract. In this paper we extended the simulator based on the TRI-ANA concept, with a model for the heat demand of households. The heat demand is determined based on factors such as building properties, user setpoints and weather conditions. The simulator exploits the flexibility of both the electricity and heat components to optimize the stream of both commodities, heat and electricity.

Keywords: TRIANA · Demand side management · Heating system

1 Introduction

Over the previous decade, there has been an increase in the amount of locally generated energy, e.g. by installing PV panels. As a result, a considerable part of the electricity needed in the local grids can be supported by these renewable energy production. However, the demand hours do not always match the production hours of renewable energies. Technologies such as electrical and thermal storage, and smart gird concepts steering controllable devices can help to balance the locally generated energy and the total demand.

This paper presents a multi-commodity simulation tool of a smart controlled micro-grid using the TRIANA simulator. As an example we show a simulation that aims to balance the supply and demand of heat and electricity for a group of houses in such a micro-grid. In the current tool, PV panels and a central combined heat and power system (CHP) are the local energy producers. Additionally, each house is equipped with time-shiftable devices, an electric battery and a floor heating system.The desired tool can be used to answer questions like e.g. under which conditions such a micro-grid with local production, storage and demand has the ability to operate independent of the grid.

2 The TRIANA Simulator

TRIANA is a three-step control methodology for energy management and has been developed at the University of Twente [2,3]. The three steps are: prediction, planning and real-time control. Prediction of the demand and production is done on device level. To match the demand and production locally as good

© Springer International Publishing Switzerland 2016
A. Remke and B.R. Haverkort (Eds.): MMB & DFT 2016, LNCS 9629, pp. 55–59, 2016.
DOI: 10.1007/978-3-319-31559-1_6

as possible, a planning is determined for a certain time horizon based on the achieved predictions. Finally, real-time control steers the system in the direction of the planning.

TRIANA optimizes the planning toward an objective using a central controller. In this work, we use the profile steering method introduced in [4] to control the devices. This methodology attempts to steer the realized profile of the system toward a desired profile. In other words, it minimizes the deviation between the realized energy usage and a desired profile.

Modeling an energy system in TRIANA is done by using suitable component models termed devices. The following three types of device are examples of device classes supported by TRIANA:

- Uncontrollable devices: Uncontrollable devices can be divided into consumers and producers. Devices such as lighting and ventilation consume electricity and have a static consumption profile. The producers, such as PV panels, have a static production profile, which is achieved by predictions based on weather data, the size, efficiency and orientation of PV panel, etc.
- Time-shiftable devices: These kinds of device, like washing machines, offer flexibility of their starting time and they have the constraint to be finished before a specific time. Based on this time specification it can be decided what the best time is to turn a device on.
- Buffer devices: Buffer devices have more flexibility, since they can be charged and discharged. Hereby, constraints such as a certain state of charge up to a specific time may have to be taken into account. Various type of devices can be categorized as a buffer with specific characteristics. Examples of buffer-typed devices include normal buffer such as a battery, buffer-converter devices such as a thermal buffer and buffer-time-shiftable devices such as electrical vehicle.

Although TRIANA is a general concept, the developed simulation tool up to now was mainly electricity oriented and did not have any components to model the heat demand of a house. E.g. in [5] just a static input is used for describing the heating demand of houses. However, a smart grid oriented control will be more effective if a sophisticated house model is used that also describes the flexibility of the heating system of a house in relation to building properties, user setpoints and weather conditions. This leads to a dynamic heat model that reveals the flexibility of the heating system.

The main contribution of this paper is to add such a heating system component to TRIANA (see Sect. 3). In this way the heat demand is no longer just static, but can be incorporated in the control of the house to match demand and supply on grid level.

3   Extending TRIANA with Heat Components

The heating system added to the TRIANA simulation tool is a floor heating system for a single house as is described in [1]. In this heating system, thermal nodes with a thermal capacitance are defined for the floor and for a zone which is affected by separation walls, inner and outer envelope walls and the ceiling. The zone node is affected by ventilation, infiltration, appliances and the presence of people. Furthermore, the solar gain through the window area is also considered.

The controller of the floor heating system is also dependent on some other variables, i.e. max floor temperature, user setpoints (T_s), acceptable deviation from setpoint (d). The heating system is modeled such that it turns on when the zone temperature (T_z) is low and deviates more than d from T_s $(T_z < T_s - d)$. It stays on until either the zone temperature passes the highest acceptable deviation $(T_z > T_s + d)$ or the maximum floor temperature is reached.

Within the implemented use case, the heat demand of the houses in a neighborhood is aggregated to a heat pool which is connected to a heat buffer and a CHP plant. Figure 1 represents the neighborhood energy system using the model described in [3].

For scheduling all flexible appliances in the house, as well as the CHP plant and the heat buffer, we use the profile steering method introduced in [4]. Hereby, the heat buffer gives the CHP plant flexibility to carry out some pre-heating by fill-

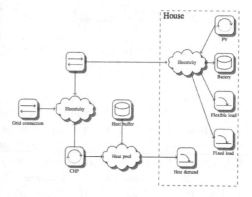

Fig. 1. The neighborhood energy system schematic [5]

ing the buffer already before the time the heat is required, when electricity is needed. The only constraints now is that the state of charge of the buffer always must be enough to provide the predicted heat consumption for the next periods.

4 Results

In this section, a case study that consists of both heat and electricity demand is presented as an example of a multi-commodity simulation in TRIANA. This case study has already been described in [5]. The model includes 16 well-insulated terraced houses, with controllable devices, namely a washing and dish washing machine, and an electric battery. The houses heated with floor heating, are equipped with solar-PV panels, and located in a typical Dutch area. Moreover, there is a central CHP plant in the neighborhood, incorporating a heat buffer (see Fig. 1). Furthermore, inflexible loads are given for each house. The aim of this case is to investigate to what extent the CHP plant can meet the electricity demand of the houses.

Two cases are compared. The first case uses the static heat demand as a direct input for the CHP (Base), and the CHP has to meet the heat demand directly. In the second case, the heating model is used, and all flexible devices in the house are controlled to adopt their energy profile to the generation of the CHP (Control). Hereby, the CHP is also controlled and uses the thermal storage to supply the heat demand.

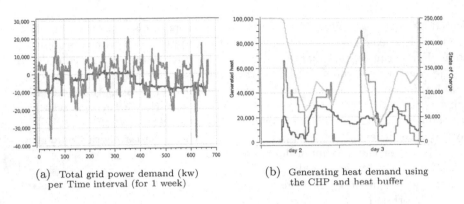

(a) Total grid power demand (kw) per Time interval (for 1 week)

(b) Generating heat demand using the CHP and heat buffer

Fig. 2. – Base – Control – State of Charge (Color figure online)

For the evaluation, a week with high heat demand and low PV generation is chosen, in which the total amount of generated electricity by the CHP is always higher than the total electricity consumption of all houses. Thus, in principle the CHP could meet all electricity demand. Such a week is ideal to investigate the effectiveness of using a control methodology for flexible devices such as CHP.

In Fig. 2a, the resulting total power profiles of the complete neighborhood are given for both cases. In the Base case, electricity generated by the CHP is often not enough to meet all the electricity demand. However, in the Control case, the profile of the CHP can meet the demand using only a minimal amount of energy from the grid. In contrast to the Base case with a large swing, the Control case has a flat profile due to the balancing.

Figure 2b shows the CHP heat production for both cases and the state of charge for the heat buffer in the Control case for 2 days. The generated heat in Control case is less spiky than the Base case, since it is using the heat buffer to meet the heat demand.

5   Conclusion and Future Work

In this paper, a first approach to extend the TRIANA simulator to networks which include both heat and electricity is presented. The resulting tool is evaluated on data obtained from a model described in [5], where the heating system is based on floor heating system of a Dutch low energy house. The control method aims to flatten the electricity profile and to minimize the import of electricity from the grid. Hereby, the flexibility of the devices is used.

Future work will aim to investigate different control methods to control the heating system. This is expected to give more flexibility to the CHP heat generation.

References

1. van Leeuwen, R.P., de Wit, J.B., Fink, J., Smit, G.J.M.: House thermal model parameter estimation method for model predictive control applications. In: IEEE PowerTech, pp. 1–6. IEEE Power and Energy Society, Eindhoven (2015)
2. Bakker, V.: TRIANA: a control strategy for smart grids - forecasting, planning and real-time control. Ph.D. dissertation, University of Twente (2012)
3. Molderink, A.: On the three-step methodology for smart grids. Ph.D. dissertation, University of Twente (2011)
4. Gerards, M.E.T., Toersche, H.A., Hoogsteen, G., van der Klauw, T., Hurink, J.L., Smit, G.J.M.: Demand side management using profile steering. In: IEEE PowerTech, pp. 1–6. IEEE Power and Energy Society, Eindhoven (2015)
5. Perez, K.X., Baldea, M., Edgar, T.F., Hoogsteen, G., van Leeuwen, R.P., van der Klauw, T., Homan, B., Fink, J., Smit, G.J.M.: Soft-islanding a group of houses through scheduling of CHP, PV and storage (2016, accepted at IEEE Energycon)

Performance and Precision of Web Caching Simulations Including a Random Generator for Zipf Request Pattern

Gerhard Hasslinger[1]([✉]), Konstantinos Ntougias[2],
and Frank Hasslinger[3]

[1] Deutsche Telekom Technik, Darmstadt, Germany
gerhard.hasslinger@telekom.de
[2] Athens Information Technology, Athens, Greece
kontou@ait.gr
[3] Darmstadt University of Technology, Darmstadt, Germany
frank.hasslinger@stud.tu-darmstadt.de

Abstract. The steadily growing Internet traffic volume for video, IP-TV and other content needs support by caching systems and architectures which are provided in global content delivery networks as well as in local networks, on home gateways or user terminals. The efficiency of caching is important in order to save transport capacity and to improve throughput and delays.

However, since analytic solutions for the hit rate as the main caching performance measure are not available even under the baseline scenario of an independent request model (IRM) with usual Zipf request pattern and caching strategies, simulation methods are used to evaluate caching efficiency. Based on promising experience with simulation approaches of caching methods in previous work, we study and verify two main prerequisites: First, a fast random Zipf rank generator is derived, which allows to extend simulations to billions of requests. Moreover, the accuracy of alternatives of the hit rate evaluation is compared based on the 2nd order statistics. The results indicate that the sum of request probabilities of objects in the cache provides a more precise estimator of the hit rate as a simple hit count.

Keywords: Simulation of caching strategies · Least Recently Used (LRU) · Score gated LRU · Least Frequently Used (LFU) · Zipf request pattern · Random zipf rank generator · 2nd order statistics · Hit rate estimators

1 Introduction: Caching Strategies and Evaluation by Simulations

Goals and Applications of Web Caching. Caching is widely used for support of IP services from global scale content delivery networks (CDNs) to local caches [2, 8–10]. Main goals and benefits are

- to shorten the transport paths and corresponding delays associated with the delivery of data from an original server to the requesting users,

© Springer International Publishing Switzerland 2016
A. Remke and B.R. Haverkort (Eds.): MMB & DFT 2016, LNCS 9629, pp. 60–76, 2016.
DOI: 10.1007/978-3-319-31559-1_7

- to reduce the traffic load, which is most valuable for ISPs on expensive links, e.g., on international transatlantic routes or on paid peering connections,
- to shift traffic load from the busy hour to low load phases by prefetching and overnight cache updates,
- to increase the throughput due to shorter round trip times in TCP connections for connections from a cache, improving the performance on links and network domains with high failure rate such as air interfaces in mobile networking,
- and to replicate data in distributed caching infrastructures for enhanced availability and for enabling higher throughput from multiple caching servers in case of flash crowds.

The cache replacement strategy is important for the efficiency of caching, measured by the cache hit rate as the fraction of requests that can be served from cached content. Least recently used (LRU) and least frequently used (LFU) are main caching principles [16]. LRU is a widely used caching strategy that simply puts each requested object on top of a cache being implemented as a double linked list, while evicting the bottom element if the storage is exhausted. Advantages of LRU are a simple update mechanism with low constant effort per request and high flexibility to adapt to changing popularity of objects. The least frequently used (LFU) principle keeps a count statistics for the number of past requests to each object and fills the cache storage with the most popular ones. LFU achieves optimum hit rates for independent requests (IRM) and reduces fluctuation of objects entering and leaving the cache, if their popularity has a monotonous trend over time. However, an unlimited count statistics can't adapt to changing popularity rendering pure LFU inapplicable in practice.

Therefore alternatives with limited statistics have been proposed and evaluated [4, 8, 10, 15]. A wide class of such strategies is attributed as LRFU spectrum by Lee et al. [14]. These caching schemes include LRU and LFU as extreme cases. Two basic variants of this family of LRFU caching policies are

- sliding window, where the LFU request count is restricted the window of the W most recent requests, and
- geometrical fading, introducing a fading or aging factor $\rho < 1$ such that the kth recent request is weighted by ρ^k and objects are ranked due to the sum of weights.

Both schemes prefer objects for caching based on an especially defined score function [10]. They include LFU as an unlimited equally weighted count of previous requests as one extreme for $W \to \infty$, $\rho \to 1$. On the other extreme, geometric fading is equivalent to LRU for $\rho \leq 0.5$, since then the most recent request dominates the weights. For sliding window implementations with $W = 1$, LRU is again resembled, if the required tie breaker for ranking the objects of the same weight is using the LRU principle.

Finally, we use and recommend score-gated (SG-)LRU [10] as an approach to implement LRFU methods combining the advantages of both, LRU and LFU. In extension of pure LRU, SG-LRU assigns a score to each object and admits an external object to enter the cache only if its score is higher than the score of the bottom object of the cache. Otherwise, the bottom object is put on top. In this way, SG-LRU preserves the low LRU update effort, avoiding more complex updates for sorted lists according to scores [14]. Nonetheless, SG-LRU collects and keeps the highest scored objects in the cache, provided that the score ranking of objects is stable over longer time. When we compare pure LRU and SG-LRU in the evaluation part of this work, we use scores based on geometric fading. In general, sliding window or any arbitrary score function with low update effort can be combined with SG-LRU, which opens a flexible class of caching strategies for object specific preferences still based on fast LRU updates.

Simulation of Caching Strategies. Efficient simulation of caching methods directly reflects in the update effort per request except for the uploading of data for objects entering the cache. LRU and SG-LRU caching strategies have low constant update effort per request. Then the random generator for choosing the next object to be requested becomes another main factor of the simulation effort. For the usual Zipf distributed request pattern we didn't find an efficient random generator in the literature or in simulation tool sets covering the relevant parameter range [5, 20].

Therefore we derived an inversion formula for a Zipf random number generator as a first part of this work which is applied in the following evaluation of SG-LRU schemes with a fixed set of objects and fixed popularity according to the independent request model (IRM). In final examples, we extend the evaluation of caching schemes for a model including varying popularity of objects with new objects appearing at a maximum and afterwards decreasing popularity level.

We focus on simulating the hit rate as basic performance measure of caching. One of the rare exact analytical results on cache hit rates is an upper bound for a cache for M objects given by the sum of M request probabilities of the most popular objects under IRM conditions. Moreover, the performance of caching strategies is investigated based on measurement traces which show hit rate deficits of LRU [15]. In previous work [10], the simulation test series for hit rate estimations showed low variability. A main goal of the current work is to control and optimize the precision of simulation results by investigating the 2nd order statistics over multiple time scales.

In the next section we proceed with a brief overview on the relevance of Zipf's law in request statistics on popular Internet platforms. A random Zipf rank generator is developed and verified in Sect. 3. Section 4 presents examples of simulation results with different run lengths showing decreasing variance and convergence to a mean estimated hit rate. Sections 5 and 6 compare two hit rate estimators by the count of hits per request and by the sum of request probabilities of objects in the cache, based on 2nd order statistic. Section 7 extends this comparison to the score gated LRU strategy and Sect. 8 shows results for another extension of the request model from IRM to dynamically changing object popularity. Finally, main conclusions from the considered case studies are summarized in Sect. 9.

2   Zipf'S Law for Access to Content on the Internet

Many studies have confirmed Zipf's law for request pattern on Internet platforms as a favourable property for caching efficiency such that a small set of popular web objects attracts most user requests. When a finite set of N objects is considered for web caching, Zipf's law assigns decreasing request probabilities $z(r)$ to each of them corresponding to their popularity rank $r \in \{1, 2, ..., N\}$:

$$z(r) = \alpha r^{-\beta} \text{ for } \alpha, \beta > 0; \ \alpha = z(1) = 1 / \sum\nolimits_{r=1}^{N} z(r) \tag{1}$$

where $\beta > 0$ is an adaptive shape parameter and α is a normalization constant. The characteristics of Zipf's law is a focus of the requests on a small fraction of most popular objects, known as 90:10- (or 80:20-)rules such that the top 10 % of the objects attract 90 % of the user requests. The shape parameter β determines the skewness of the distribution, where an 80:20-rule roughly corresponds to $\beta \approx 0.85$ [18]. Access probabilities are becoming more unbalanced for $\beta \to 1$ or $\beta > 1$. Cases for $\beta > 1$ are modeled in [7] but we only found estimations of $\beta \leq 1$ in measurement studies of web content requests. In particular,

- Breslau et al. [2] obtained $0.64 \leq \beta \leq 0.83$ in six web proxy and HTTP request traces over up to three months duration,
- Che et al. [4] obtained $0.64 \leq \beta \leq 0.75$ for eight single day traces,
- Fricker et al. [7] obtained $\beta \approx 0.75$ and $\beta \approx 0.82$ from two Torrent web sites and $0.56 \leq \beta \leq 0.88$ referring to a collection of other papers including Cha et al. [3], and
- Hefeeda and Saleh [13] obtained $0.6 \leq \beta \leq 0.78$ for request traces in P2P systems.

Therefore, caching simulations for Zipf distributed requests seem relevant in the range $0.5 \leq \beta \leq 1$. Moreover, infinite object sets can be considered for $\beta > 1$, whereas the sum of probabilities $z(r)$ in Eq. (1) does not converge for $\beta \leq 1$, which imposes a restriction to a finite set of N objects in the relevant range $\beta < 1$.

3   An Inversion Method for a Random Zipf Rank Generator

Owing to the relevance of Zipf request pattern, an efficient random generator for Zipf distributed ranks is essential for web cache simulations. The random selection of an object to be addressed next is a time-critical simulation step which must be performed as part of an (SG-)LRU update step at low constant effort per request.

As a basis, the cumulative distribution function (CDF)

$$Z_{CDF}(n) = \sum\nolimits_{r=1}^{n} z(r) = \sum\nolimits_{r=1}^{n} r^{-\beta} / \sum\nolimits_{r=1}^{N} r^{-\beta} \tag{2}$$

is calculated and stored at the start of the simulation. Then for each request we have to compute a Zipf distributed rank $r \in \{1, ..., N\}$ from a uniform random number $R \in [0, 1]$, such that

$$Z_{CDF}(r - 1) < R \leq Z_{CDF}(r) \text{ assuming } Z_{CDF}(0) = 0. \tag{3}$$

To the authors' knowledge, there is no useful recommendation for an efficient Zipf random generator for web caching purposes available in literature. The Mathematica tool set documentation [20] refers to an acceptance-rejection method proposed by

Devroye [5], which is restricted to infinite object sets and excludes the most relevant range $\beta \leq 1$ for web caching. Instead, we derive a direct inversion formula covering Zipf distributions of finite support over the entire range $\beta \geq 0$.

Explicit upper and lower bounds of $Z_{CDF}(n)$ are obtained from a comparison of the sum of Zipf probabilities as a step function with the integral over the corresponding continuous function, which is strictly monotonous:

$$\int_{x=1}^{n+1} x^{-\beta} dx = \frac{x^{1-\beta}}{1-\beta} \Big|_1^{n+1}$$

$$= \frac{(n+1)^{1-\beta} - 1}{1-\beta} \leq \sum_{r=1}^n r^{-\beta} < \frac{(n+1)^{1-\beta} - \beta}{1-\beta} \text{ for } \beta > 0; \beta \neq 1. \quad (4)$$

When we try an approximate Zipf rank generator based on the arithmetic mean of the upper and lower bound, we experience only partially sufficient precision. The right hand curves of Fig. 3 show results for an example for $N = 10^5$ objects and for different values of the Zipf shape parameter β. The deviations in the rank r are checked by the condition (3). Small rank deviations $\leq \pm 1$ are confirmed only for $\beta \leq 0.2$ and when β is close to 1. Rank deviations > 50 are visible for $\beta = 0.9$ and even much larger ones for $\beta > 1$, although this range is not observed for Zipf like web request pattern.

The deviation between the step function for $Z_{CDF}(n)$ and the integral in Eq. (4) is large for the top ranks r but on the other hand it is diminishing with smaller steps for large r. Therefore, we expect the integral to provide a good approximation especially for the second half $N/2 \leq r \leq N$, which leads to an almost perfect rank generator:

$$Z_{CDF}(r) \approx Z_{CDF}\left(\frac{N}{2}\right) + \left(1 - Z_{CDF}\left(\frac{N}{2}\right)\right) \int_{N/2}^r x^{-\beta} / \int_{N/2}^N x^{-\beta}$$

$$\text{for } N/2 \leq r \leq N.$$

$$= Z_{CDF}\left(\frac{N}{2}\right) + \left(1 - Z_{CDF}\left(\frac{N}{2}\right)\right) \frac{r^{1-\beta} - \left(\frac{N}{2}\right)^{1-\beta}}{N^{1-\beta} - \left(\frac{N}{2}\right)^{1-\beta}}$$

We obtain the random Zipf rank generator by replacing $Z_{CDF}(r)$ with a random value R ($Z_{CDF}(N/2) \leq R \leq 1$) and then invert the formula to obtain the rank r from given R:

$$\Rightarrow \frac{R - Z_{CDF}\left(\frac{N}{2}\right)}{1 - Z_{CDF}\left(\frac{N}{2}\right)} = \frac{r^{1-\beta} - \left(\frac{N}{2}\right)^{1-\beta}}{N^{1-\beta} - \left(\frac{N}{2}\right)^{1-\beta}}$$

$$\Rightarrow \quad r = \left[\left(\frac{N}{2}\right)^{1-\beta} + \left[N^{1-\beta} - \left(\frac{N}{2}\right)^{1-\beta}\right] \frac{R - Z_{CDF}\left(\frac{N}{2}\right)}{1 - Z_{CDF}\left(\frac{N}{2}\right)}\right]^{\frac{1}{1-\beta}}$$

$$= N\left[\left(\frac{1}{2}\right)^{1-\beta} + \left[1 - \left(\frac{1}{2}\right)^{1-\beta}\right] \frac{R - Z_{CDF}\left(\frac{N}{2}\right)}{1 - Z_{CDF}\left(\frac{N}{2}\right)}\right]^{\frac{1}{1-\beta}} = N\left[1 - \frac{(1-R)(1 - \left(\frac{1}{2}\right)^{1-\beta})}{1 - Z_{CDF}\left(\frac{N}{2}\right)}\right]^{\frac{1}{1-\beta}}.$$

$$(5)$$

When we check $Z_{CDF}(r) \le R \le Z_{CDF}(r + 1)$ to confirm the correctness of the rank computed by Eq. (5) we observe an almost perfect match, such that r deviates from the correct rank by less than ± 1.

Moreover, although formula (5) is justified only for ranks $r \ge N/2$ and thus for random values R in the range $Z_{CDF}(N/2) \le R \le 1$, we applied the Zipf generator over the total range $0 \le R \le 1$ for all ranks $1 \le r \le N$. As a result, which is surprising on first glance, the accuracy of Eq. (5) holds over the entire range $0 \le R \le 1$ with deviations less than ± 1 in all examples and test series we investigated. The precision of the Zipf rank generator is shown in Fig. 1 for an example of the following Zipf distribution:

$$z(r) = 0.2503133 r^{-0.999999} \approx \frac{1}{4r} \text{ for } N = 30.$$

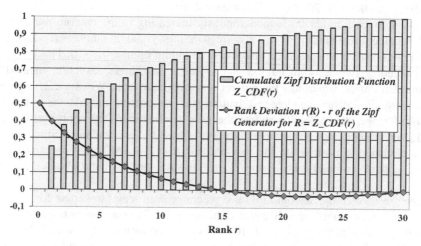

Fig. 1. Deviations $\Delta(r)$ of the Zipf rank generator of formula (5)

Therefore we check the deviations

$$\Delta(r) = N[1 - (1 - Z_{CDF}(r)) \frac{1 - (\frac{1}{2})^{1-\beta}}{1 - Z_{CDF}(\frac{N}{2})}]^{\frac{1}{1-\beta}} - r \qquad (6)$$

of ranks computed by Eq. (5) for $R = Z_{CDF}(r)$ over the distribution range $r = 0,\ldots, N$.

Figure 2 shows the deviations in a wider range of case studies for $0 \le \beta \le 3$ and larger object sets $N = 100$ and $N = 10^6$. The graphs confirm very similar and limited deviations below a maximum deviation $\Delta(r) < 0.6$ at the top rank $r = 1$. In the first half of the distribution range $r \le N/2$, deviations are monotonously decreasing to 0 at $r = N/2$. In the second half $N/2 \le r \le N$, deviations $\Delta(r)$ are negative but do not fall below -0.1.

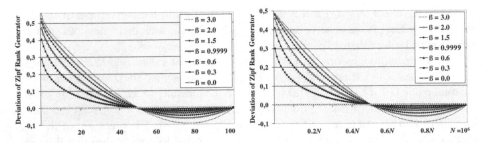

Fig. 2. Deviations $\Delta(r)$ of the Zipf rank generator of formula (5) in the range $[1, N]$ for $N = 100$ (left figure) and $N = 10^6$ (right figure)

Finally, we extended our checks of $\Delta(r)$ to a set of Zipf distribution functions for all values of $\beta = 0$, 0.1, 0.2, ..., 3 combined with all $N = 1, 2, 3, ..., 10^5$ as well as $N = 10^5 + 100$, $10^5 + 200$, ..., 10^6. In each case $\forall r \in [1, ..., N]$: $-1 < \Delta(r) < 1$ is confirmed. Since formula (5) is monotonously increasing in the random number R, a check for all discrete ranks $r = 1, ..., N$ corresponding to random numbers $R = Z_{CDF}(r)$ is sufficient to confirm the precision also for any random number $R \in [0, 1]$.

Concluding, we recommend formula (5) as a fast direct inversion method for random Zipf ranks, which hits the correct or a neighbor rank. When a caching simulation with Zipf distributed request pattern has parameters outside the previously evaluated range, we can still validate the rank generator (5) by applying the same checks according to Eqs. (3) and (6) in the start phase of the simulation. Since the sign of the deviation is positive on the first half for $R < Z_{CDF}(N/2)$ and negative on the second, a single comparison of R and $Z_{CDF}(r)$ is sufficient to finally obtain the correct rank.

The precision of the random Zipf rank generator even seems to pertain for $\beta > 3$ and for $N > 10^6$, but we only sparsely covered the range $\beta > 3$ in our checks because it is not relevant for web caching. For $N > 10^6$ numerical problems are indispensible when standard double real number representation is employed for computations, because a uniform distribution over $N = 10^6$ objects already leads to small request probabilities of 10^{-6}, which are becoming much smaller for skewed Zipf distributions for $\beta > 0.5$ in the ranks $r > N/2$. As a consequence, the smallest resolution unit between real numbers in double precision already maps into rank differences > 1. An extended real number representation or a refined random rank generator has to be established for objects with request probabilities $< 10^{-10}$, which we haven't implemented yet. However, we can ignore objects that are seldom requested over long time and exclude them. In this way, the size of relevant object sets for web caching can be kept below $N = 10^6$.

The rank generator could be modified or generalized regarding our initially considered range $N/2 \leq r \leq N$. Instead of $N/2$ we can take any value between 1 and N for the lower bound of the range and we may optimize this value with regard to the precision. Figure 3 shows an example with range $N/10 \leq r \leq N$, whose deviations are more than 10-fold larger on the negative part than for $N/2 \leq r \leq N$. In fact, we experienced close to optimum precision for $N/2 \leq r \leq N$.

However, beyond a dense computational check over the most relevant range, we lack a mathematical confirmation of the favourable properties except for $\Delta(N/2) = \Delta(N) = 0$.

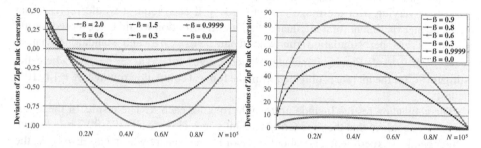

Fig. 3. Deviations of the Zipf rank generator over the range $[1, 10^5]$ for alternatives using Eq. (5) with $N/10$ replacing $N/2$ (left fig.) and based on Eq. (4) (right fig.)

For simulations with a specific Zipf distribution, the random rank generator of Eq. (5) is used in the format $(a + bR)^c$ with pre-computed constants a, b, c depending on N, $Z_{CDF}(N/2)$ and β. Alternatively, a binary search can be implemented to find r such that $Z_{CDF}(r) \leq R \leq Z_{CDF}(r + 1)$ as a standard random generator for a discrete distribution. Search methods require a number of steps which is increasing in the order of $\ln(N)$ and thus are less efficient than the inversion formula especially for large object sets.

4   Simulation of Caching Strategies: Run Time Versus Precision

An efficient Zipf rank generator is helpful to order to investigate how the precision of the hit rate is developing with the run time in terms of the number of simulated requests. In simulation studies comparing different caching strategies in the LRU/LFU spectrum, i.e. caching schemes combining LRU with LFU, we experienced low variability in the simulation results indicating high precision and finally noticed large differences in the achievable hit rate of different caching schemes [10]. Therefore we would like to get better insight into the simulation statistics in order to verify the precision. We start with simulations comparing pure LRU and SG-LRU caching methods based on Zipf distributed independent requests (IRM).

We evaluate the hit rate as the fraction of requests to objects in the cache. The simulations start with an empty cache. While the cache is filling, the score-gated and pure LRU caching strategies behave identical. As soon as the cache is full, pure LRU already has entered steady state regarding the statistics of objects in the cache. Consequently, the mean hit rate per simulated request with a full cache equals the long term LRU hit rate. Thus, it is sufficient to exclude the cache filling phase as a non-representative start phase for pure LRU simulations.

Figure 4 demonstrates how the variability in simulation results is reducing with longer run time. An example of Zipf distributed requests to $N = 10^6$ objects is considered with $\beta = 0.9999$ and a small cache size of $M = 200$ which already achieves more than 27 % LRU hit rate.

Each dot in the figure refers to a simulated hit rate result. The number K of simulated requests is varying over the range $[10^6, 1.6 \cdot 10^{10}]$. If each request would represent an independent experiment for a hit, then a binomial distribution would be observed for the number of hits per simulation run with mean $\mu_h = hK$ and standard deviation $\sigma_h = \sqrt{h(1-h)K}$. Figure 4 includes dotted curves for $(\mu_h \pm \sigma_h)/K$, where the estimate μ_h for the hit rate is obtained from the longest simulation run over $K = 1.6 \cdot 10^{10}$ requests.

The simulation results include up to eight runs for each K. The results of the simulation series confirm that the long term mean hit rate is close to a 68-95-99.7 rule known for independent experiments, i.e. about 68 % of the results are within $(\mu_h \pm \sigma_h)/K$, the 95 % confidence interval is around $(\mu_h \pm 2\sigma_h)/K$ and about 99.7 % are within $(\mu_h \pm 3\sigma_h)/K$. However, hit rates are not independent for successive requests because the LRU cache content is changing in no more than one object per simulated request.

Corresponding results of a case study for SG-LRU are shown in Fig. 5. The convergence to a steady state now depends on stabilizing scores for the objects, which takes much longer than the cache filling phase. In order to reach steady state conditions, we exclude the first quarter of each simulation run from the evaluations, which covers the phase for stabilizing scores, provided that the run time pertains sufficiently long.

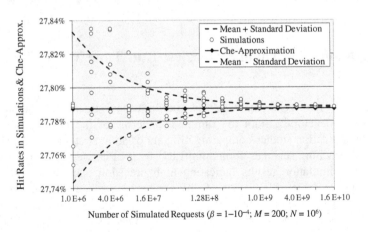

Fig. 4. Simulated LRU hit rates for different run times

Figure 5 presents SG-LRU results for the same Zipf distributed IRM case as in Fig. 4. A geometrical fading score function is applied with $\rho = 0.9999$. Again, up to eight simulation results are shown with $10^6 \le K \le 1.6 \cdot 10^{10}$ requests in the evaluation phase and the deviations are in the range $(\mu_h \pm \sigma_h)/K$ of independent requests.

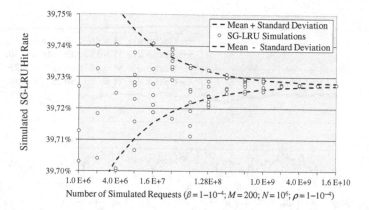

Fig. 5. Simulated SG-LRU hit rates for different run times

The LRU simulation results in Fig. 4 are close to the Che approximation for the LRU hit rate $h_{Che} \approx 27.787$ % [4]. The SG-LRU simulations yield $h_{SG\text{-}LRU} \approx 39.728$ %, which exploits most of the optimum LFU hit rate $h_{LFU} = z(1) + \ldots + z(M) \approx 40.667$ % as the maximum achievable hit rate under IRM conditions.

5 Hit Count Versus Sum of Cached Objects' Request Probabilities

For studying the variability of the hit rate during an LRU caching simulation, the sum of the request probabilities of all objects in the cache after the kth simulated request is essential, which equals the cache hit probability $\pi(k)$ of the next request:

$$\pi(k) = \sum\nolimits_{j:\text{Object } j \text{ is in the cache}} z(j).$$

Figure 6 shows excerpts $\pi(K+1), \ldots, \pi(K+1000)$ of the stochastic process $\pi(k)$ for an LRU caching simulation with Zipf distributed requests ($\beta = 0.8$; $N = 1000$ objects) in steady state IRM conditions with a full cache. Four cases of different cache sizes are considered, which are sufficient to achieve 10 %, 25 %, 50 % and 75 % cache hit rate. The curves show that the variability of $\pi(k)$ is decreasing with the cache size. The fluctuations in $\pi(k)$ are caused by objects dropping off and re-entering the cache. A larger cache can hold the top popular objects for longer time such that the objects dropping off the cache have smaller request probabilities and therefore have smaller impact on $\pi(k)$. Moreover, the cache content remains unchanged after a cache hit, i.e. $\pi(k)$ remains constant for a fraction of requests equal to the hit rate.

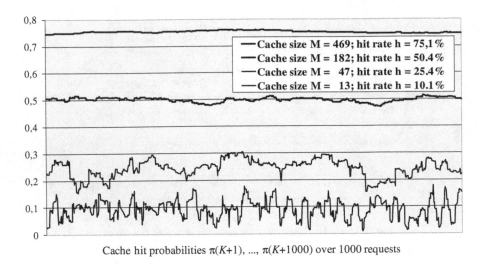

Cache hit probabilities π(K+1), ..., π(K+1000) over 1000 requests

Fig. 6. Variability of the sum of the request probabilities of objects in an LRU cache

6 2nd Order Statistics for the Precision in Multiple Time Scales

In order to characterize the variability in hit rate simulations, we evaluate the second order statistics $\sigma(\pi_{(K)})$ that indicates the standard deviation of a stochastic process over sequences of requests of different length K. $\sigma(\pi_{(K)})$ is defined and computed from the mean values over K successive requests of the process $\pi(k)$ [11, 12]:

$$\pi_{(K)}(j) = \frac{1}{K}\sum\nolimits_{k=(j-1)K+1}^{jK} \pi(k); \;\; \sigma(\pi_{(K)})) = \sqrt{E(\pi_{(K)}^2(j)) - \mu^2(\pi)}; \;\; \mu(\pi) = E(\pi_{(K)})(j)) = E(\pi(k)).$$

Note, that the expectation $\mu(\pi_{(K)}) = \mu(\pi)$ is constant over all time scales K for a process in steady state, whereas $\sigma(\pi_{(K)})$ is expected to decrease with K, e.g. for a process of independent and identically distributed random values we have $\sigma(\pi_{(K)})=\sigma(\pi)/\sqrt{K}$.

In order to evaluate $\sigma(\pi_{(K)})$ during the caching simulation, we consider successive request sequences of length $K = 10, 10^2, ..., 10^R$ of a simulation run over 10^{R+1} requests and compute the usual estimate of the standard deviation:

$$\sigma(\pi_{(K)}) = \sqrt{\sum\nolimits_{j=1}^{10^{R+1}/K} \pi_{(K)}^2(j) - \mu^2(\pi)/(\frac{10^{R+1}}{K} - 1)}; \;\; \mu(\pi) = \frac{1}{10^{R+1}}\sum\nolimits_{j=1}^{10^{R+1}} \pi(j).$$

For hit rates estimated via cache probabilities $\pi(k)$, Fig. 7 shows the second order statistics for the same example as in Fig. 6 in time scales up to $10^R = 10^7$. On the time scale $K = 1$, i.e. for single requests, the variability corresponding to the curves shown in Fig. 6 is reflected. In the time scales for $K > 10^3$ the second order statistics develops very similar in all four cases such that $\mu(\pi_{(K)}) \approx \mu(\pi_{(10^3)}) = \sqrt{10^3/K}$.

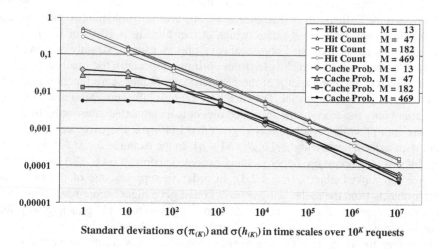

Standard deviations $\sigma(\pi_{(K)})$ and $\sigma(h_{(K)})$ in time scales over 10^K requests

Fig. 7. Second order statistics for LRU caching simulations ($N = 1000$)

Next, we compare the previous 2nd order statistics of the sum of request probabilities of the objects in the cache $\sigma(\pi_{(K)})$ with the 2nd order statistics $\sigma(h_{(k)})$ of the hit rate h, when h is basically computed via the number of hits over the same sequence of requests. On the single request time scale ($K = 1$) we obtain $\sigma(h_{(1)})$ as the standard deviation of a Bernoulli variable

$$\sigma(h_{(1)}) = \sqrt{\sum_p \Pr ob\{\pi(j) = p\} \cdot p \cdot (1 - p)}.$$

In the four cases we obtain $\sigma(h_{(1)}) \approx 0.3006, 0.4335, 0.4998, 0.433$ for $h \approx 0.1$, 0.25, 0.5 and 0.75, respectively. These are the starting points of the set of almost linear curves $\sigma(h_{(k)}) \approx \sigma(h_{(1)})/\sqrt{K}$ in Fig. 7 for 2nd order statistics $\sigma(h_{(k)})$ of the hit count.

We observe that the 2nd order statistic curves $\sigma(h_{(k)})$ stay above the 2nd order statistics of $\sigma(\pi_{(K)})$ on all time scales, although the differences decrease from factors in the range 10-75 on the smallest time scale down to factors 1.5-4 on the largest. Concluding, $\pi_{(K)}$ provides a more precise estimate of the hit rate than the fraction $h_{(k)}$ of hits counted over K requests. This is not surprising because the sum of probabilities of cached objects is a measure based on more detailed information than the hit count.

7 Evaluation Comparing Pure LRU and SG-LRU

Next, we again compare both alternative estimators, the sum of cache probabilities versus the fraction of hits, now for the score-gated SG-LRU caching strategy using the same example ($\beta = 0.8$; $N = 1000$ objects) with independent requests (IRM). The required SG-LRU cache sizes to obtain 10 %, 25 %, 50 % and 75 % hit rate are 2, 13, 87 and 342, respectively. Thus more than half of the LRU cache size is saved by SG-LRU for hit rates ≤ 50 %. In the 10 % examples, SG-LRU is able to hold the two most popular objects almost constantly in a cache, which attract already > 10 % of the requests. Pure LRU puts newly requested objects always on top, causing steadily ongoing fluctuation of cached objects, which is far from optimum especially for small caches.

For SG-LRU, the parameter ρ of the geometrically fading score function has main impact on the 2nd order statistics. For each new request, all scores are reduced by the factor ρ and only the score of the requested object is incremented afterwards. In steady state, the sum of scores of all objects is given by $1/(1 - \rho)$. The expected score of an object with request probability $z(r)$ is $z(r) /(1 - \rho)$. In the example for $M = 2$ with 10 % cache hit rate we choose $\rho = 0.999$ yielding expected scores of 64.6, 37.1 and 26.8 for the three top ranked objects ($r = 1,2,3$). In order to suppress one of the two most popular objects from the cache, another object must get a higher score when requested, which rarely happens. For $\rho \to 1$, SG-LRU converges to the LFU principle such that the most popular objects are kept almost constantly in the cache.

Therefore, the variance in the sum of cache probabilities is diminishing $\sigma(\pi_{(K)}) \to 0$ for $\rho \to 1$, whereas the 2nd order statistics of the hit count for pure LRU is almost unchanged in Fig. 8. Consequently, the difference in the 2nd order statistics between both alternative estimators is much larger, starting from factors in the range 100-1000 on the single request time scale and still having factors 4-10 on the longest time scale. The simulations would need 16-100-fold longer run time in order to compensate for factors 4-10. In general, simulation runs over 10^7 requests turn out to be sufficient to reduce the standard deviation of the hit rate estimator below 0.01 %.

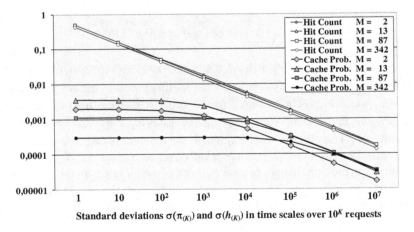

Fig. 8. Second order statistics for SG-LRU caching simulations ($N = 1000$)

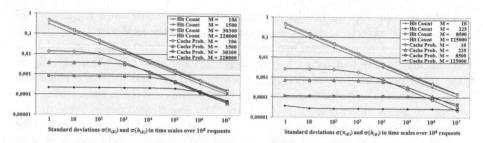

Fig. 9. Second order statistics for LRU and SG-LRU caching simulations ($N = 10^6$)

We consider another example for comparing the hit count and cache probability estimators of the cache hit rate for one million objects ($\beta = 0.9$; $N = 10^6$), which demands for larger caches. Popular web platforms often offer an even larger set of videos, pictures, files or other objects.

The required cache sizes for 10 %, 25 %, 50 % and 75 % hit rate are $M \approx 106$, 1500, 30300 and 228000 with pure LRU and $M \approx 10$, 225, 8500 and 125000 for score-gated LRU, respectively. The ratios 10/106; 225/1500 etc. indicate that the saving potential of SG-LRU cache size is even increasing with the object set. While the hit count estimator again resembles the 2nd order statistics of Figs. 7 and 8, the sum of the cache probabilities often starts already at very low variance. Figure 9 shows that this effect is valid on the single request time scale for both, pure and score gated LRU. For pure LRU, larger cache size has the effect that a set of most popular objects is staying longer in the cache and objects that frequently leave and re-enter the cache have smaller request probabilities. For SG-LRU, we have to choose fading factors $1-10^{-4} \le \rho \le 1-10^{-8}$ in order to get close to the optimum LFU hit rate. As a consequence, the cache content is stabilizing with most top popular objects included when the scores are approaching steady state, thus making the variability of $\sigma(\pi_{(K)})$ very low.

8 Simulations Including Profiles of Varying Popularity of Objects

The independent request model (IRM) ignores changes in the popularity of objects and the emergence of new objects over time. A popularity profile of an object usually starts with a fast growth phase until a maximum request frequency is reached, followed by a longer phase of slow decrease [1, 5, 17, 19]. Therefore we extend the IRM by introducing new objects at a fixed rate, such that a new object is introduced and addressed with probability p_{new} per request. Otherwise, with probability $1 - p_{new}$, the next request is addressing an "old" object of the current object set according to a Zipf distribution. The new object is assigned a popularity rank r_{new} which is uniformly chosen between 1 and N with initial Zipf request probability $z(r_{new})$. In order to preserve unique ranks, all objects in the ranks r_{new}, $r_{new} + 1$, ..., $N - 1$ are shifted to the next rank $r \rightarrow r + 1$ and finally the object in rank N is removed.

In this way, the Zipf distribution is preserved over the whole range 1, ..., N for all requests to "old" objects, such that the model approaches the IRM case for $p_{new} \to 0$. In this model, new objects start at maximum popularity on their smallest rank, which is then steadily incremented for each new object starting from a lower rank. Higher dynamics in popularity, i.e. higher p_{new}, is expected to reduce the cache efficiency, because requests to new objects do not result in cache hits and it can last a while, until the score of a new object reflects its popularity. The investigated model overestimates the impact of new objects on the hit rate in a worst case scenario due to the fact that the phase of growing popularity is skipped and new objects immediately appear on their top rank. On the other hand, the typically observed long phase of slowly decreasing popularity is reflected while the rank of an object is incremented from r_{new} to N. As another realistic effect, highly popular objects starting on a top rank stay essentially longer in the set of relevant objects for caching due to long sojourn times $N/(r \cdot p_{new})$ in top ranks r.

Figure 10 shows the 2nd order statistics of the extended model with new objects emerging with probability $p_{new} = 0.05$ per request for an example with the same Zipf request pattern ($\beta = 0.8$; $N = 1000$ objects) for old objects as in Figs. 7 and 8 (pure LRU, left part of Fig. 10, SG-LRU, right part of Fig. 10). The rate $p_{new} = 0.05$ of requests to new objects for a set of $N = 1000$ objects implies that each object rank r is renewed after a geometrically distributed period with a mean of $N / p_{new} = 20\,000$ requests. In practice, object dynamics and the corresponding rate p_{new} depend on the object type as well as the user population. Caches for a large population attract thousands or even millions of user requests per day, whereas the dynamics in top-10 or top-100 objects per day is estimated to be low in the range of a few percent [1, 6]. Thus the renewal rate of 1/20 000 requests in the example is higher than experienced for large caches.

On the whole, the curves for the 2nd order statistics for the hit rate (almost linear curves) and for the estimator based on the sum of request probabilities of caches objects show similar behaviour as in case of independent requests (IRM) and the required sizes of the cache corresponding to 10 %, 25 %, 50 % and 75 % hit rate only differ for 50 % and 75 % hit rate from the IRM case of Figs. 7 and 8.

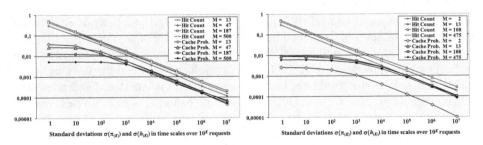

Fig. 10. 2nd order statistics for LRU and SG-LRU for requests with dynamic popularity

9 Conclusions and Outlook

This study on performance and precision of web caching simulations basically confirms the efficiency of simulative caching evaluations. We derived a fast inversion method for a random Zipf rank generator addressing the usual Zipf request pattern for web objects, which seems missing in literature and in tool sets like Mathematica. The 2nd order statistics of variability over multiple time scales is evaluated to control the accuracy of simulation results. In this way, the sum of request probabilities of objects in the cache is confirmed to provide a more precise estimator of the cache hit rate than counting the hits.

The reduction of the standard deviation is often extreme on short time scales and less significant but still present on long time scales. For both estimators, the 2nd order statistics shows a decrease of the standard deviation and corresponding confidence intervals comparable to a set of independent events. Therefore, long simulation runs can efficiently improve the precision of the hit rate estimation in all considered scenarios for different caching strategies in the LRFU spectrum.

Acknowledgements.   This work has received funding from the European Union's Horizon 2020 research and innovation programme 2014-2018 under grant agreement No. 644866. This work reflects only the authors' views and the European Commission is not responsible for any use that may be made of the information it contains.

References

1. Borghol, Y., et al.: Characterizing and modeling popularity of user-generated videos. Perform. Eval. **68**, 1037–1055 (2011)
2. Breslau, L., et al.: Web caching and Zipf-like distributions: Evidence and implications. In: Proceedings of the IEEE INFOCOM, New York, USA (1999)
3. Cha, M., et al.: I tube, you tube, everybody tubes: Analyzing the world's largest user generated content video system, Internet measurement conference IMC 2007. San Diego, USA (2007)
4. Che, H., Tung, Y., Wang, Z.: Hierarchic web caching systems: modeling, design and experimental results. IEEE JSAC **20**(7), 1305–1314 (2002)
5. Devroye, L.: Non-uniform random variate generation. Springer, Heidelberg (1986)
6. Figueiredo, F., et al.: TrendLearner: Early prediction of popularity trends of user generated content (2014). http://arxiv.org/abs/1402.2351
7. Fricker, C., Robert, P., Roberts, J., Sbihi, N.: Impact of traffic mix on caching performance in a content-centric network. In: IEEE INFOCOM Workshops, pp. 310–315 (2012). http://arxiv.org/abs/1202.0108
8. Hasslinger, G.: Efficiency of caching and content delivery in broadband access networks. In: Mukkadim, P. et al. (ed.) Chapter 4 in Advanced Content Delivery, Streaming & Cloud Services, pp. 71–90. Wiley (2014)
9. Hasslinger, G., Hartleb, F.: Content delivery and caching from a network provider's perspective. Spec. Issue Int. Content Delivery, Comput. Netw. **55**, 3991–4006 (2011)

10. Hasslinger, G., Ntougias, K., Hasslinger, F.: A new class of web caching strategies for content delivery. In: Proceedings of the Networks Symposium, Funchal, Madeira, Portugal, pp. 1–7 (2014)
11. Haßlinger, G., Mende, J., Geib, R., Beckhaus, T., Hartleb, F.: Measurement and characteristics of aggregated traffic in broadband access networks. In: Mason, L.G., Drwiega, T., Yan, J. (eds.) ITC 2007. LNCS, vol. 4516, pp. 998–1010. Springer, Heidelberg (2007)
12. Hasslinger, G., Schwahn, A., Hartleb, F.: 2-state (semi-)Markov processes beyond Gilbert-Elliot: Traffic models based on 2nd order statistics. In: Proceedings of the IEEE INFOCOM, Turin, Italy, pp. 1438–1446 (2013)
13. Hefeeda, M., Saleh, O.: Traffic modeling and proportional partial caching for peer-to-peer systems. IEEE/ACM Trans. Netw. **16**(6), 1447–1460 (2008)
14. Lee, D., et al.: LRFU: A spectrum of policies that subsumes the least recently used and least frequently used policies. IEEE Trans. Comput. **50**(12), 1352–1361 (2001)
15. Megiddo, N., Modha, S.: Outperforming LRU with an adaptive replacement cache algorithm. IEEE Comput. **5**, 4–11 (2004)
16. Podlipnik, S., Böszörmenyi, L.: A survey of web cache replacement strategies. ACM Comput. Surv. **35**, 374–398 (2003)
17. Qiu, T., et al.: Modeling channel popularity dynamics in a large IPTV system. In: Proceedings of the 11th ACM SIGMETRICS, Seattle, WA, USA (2009)
18. Shi, et al.: An applicative study of Zipf's law on web caches. Int. J. Inf. Technol. **12**(4), 49–58 (2006)
19. Szabo, G., Huberman, B.A.: Predicting the popularity of online content. ACM Commun. **53**(8), 80–88 (2010)
20. Wolfram Research, Wolfram Language Tutorial (2015). https://reference.wolfram.com/language/tutorial/RandomNumberGeneration.html

PSTeC: A Location-Time Driven Modelling Formalism for Probabilistic Real-Time Systems

Kangli He[1], Yixiang Chen[1(✉)], Min Zhang[2], and Yuanrui Zhang[1]

[1] MoE Engineering Research Center for Software/Hardware Co-design Technology
and Application, East China Normal University, Shanghai, China
kenhkl11@hotmail.com, yxchen@sei.ecnu.edu.cn
[2] Shanghai Key Laboratory of Trustworthy Computing,
East China Normal University, Shanghai, China
mzhang@sei.ecnu.edu.cn

Abstract. Internet of Things (IoT) and Cyber-Physical Systems (CPS) have become important topics in both theory and industry. In some application domains, such as when specifying the behaviour of precision mechanics, we need to include features of spatial-temporal consistency. How to model probabilistic real-time systems in such domains is a challenge. This paper presents a modelling formalism, called PSTeC, for describing the behaviour of probabilistic real-time systems focusing on spatial-temporal consistency with nondeterministic, probabilistic and real-time aspects. The consistency restricts a process to start and finish at the required location and time. Communications between agents is specified by interactive actions. The language we propose is an extension of STeC, which is a specification language for location-aware real-time systems, adding probabilistic operations so as to support the incorporation of probabilistic aspects. We first give a formal definition of the syntax for PSTeC, then focus on the details of its operational semantics, which maps a PSTeC term onto a Probabilistic Spatial-Temporal Transition System (PSTTS) following the structured operational semantics style. A simple example demonstrates the expressiveness of PSTeC.

1 Introduction

Real-time systems are everywhere, spreading from tiny micro chips to continent-spanning power grids. Internet of Things and Cyber-Physical Systems are *en vogue* incarnations of real-time systems featuring nondeterministic, probabilistic and real-time aspects. Often, we need to consider not only the time aspect but also the location of one agent, i.e., we want the behaviour of an agent to start and finish at the required location and time. During the system design phase, we usually use formal methods to model the system and then check whether requirements on correctness do hold. If that is not the case, one tries to fix the model so as to eventually guarantee the absence of errors before beginning implementation. Chen [2] proposes a location-triggered specification language for real-time systems, called STeC, which emphasizes *location*, *time*, and especially on the

© Springer International Publishing Switzerland 2016
A. Remke and B.R. Haverkort (Eds.): MMB & DFT 2016, LNCS 9629, pp. 77–91, 2016.
DOI: 10.1007/978-3-319-31559-1_8

consistency between them. The *location* describes the physical location (e.g., a particular bus station in Münster, Germany) or a state (e.g., "closed") of agents, the *time* focuses on exact physical time (e.g., 5:22pm) at which the behaviour starts or finishes, together with the duration expressing how long the behaviour executes or persists. Intuitively, we aim at allowing such a process to take place and finish at the required location and time, and with the specified execution time, so as to guarantee the spatial-temporal *consistency*. This is very important to ensure the success of tasks in real-time systems concerning precision, such as railway crossing systems or robot hands. The syntax of STeC [2] resembles some classical process algebras, such as CSP and CCS, it uses processes to describe the behaviours of agents and systems, but STeC restricts each atomic or compositional process by a pair of (starting) location and time, and also a duration, i.e., all the processes are triggered by location and time.

STeC has been extended with a hybrid clock to specify both logical and chronometric time aspects of real-time system [4], and is powerful enough for real-time systems, yet it does not support the description or specification of probabilistic aspect as they prevail in probabilistic real-time systems. In this paper, we address this challenge. Formalization of probabilistic systems has become an important topic of investigations in theoretical computer science. Segala [16] defines several probabilistic models and simulation relations for probabilistic processes, and He [10] has extended the Dijkstra's guarded command languages [5] with a probabilistic choice operator to express randomized algorithms. Ying [19] develops formal methods and mathematical tools for modeling and reasoning about programs containing probability information, and Chen [3] has extended probabilistic choice in probabilistic programs to sub-probabilistic choice. In recent decades, model checking methods for probabilistic and probabilistic timed automata have been developed, and implemented among others by Kwiatkowska et al. [13,14]. Hermanns et al. [7,9,11] have developed various model checkers for probabilistic systems, and He [8] uses the probabilistic model checker PRISM [12] to verify a communication protocol under a specific Internet of Things (called WInternet).

As mentioned above, the modelling mechanisms for probabilistic systems are not new, but lack of a formalism for precision real-time systems, in which location and time are the two most important keys to success for tasks. Modern languages, such as Modest [1] and the PRISM language (i.e., guarded commands), are easy for users to learn and are capable to express a probabilistic real-time system model focusing on time, not on locality. This means that the model is driven by (discrete or continuous) time without considering the physical location of each agent. Location and the spatial-temporal consistency are not considered of interest. In contrast, PSTeC not only deals with the basic modelling of probabilistic, nondeterministic and real-time characteristics, but also takes location and spatial-temporal consistency aspects into account. PSTeC is also an easy-to-learn language for non-scientist users such as engineers. Inspired by the general approach to reason about probabilistic systems, we extend the syntax of STeC with additional probabilistic operators equipped with an operational semantics.

This has already proved successful for non-probabilistic real-time system, with the inclusion of probabilistic distributions. Notably, adding a probabilistic feature to the STeC syntax will change the original semantics in its entirety (i.e., not just simply appending additional semantics for the probabilistic features), and also we need to find a suitable way to integrate the features semantically. To do so, we take inspiration from the way the operational semantics of Modest [1,6] lifts structural operational semantics to work with probabilistic distributions over complex structures.

Organisation of the Paper. Section 2 first defines the syntax of PSTeC formally with some useful shorthands to help modelling, and then develops the operational semantics of PSTeC in full detail. A model of a smart spray painting factory is presented as a case in Sect. 3 to show how to use PSTeC to specify location-aware probabilistic real-time systems. Finally, Sect. 4 concludes the paper.

2 Formal Definition of PSTeC

In this section, we present the formalism of PSTeC, as an extension of STeC [2]. To be clear with respect to the description of behaviours of individual **Agent**, respectively the concurrent **System**, we give the definition of PSTeC syntax for agents and systems separately. Processes P for **Agent** and S for **System** are constructed according to the grammar given in Eqs. 1 and 2 respectively.

2.1 Syntax

(1) For each **Agent**:

$$
\begin{aligned}
A &::= \mathrm{Send}_{(l,t)}^{\rightarrow G'}(m,\delta) \mid \mathrm{Get}_{(l,t)}^{\leftarrow G'}(m,\delta) \\
B &::= \mathrm{Act}_{(l,t)}(l',\delta) \mid \mathrm{Stat}_{(l,t)}(\delta) \\
C &::= A \mid B \\
P &::= \mathrm{Stop}_{(l,t)}(\infty) \mid \mathrm{Skip}_{(l,t)}(0) \mid C \mid \\
&\quad P;P \mid P \parallel P \mid P \mathbin{\|} P \mid B \to P \mid \\
&\quad P \trianglerighteq_\delta P \mid P \trianglerighteq \|_{i \in I}\mathrm{Get}_{(l,t)}^{\leftarrow G'}(m_i,\delta) \to P_i \mid \\
&\quad C \to +_{i \in I}\, p_i : \{as_i\}\, P_i
\end{aligned}
\tag{1}
$$

In order to track and record the messages concerned in the system, we define a *storage* for each agent, denoted by $\sigma \subseteq 2^{\mathcal{M}}$ (if necessary, we use $\sigma_{G'}$ to denote the *storage* for agent G'), where $\mathcal{M}$ is the set of messages with the form $m_{G'\upharpoonright G'}$ or m, and $\sum$ as the set of storages (i.e., $\sigma \in \sum$). Note that, $m_{G'\upharpoonright G'}$ represents the message from G to G', and we use $\bot$ to describe unknown agent, i.e., $m_{\bot\upharpoonright G}$ stands for the message from some unknown agent to agent G. The duration δ takes the non-negative real numbers as well as the infinite ∞. If δ takes the ∞ value then it means the process will continue to execute and will not stop, and if δ is 0 then it means that the execution of the process takes no time.

Atomic Processes. We assume that the set of atomic processes $\mathcal{AP}$ are partitioned into a set of *interactions* $\mathcal{A}$, a set of *guards* $\mathcal{B}$, Stop and Skip.

Two interaction processes Send and Get are involved in our language, they are used to describe the communication between two agents through messages without changing locations. Informally, the atomic process $\text{Send}_{(l,t)}^{\to G'}(m,\delta)$ shows that agent G sends message m (i.e., $m_{G\cap G'}$) to the destination agent G' at location l and at time t, taking time δ. Similarly, agent G executes $\text{Get}_{(l,t)}^{\leftarrow G'}(m,\delta)$ to get message m (i.e., $m_{G'\cap G}$) from agent G' by δ duration.

Two most common atomic processes are action Act and state Stat, which are also called *guards* of the Dijkstra's guarded type denoted by B. $\text{Act}_{(l,t)}(l',\delta)$ represents that the action Act is executed at location l and at time t, taking δ duration, when the action finishes, the agent arrives at location l'. $\text{Stat}_{(l,t)}(\delta)$ represents that at location l and at time t, the agent keeps state Stat for δ unit times. Note that, l and l' in B can either represent the location (e.g., $Lapp$) or state (e.g., $Open$) according to different real situations. The *guard* B takes the Boolean/truth values: True T and False F. We use $\mathcal{B}$ to denote the set of guards, i.e., $B \in \mathcal{B}$, then a *truth assignment* for guard B is a function $\nu : \mathcal{B} \to \{T, F\}$, if action $\text{Act}_{(l,t)}(l',\delta)$ finishes within the δ time units and moves to location l', then $\nu(\text{Act}_{(l,t)}(l',\delta)) = T$ (i.e., True), else $\nu(\text{Act}_{(l,t)}(l',\delta)) = F$ (i.e., False). Similarly, if state $\text{Stat}_{(l,t)}(\delta)$ keeps δ time units, then $\nu(\beta_{(l,t)}(\delta)) = T$, else $\nu(\text{Stat}_{(l,t)}(\delta)) = F$. Typically, the valuation **False** formally specify such situation: (1) Action $\text{Act}_{(l,t)}(l',\delta)$ finishes less than or more than δ duration. (2) State $\text{Stat}_{(l,t)}(\delta)$ lasts less than or more than δ time units. 3) When action $\text{Act}_{(l,t)}(l',\delta)$ or state $\text{Stat}_{(l,t)}(\delta)$ finishes, the agent is not at location l'.

Process $\text{Stop}_{(l,t)}(\infty)$ will never finish unless it is interrupted. $\text{Skip}_{(l,t)}(0)$ will finish immediately without taking any time.

Compositional Processes. $P; P$ is the sequential composition. $P_1 \parallel P_2$ represents the parallel, since we only consider the handshake above Send-Get interactions and there is no possible that same message m is sent and got by agent G at the same time, P_1 and P_2 just behave independently. Note that because we have to restrict each atomic process with the triggered location and time as well as the execution duration, so P_1 and P_2 will behave following their own procedure instead of interleaving. $P \parallel P$ represents nondeterministic choice and executes if one of the sub processes executes. $B \to P$ stands for the If-Then statement that if guard B is True (i.e., $\nu(B) = T$) then agent behaves like process P.

Timeout process $P_1 \unrhd_\delta P_2$ behaves as P_1 for δ time units and then behaves as P_2, in another word, process P_1 is interrupted by duration δ. $P \unrhd \parallel_{i\in I} \text{Get}_{(l,t)}^{\leftarrow G'}(m_i,\delta) \to P_i$ is another type of interruption that P executes until agent G finishes Get, which starts at location l and at time t, and gets message m_i, then agent behaves like process P_i.

$C \to +_{i\in I} p_i : \{as_i\} P_i$, which makes the main difference from STeC to PSTeC, represents a probabilistic choice that after C is executed the process behaves as P_i with probability p_i, where C can be arbitrary atomic process except Stop and Skip. p_i denotes the probability measure for process P_i and $\sum_{i\in I} p_i = 1$.

as_i represents a set of assignments with the form: $x_1 = e_1, \ldots, x_n = e_n$, where $x_i \in Var(0 < i \leq n)$ are different variables and e_i can be constants (e.g., $5, closed$), variables (e.g., x_1), or arithmetic expressions (e.g., $x_1 - 5$). The set of as_i is denoted by $\mathbb{A}$. Similarly, we use $\mathcal{C}$ to denote the set of C, and have the *truth assignment* for *probabilistic* guard C, i.e., a function $\rho : \mathcal{C} \rightarrow \{T, F\}$. The truth assignment for the subset $\mathcal{B} \subseteq \mathcal{C}$ is the same as that described in Sect. 2.1. Now we only consider the part composed by A: If action $\mathrm{Get}_{(l,t)}^{\leftarrow G'}(m, \delta)$ finishes successfully within δ time units and there exists m (specifically $m_{G' \upharpoonright G}$) in the storage of G' (i.e., $m_{G' \upharpoonright G} \in \sigma_{G'}$), $\rho(\mathrm{Get}_{(l,t)}^{\leftarrow G'}(m, \delta)) = T$ (i.e., True). If action $\mathrm{Send}_{(l,t)}^{\rightarrow G'}(m, \delta)$ finishes successfully within δ time units and m (specifically $m_{G \upharpoonright G'}$) exists in the storage of G (i.e., $m_{G \upharpoonright G'} \in \sigma_G$), $\rho(\mathrm{Send}_{(l,t)}^{\rightarrow G'}(m, \delta)) = T$ (i.e., True). Considering probabilistic choice process:

$$\mathrm{Closing}_{(L,t)}(L, \theta_1) \rightarrow$$

$$\begin{pmatrix} 0.8 : \{st = closed\}(\mathrm{Send}_{(L,t+\theta_1)}^{\rightarrow T}(CR, 2) \parallel \mathrm{Closed}_{(L,t+\theta_1)}(\theta_2)) \\ + \\ 0.2 : \{st = nclosed\}(\mathrm{Send}_{(L,t+\theta_1)}^{\rightarrow T}(NC, 2) \parallel \mathrm{Closing}_{(L,t+\theta_1)}(L, \theta_3)) \end{pmatrix}$$

where the variable st stands for the state of **Gate** with initial value *open*. **Gate** takes action Closing to try to close itself, and when this action is done after θ_1 time units: (1) The state of **Gate** is closed with probability 0.8, then **Gate** sends message $CROSS$ to **Train** and meanwhile it stays Closed. Or (2) the state is non-closed with 0.2, then **Gate** sends message $NONCROSS$ to **Train** and meanwhile it continues to close.

(2) For the **System**:

$$S ::= P_G \mid S \bowtie S \tag{2}$$

The system process consists of $n(\geq 1)$ agent processes behaving concurrently (i.e., $P_{G_1} \bowtie P_{G_2} \bowtie \ldots \bowtie P_{G_n}$). If there are two different agents G_1 and G_2 in the system, then they handshake on interactions (i.e., if $\mathrm{Send}_{(l_{G_1}, t_{G_1})}^{\rightarrow G_2}(m_{G_1 \upharpoonright G_2}, \delta_{G_1})$ and $\mathrm{Get}_{(l_{G_2}, t_{G_2})}^{\leftarrow G_1}(m_{G_1 \upharpoonright G_2}, \delta_{G_2})$ are ingredients of P_{G_1} and P_{G_2} respectively, and $t_{G_1} = t_{G_1}$, $\delta_{G_1} = \delta_{G_2}$, then P_{G_1} and P_{G_2} should execute the above interactions at the same time), otherwise they behave independently. Similarly, for n agents, if $\mathrm{Send}^{\rightarrow G_i}$ and $\mathrm{Get}^{\leftarrow G_j}$ with the same message (note that we use $m_{G_i \upharpoonright G_j}^k$ to represent $m_{G_i \upharpoonright G_j}$ from G_i to G_j at kth time, where $k \geq 1$, which means different time-stamped messages from the same sender and receiver G_i to G_j) exist in sub processes P_{G_j} and P_{G_i} respectively, then the above restrictions should be guaranteed, otherwise they behave independently.

We use $\mathcal{P}$ to denote the set of agent processes (i.e., $P \in \mathcal{P}$) and $\mathcal{S}$ as the set of system processes (i.e., $S \in \mathcal{S}$). Notation E is used to describe a successful termination, and considering P we always rewrite processes of form $E; P, P; E$, $E \parallel P, P \parallel E$ as P. The extended set of processes are denoted by $\mathcal{P}^E = \mathcal{P} \cup E$. Note that the structure $(\mathcal{P}^E, E, ;, \parallel)$ is a bimonoid, and $(\mathcal{P}^E, E, \parallel)$ is a commutative monoid.

Reed and Roscoe [17] defined a process WAIT t to specify the waiting state lasting for t time units. Same as in [2], we define agent process Wait as:

$$\text{Wait}_{(l,t)}(\delta) \overset{def}{=} \text{Stop}_{(l,t)}(\infty) \unrhd_\delta \text{Skip}_{l,t+\delta}(0) \tag{3}$$

to describe agent G waits for δ time units and does nothing, and

$$\text{Wait}_{(l,t)}^{\leftarrow G'}(m) \overset{def}{=} \text{Stop}_{(l,t)}(\infty) \unrhd \text{Get}_{(l,t')}^{\leftarrow G'}(m,\delta) \rightarrow \text{Skip} \tag{4}$$

to describe agent G waits for the message m coming from G' without changing the location, where $t < t'$.

2.2 Some Constraints

Since giving the syntax of PSTeC, we need to clarify some constraints that ensure the statements are meaningful and practical.

1. For $P_1; P_2$, $P_1 \parallel P_2$ and $P_1 \mid P_2$, the starting location and time of P_2 should be the same as those of P_1 respectively.
2. For $P = P_1 \mid P_2$, If P has successive processes, the finishing location and time of P_1 and P_2 are the same respectively.

2.3 Operational Semantics

An *environment* e for each **Agent** is a triple (a, u, σ), where (a, u) is a *spatial-temporal point*, in which a stands for the location or state, and u is a global clock in the system. We use $\mathcal{E} : \mathcal{L} \times \mathcal{T} \times \sum$ to denote the set of environments, where $\mathcal{L}$ represents the set of location variables and $\mathcal{T}$ represents the set of time variables. We define functions $t(P) : \mathcal{P} \rightarrow \mathcal{T}$ to extract the triggered time ingredient of process P and $l(P) : \mathcal{P} \rightarrow \mathcal{L}$ to extract the triggered location ingredient of process P. Based on the environment (a, u, σ), we give the *truth assignment* for the probabilistic guards C as a function $\mathfrak{T} : \mathcal{C} \times \mathcal{E} \rightarrow \{T, F\}$. $\mathfrak{T}(C)(a, u, \sigma) = T$ if and only if $(l(C), t(C)) = (a, u)$ and $\rho(C) = T$.

We define the set of configurations **Stconf** as $\mathcal{P}^E \times \mathcal{E}$. A configuration is of the form $\langle P, (a, u, \sigma) \rangle$ denoted by π, where P is a agent process or E. The operational semantics for agent process P is given in terms of the *probabilistic spatial-temporal transition system* following the structured operational semantics style (SOS) [15], in which the operational semantic is described as the individual step of its operands. To handle the probabilistic aspects (induced by the probabilistic choice operator, but affecting the entirety of the semantics) we take inspirations from the Modest operational semantics [1,6].

We define *spatial-temporal probability measure* (st-probability measure for short) as a function $\mathbf{P} : \mathbb{A} \times \textbf{Stconf} \rightarrow [0, 1]$ to map an assignment and a configuration onto a probability.

Definition 1. *A probabilistic spatial-temporal transition system (PSTTS) is defined as a subset* $\rightarrow \subseteq \textbf{Stconf} \times \mathbf{P}(\mathbb{A} \times \textbf{Stconf})$.

where $\mathbf{P}$ is a kind of "symbolic" probabilistic distribution over pairs of assignments and target configurations. Intuitively speaking, for $\langle \pi, \mathbf{P}(as_i, \pi_i) \rangle \in \rightarrow$, we write $\pi \rightarrow \mathbf{P}(as_i, \pi_i)$, and once $\pi \rightarrow \mathbf{P}(as_i, \pi_i)$ is executed, the configuration is changed to π_i assigning variables values according to as_i with probability $\mathbf{P}(as_i, \pi_i)$, satisfying for all target pairs of (as_i, π_i) that $\sum_{i \in I} \mathbf{P}(as_i, \pi_i) = 1$.

Let $\mathcal{D}(as, \pi)$ denote the *deterministic* (often called *Dirac*) probability measure that is defined by $\mathcal{D}(as, \pi)(as, \pi) = 1$ and $\mathcal{D}(as, \pi)(as', \pi') = 0$ for all $(as', \pi') \neq (as, \pi)$. Intuitively, the assignment as and configuration π are chosen with probability 1.

Before presenting the operational semantics, we first define some functions. $\iota(P), \tau(P), \kappa(P)$ are extended from [18]: $\iota(P)$ denotes the location where P is finished, $\tau(P)$ denotes the duration that P is executed successfully, and $\kappa(P)$ records the store of messages after process P finished. We use $\ominus(P)(a, u, \sigma) :$ $\mathcal{P} \times \mathcal{L} \times \mathcal{T} \times \mathcal{M} \rightarrow \mathcal{M}$ to record the set of messages that are going to be removed from σ after the execution of process P under the environment (a, u, σ). Function Last is defined to find the max location (which can only be comparable with the same agent). $\iota(P)^{t+\delta}$ and $\kappa(P)^{t+\delta}$ record the location and storage of process P at time $(t + \delta)$ respectively. $\ominus(P)^{t+\delta}$ records the set of messages that are produced at time $(t + \delta)$ in $\ominus(P)$. These functions will be used in the following subsections.

Time Function. The execution time $\tau(P)$ of a process P is defined in Table 1, where [1]: **if** the process has no successive process we simply omit the time of this process since we really don not care under this condition, **else** we restrict $\tau(P_1) = \tau(P_2)$, **so** $1 = \tau(P_1)$, [2]: similarly **if** there is no successors we omit it **else** we restrict $\tau(P_i) = \tau(P_{i+1})$, **so** $2 = t - t(P) + \delta + \tau(P_i)$.

Location Function. We define the location function $\iota(P)$ under the environment (l, t, σ) as in Table 2, where [3]: **if** the process has no successor we omit it **else** we restrict $\iota(P_1) = \iota(P_2)$, **so** $3 = \iota(P_1)$, [4]: **if** no successor we omit it **else** we restrict $\iota(P_1) = \iota(P_2)$, **so** $4 = \iota(P_i)(\iota(P)^{t'+\delta}(l, t, \sigma), t' + \delta, \kappa(P)^{t'+\delta}(l, t, \sigma) \cup \{m_{G'\upharpoonright G}\})$, [5]: $= \text{Last}\{\iota(P_i)(\iota(C)(l, t, \sigma), t + \tau(C), \kappa(C)(l, t, \sigma))\} \mid i \in I$.

Message Function. The message function $\kappa(P)$ under the environment (l, t, σ) is defined in the Table 3, where [6]: notice that, we allow message redundancy, i.e., if the parallel process is chosen to behave as P_1, then $\kappa(P_1) \subseteq \kappa(P_1 \| P_2)$, or if P_2 is chosen, then $\kappa(P_2) \subseteq \kappa(P_1 \| P_2)$, [7]: $= \cup_{i \in I} \kappa(P_i)(\iota(P)^{t'+\delta}(l, t, \sigma), t' + \delta, \kappa(P)^{t'+\delta}(l, t, \sigma) \cup \{m_{G'\upharpoonright G}\})$.

Now we first present the operational semantics of agent process and then the operational semantics for a more complex system process.

Basic Processes. Behaviour $\text{Stop}_{(l,t+1)}(\infty)$ will not terminate before it is interrupted and $\text{Skip}_{(l,t)}(0)$ terminates immediately, both of them will neither change the value of any variable nor the storage of the agent. When the spatial-temporal

Table 1. Time function $\tau(P)$.

$\tau(\text{Stop}_{(l,t)}(\infty)) = \infty$	$\tau(\text{Skip}_{(l,t)}(0)) = 0$
$\tau(\text{Send}_{(l,t)}^{\to G'}(m,\delta)) = \delta$	$\tau(\text{Get}_{(l,t)}^{\leftarrow G'}(m,\delta)) = \delta$
$\tau(\text{Act}_{(l,t)}(l',\delta)) = \delta$	$\tau(\text{Stat}_{(l,t)}(\delta)) = \delta$
$\tau(P_1; P_2) = \tau(P_1) + \tau(P_2)$	$\tau(P_1 \parallel P_2) = max\{\tau(P_1), \tau(P_2)\}$
$\tau(P_1 \mid P_2)^1$	$\tau(B \to P) = \tau(B) + \tau(P)$
$\tau(P_1 \trianglerighteq_\delta P_2) = \delta + \tau(P_2)$	$\tau(P \trianglerighteq \parallel_{i \in I} \text{Get}_{(l,t)}^{\leftarrow G'}(m_i,\delta) \to P_i)^2$
$\tau(C \to +_{i \in I}\ p_i : \{as_i\}\ P_i) = \tau(C) + max\{\tau(P_i)\} \mid i \in I$	

Table 2. Location function $\iota(P)$.

$\iota(\text{Stop}_{(l,t)}(\infty))(l,t,\sigma) = l$	$\iota(\text{Skip}_{(l,t)}(0))(l,t,\sigma) = l$
$\iota(\text{Send}_{(l,t)}^{\to G'}(m,\delta))(l,t,\sigma) = l$	$\iota(\text{Get}_{(l,t)}^{\leftarrow G'}(m,\delta))(l,t,\sigma) = l$
$\iota(\text{Act}_{(l,t)}(l',\delta))(l,t,\sigma) = l'$	$\iota(\text{Stat}_{(l,t)}(\delta))(l,t,\sigma) = l$
$\iota(P_1; P_2)(l,t,\sigma) = \iota(P_2)(\iota(P_1)(l,t,\sigma), t + \tau(P_1), \kappa(P_1)(l,t,\sigma))$	
$\iota(P_1 \parallel P_2)(l,t,\sigma) = \text{Last}\{\iota(P_1)(l,t,\sigma), \iota(P_2)(l,t,\sigma)\}$	
$\iota(P_1 \mid P_2)(l,t,\sigma)^3$	$\iota(B \to P) = \iota(P)(\iota(B)(l,t,\sigma), t + \tau(B), \sigma)$
$\iota(P_1 \trianglerighteq_\delta P_2)(l,t,\sigma) = \iota(P_2)(\iota(P_1)^{t+\delta}(l,t,\sigma), t + \delta, \kappa(P_1)^{t+\delta}(l,t,\sigma))$	
$\iota(P \trianglerighteq \parallel_{i \in I}\text{Get}_{(l',t')}^{\leftarrow G'}(m_i,\delta) \to P_i)(l,t,\sigma)^4$	$\iota(C \to +_{i \in I}\ p_i : \{as_i\}\ P_i)(l,t,\sigma)^5$

Table 3. Message function $\kappa(P)$.

$\kappa(\text{Stop}_{(l,t)}(\infty))(l,t,\sigma) = \sigma$	$\kappa(\text{Skip}_{(l,t)}(0))(l,t,\sigma) = \sigma$
$\kappa(\text{Send}_{(l,t)}^{\to G'}(m,\delta))(l,t,\sigma) = \sigma \setminus \{m_{G'^\uparrow G'}\}$	$\kappa(\text{Get}_{(l,t)}^{\leftarrow G'}(m,\delta))(l,t,\sigma) = \sigma \cup \{m_{G'^\uparrow G}\}$
$\kappa(\text{Act}_{(l,t)}(l',\delta))(l,t,\sigma) = \sigma$	$\kappa(\text{Stat}_{(l,t)}(\delta))(l,t,\sigma) = \sigma$
$\kappa(P_1; P_2)(l,t,\sigma) = \kappa(P_2)(\iota(P_1)(l,t,\sigma), t + \tau(P_1), \kappa(P_1)(l,t,\sigma))$	
$\kappa(P_1 \parallel P_2)(l,t,\sigma) = \kappa(P_1)(l,t,\sigma) \cup \kappa(P_2)(l,t,\sigma) \setminus (\ominus(P_1)(l,t,\sigma) \cup \ominus(P_2)(l,t,\sigma))$	
$\kappa(P_1 \mid P_2)(l,t,\sigma) = \kappa(P_1)(l,t,\sigma) \cup \kappa(P_2)(l,t,\sigma)^6$	
$\kappa(B \to P) = \kappa(P)(\iota(B)(l,t,\sigma), t + \tau(B), \sigma)$	
$\kappa(P_1 \trianglerighteq_\delta P_2)(l,t,\sigma) = \kappa(P_2)(\iota(P_1)^{t+\delta}(l,t,\sigma), t + \delta, \kappa(P_1)^{t+\delta}(l,t,\sigma))$	
$\kappa(P \trianglerighteq \parallel_{i \in I}\text{Get}_{(l',t')}^{\leftarrow G'}(m_i,\delta) \to P_i)(l,t,\sigma)^7$	
$\kappa(C \to +_{i \in I}\ p_i : \{as_i\}\ P_i)(l,t,\sigma) = \cup_{i \in I}\kappa(P_i)(\iota(C)(l,t,\sigma), t + \tau(C), \kappa(C)(l,t,\sigma))$	

point coincides the triggered location and time of the processes, the operational semantics read:

$$\frac{(a, u) = (l, t)}{\langle \text{Stop}_{(l,t)}(\infty), (a, u, \sigma) \rangle \to \mathcal{D}(\emptyset, \pi)}$$

where $\pi = \langle \text{Stop}_{(l,t)}(\infty), (l, t, \sigma) \rangle$, and

$$\frac{(a, u) = (l, t)}{\langle \text{Skip}_{(l,t)}(0), (a, u, \sigma) \rangle \to \mathcal{D}(\emptyset, \pi)}$$

where $\pi = \langle E, (l, t, \sigma) \rangle$.

Since the assignments are partial functions, $\emptyset$ stands for the empty assignment that no variable changes its value.

Interactions Send and Get specify the interaction or handshaking between two agents by messages. Send sends a message m (specifically $m_{G \vdash G'}$) from storage G to the storage of G'. Note that the procedure that m is added into $\sigma_{G'}$ is not presented here but in the operational semantics of Get process in agent G'. Whilst, Get gets a message m (specifically $m_{G' \vdash G}$) from $\sigma_{G'}$. Similarly, the procedure of judgement for $m_{G' \vdash G} \in \sigma_{G'}$ is presented in the operational semantics of Send in G. In fact the above two procedures will be presented in the operational semantics of system process in later subsection. No assignments are executed:

$$\frac{(a, u) = (l, t) \wedge m_{G \vdash G'} \in \sigma}{\langle \text{Send}_{(l,t)}^{\to G'}(m, \delta), (a, u, \sigma) \rangle \to \mathcal{D}(\emptyset, \pi)}$$

where $\pi = \langle E, (l, t + \delta, \sigma \setminus \{m_{G \vdash G'}\}) \rangle$, and

$$\frac{(a, u) = (l, t)}{\langle \text{Get}_{(l,t)}^{\leftarrow G'}(m, \delta), (a, u, \sigma) \rangle \to \mathcal{D}(\emptyset, \pi)}$$

where $\pi = \langle E, (l, t + \delta, \sigma \cup \{m_{G' \vdash G}\}) \rangle$.

We require that action Act takes δ time units to execute successfully moving to location l' and Stat keeps δ without changing the location. No message are involved and both processes execute no assignments:

$$\frac{(a, u) = (l, t)}{\langle \text{Act}_{(l,t)}(l', \delta), (a, u, \sigma) \rangle \to \mathcal{D}(\emptyset, \pi)}$$

where $\pi = \langle E, (l', t + \delta, \sigma) \rangle$, and

$$\frac{(a, u) = (l, t)}{\langle \text{Stat}_{(l,t)}(\delta), (a, u, \sigma) \rangle \to \mathcal{D}(\emptyset, \pi)}$$

where $\pi = \langle E, (l, t + \delta, \sigma) \rangle$.

Sequential Composition. $P_1; P_2$ executes P_1 until it successfully terminates, then it continues with the execution of P_2. When sequential process executes $\delta_0 \leq \tau(P_1; P_2)$ time units, like in [1], we define the operational semantics as:

$$\frac{\langle P_1, (a, u, \sigma)\rangle \rightarrow \mathbf{P}}{\langle P_1; P_2, (a, u, \sigma)\rangle \rightarrow \mathbf{P} \circ \mathbf{M}_;^{-1}}$$

where

$$\mathbf{M}_;(as, \langle P_1', e\rangle) \stackrel{def}{=} \begin{cases} \langle as, \langle P_1'; P_2, e\rangle\rangle & \text{if } P_1' \neq E \\ \langle as, \langle P_2, e\rangle\rangle & \text{if } P_1' = E \end{cases}$$

and $e = (\iota(P_1)^{u+\delta_0}(a, u, \sigma), u + \delta_0, \kappa(P_1)^{u+\delta_0}(a, u, \sigma))$. The inverse of $\mathbf{M}_;$ is used in $\mathbf{P} \circ \mathbf{M}_;^{-1}$ to retrieve the st-probability measure for the sequential composition from the st-probability measure assigned by $\mathbf{P}$ to the first component of a sequential composition.

Parallel Composition. As mentioned in Sect. 2.1, parallel composition $P_1 \parallel P_2$ in agent process simply behaves independently:

$$\frac{\langle P_1, (a, u, \sigma)\rangle \rightarrow \mathbf{P}_1 \wedge \langle P_2, (a, u, \sigma)\rangle \rightarrow \mathbf{P}_2}{\langle P_1 \parallel P_2, (a, u, \sigma)\rangle \rightarrow (\mathbf{P}_1 \times \mathbf{P}_2) \circ \mathbf{M}_\parallel^{-1}}$$

where $(\mathbf{P}_1 \times \mathbf{P}_2)(\Omega_1, \Omega_2) \stackrel{def}{=} \mathbf{P}_1(\Omega_1) \cdot \mathbf{P}_2(\Omega_2)$ for all Ω_1 and Ω_2, corresponding to the product of two probability spaces, and

$$\mathbf{M}_\parallel(\langle as_1, \langle P_1', e_1\rangle\rangle, \langle as_2, \langle P_2', e_2\rangle\rangle)$$
$$\stackrel{def}{=} \begin{cases} \langle as_1 \cup as_2, \langle P_1' \parallel P_2', e\rangle\rangle & \text{if } P_1' \neq E \text{ or } P_2' \neq E \\ \langle as_1 \cup as_2, \langle E, e\rangle\rangle & \text{if } P_1' = E \text{ and } P_2' = E \end{cases}$$

where $e_1 = (l_1, u + \delta_0, \sigma_1), e_2 = (l_2, u + \delta_0, \sigma_2), e = (\text{Last}\{l_1, l_2\}, u + \delta_0, \sigma_\parallel)$, in which $l_1 = \iota(P_1)^{u+\delta_0}(a, u, \sigma), \sigma_1 = \kappa(P_1)^{u+\delta_0}(a, u, \sigma), l_2 = \iota(P_2)^{u+\delta_0}(a, u, \sigma), \sigma_2 = \kappa(P_2)^{u+\delta_0}(a, u, \sigma), \sigma_\parallel = \sigma_1 \cup \sigma_2 \setminus (\ominus(P_1)^{u+\delta_0}(a, u, \sigma) \cup \ominus(P_2)^{u+\delta_0}(a, u, \sigma))$.

Nondeterministic Choice. $P_1 \| P_2$ is the usual alternative composition, only one alternative is chosen nondeterministically, the operational semantics is:

$$\frac{\langle P_i, (a, u, \sigma)\rangle \rightarrow \mathbf{P}_i \quad (i \in \{1, 2\})}{\langle P_1 \| P_2, (a, u, \sigma)\rangle \rightarrow \mathbf{P}_i}.$$

If-Then. When the guard B is true under environment (a, u, σ), agent behaves as process P:

$$\frac{\langle B, (a, u, \sigma)\rangle \rightarrow \mathbf{P} \wedge \mathfrak{T}(B)(a, u, \sigma) = T}{\langle B \rightarrow P, (a, u, \sigma)\rangle \rightarrow \mathbf{P} \circ \mathbf{M}_\rightarrow^{-1}}$$

where $\mathbf{M}_\rightarrow(\langle as, \langle E, e\rangle\rangle) \stackrel{def}{=} \langle as, \langle P, e\rangle\rangle$, and $e = (\iota(B)(a, u, \sigma), t(B) + \tau(B), \sigma)$.

Interruption. Timeout interruption $P_1 \trianglerighteq_\delta P_2$ will behave like P_1 before δ time units and then as P_2. When the process executes $\delta_0 \leq \delta$ time units:

$$\frac{\langle P_1, (a, u, \sigma)\rangle \to \mathbf{P}}{\langle P_1 \trianglerighteq_\delta P_2, (a, u, \sigma)\rangle \to \mathbf{P} \circ \mathbf{M}_{\trianglerighteq_\delta}^{-1}}$$

where

$$\mathbf{M}_{\trianglerighteq_\delta}(\langle as, \langle P_1', e\rangle\rangle) \stackrel{def}{=} \begin{cases} \langle as, \langle P_1' \trianglerighteq_{\delta-\delta_0} P_2, e\rangle\rangle & \text{if } \delta_0 < \delta \\ \langle as, \langle P_2, e\rangle\rangle & \text{if } \delta_0 = \delta \end{cases}$$

where $e = (\iota(P_1)^{u+\delta_0}(a, u, \sigma), u + \delta_0, \kappa(P_1)^{u+\delta_0}(a, u, \sigma))$.

Let

$$Q_i \equiv \mathrm{Get}_{(l,t)}^{\leftarrow G'}(m_i, \delta)$$

Get interruption $P \trianglerighteq \|_{i \in I} \mathrm{Get}_{(l,t)}^{\leftarrow G'}(m_i, \delta) \to P_i$ behaves like P_1 until the agent receives one message m_i successfully, then it behaves as P_i. When get interruption process executes δ_0 time units:

$$\frac{\langle P, (a, u, \sigma)\rangle \to \mathbf{P}_1 \wedge \langle Q_i, (l, t, \sigma')\rangle \to \mathbf{P}_2 \wedge m_{iG' \upharpoonright G} \in \sigma_{G'}}{\langle P \trianglerighteq \|_{i \in I} Q_i \to P_i, (a, u, \sigma)\rangle \to (\mathbf{P}_1 \times \mathbf{P}_2) \circ \mathbf{M}_{\trianglerighteq_{Get}}^{-1}}$$

where $\sigma' = \kappa(P)^t(a, u, \sigma)$ and

$$\mathbf{M}_{\trianglerighteq_{Get}}(\langle as_1, \langle P', e_1\rangle\rangle, \langle as_2, \langle Q_i', e_2\rangle\rangle)$$

$$\stackrel{def}{=} \begin{cases} \langle as_1 \cup as_2, \langle P' \trianglerighteq Q_i \to P_i, e\rangle\rangle & \text{if } u + \delta_0 < t \\ \langle as_1 \cup as_2, \langle P' \trianglerighteq Q_i' \to P_i, e\rangle\rangle & \text{if } u + \delta_0 \geq t \text{ and } Q_i' \neq E \\ \langle as_1 \cup as_2, \langle P_i, e\rangle\rangle & \text{if } u + \delta_0 \geq t \text{ and } Q_i' = E \end{cases}$$

where $e_1 = (l_1, u + \delta_0, \sigma_1), e_2 = (l_2, u + \delta_0, \sigma_2), e = (\mathrm{Last}\{l_1, l_2\}, u + \delta_0, \sigma_{\trianglerighteq_{Get}})$, in which $l_1 = \iota(P)^{u+\delta_0}(a, u, \sigma), \sigma_1 = \kappa(P)^{u+\delta_0}(a, u, \sigma), l_2 = \iota(Q_i)^{u+\delta}(l, t, \sigma'), \sigma_2 = \kappa(Q_i)^{u+\delta_0}(l, t, \sigma'), \sigma_{\trianglerighteq_{Get}} = \sigma_1 \cup \sigma_2 \setminus (\ominus(P)^{u+\delta_0}(a, u, \sigma) \cup \ominus(Q_i)^{u+\delta_0}(l, t, \sigma'))$.

Probabilistic Choice. Process $C \to +_{i \in I} p_i : \{as_i\} P_i$ first behaves as C and when C terminates successfully it randomly selects an alternative $i \in I$ according to the probability p_i, performs an assignment according to as_i, and continues executing P_i:

$$\frac{(a, u) = (l(C), t(C)) \wedge \mathfrak{T}(C)(a, u, \sigma) = T}{\langle C \to +_{i \in I} p_i : \{as_i\} P_i, (a, u, \sigma)\rangle \to \mathbf{P}}$$

where $\mathbf{P}(\langle as_i, \pi_i\rangle) = p_i$, in which π_i stands for the ith configuration with ith process P_i and ith environment e_i (i.e., $\pi_i = \langle P_i, e_i\rangle$), note that $\sum_{i \in I} p_i = 1$.

Operational Semantics for System Process. When different agents behave concurrently in the system, they have their own traces of location and storages but the same global time. The concurrent operation between two processes will be like handshaking over the interactions (i.e., Send and Get) or behave independently otherwise. Similarly, unlike interleaving, since each process has to follow the specification, the operational semantics for the system process is actually combined by the operational semantics of sub agent processes with checking whether the handshaking is legal (i.e., $\text{Send}_{(l,t)}^{\rightarrow G_1}(m,\delta)$ and $\text{Get}_{(l,t)}^{\leftarrow G_2}(m,\delta)$ in P_{G_2} and P_{G_1} respectively with the same triggered time, duration and message) if there exists one. We define a configuration $\textbf{Stconf}_S$ for a system process as $\mathcal{S} \times \mathcal{E}^n$, where n stands for the number of sub agent processes in S, a system configuration of the form $\langle S, EN^n \rangle$ is denoted by π_S, where $S = P_{G_1} \bowtie P_{G_2} \bowtie \ldots \bowtie P_{G_n}$ and $EN^n = (e_1, e_2, \ldots, e_n)$. We use $\pi_{S_i} = \langle P_{G_i}, e_i \rangle$ to denote the configuration for ith sub agent process, where $e_i = (a_i, u, \sigma_i)$ (they have the same u since it stands for the global time).

Definition 2. *The* operational semantics for system process S *with* n *sub agent processes is defined as a subset* $\rightarrow_S \subseteq \textbf{Stconf}_S \times \textbf{P}_S(\mathbb{A}^n \times \textbf{Stconf}_S)$.

where $\textbf{P}_S : \mathbb{A}^n \times \textbf{Stconf}_S \rightarrow [0,1]$ is a function to map n-element set of assignments and n-element configurations onto a probability.

For $\langle \pi_S, \textbf{P}_S(AS^n, \pi'_S) \rangle \in \rightarrow_S$, where $AS^n = (as_1, as_2, \ldots, as_n)$, we write $\pi_S \rightarrow_S \textbf{P}_S(AS^n, \pi'_S)$, where $\pi_{S_i} \rightarrow \textbf{P}(as_i, \pi'_{S_i})$. Once $\pi_S \rightarrow_S \textbf{P}_S(AS^n, \pi'_S)$ is executed, the system configuration is changed to π'_S with sub agent process P_{G_i} assigning its variables values according to as_i with probability $\textbf{P}_S(\langle AS^n, \pi'_S \rangle) = \prod_{i \in n} \textbf{P}(\langle as_i, \pi'_{S_i} \rangle)$. Particularly, the operational semantics of system process with one agent process is same as that of the latter, i.e., we simply rewrite $\rightarrow_S$ as $\rightarrow$. The operational semantics for system process S with $n(\geq 2)$ sub agent processes $P_{G_1}, \ldots, P_{G_n}$ is presented as follows:

$$\frac{\langle P_{G_1}, e_1 \rangle \rightarrow \textbf{P}_{G_1} \wedge \ldots \wedge \langle P_{G_n}, e_n \rangle \rightarrow \textbf{P}_{G_n} \wedge \textbf{CheckLegal}}{\langle P_{G_1} \bowtie \ldots \bowtie P_{G_n}, EN^n \rangle \rightarrow_S (\textbf{P}_{G_1} \times \ldots \times \textbf{P}_{G_n}) \circ \textbf{M}_{\bowtie}^{-1}}$$

where

$$\textbf{M}_{\bowtie}(\langle as_1, \langle P'_{G_1}, e'_1 \rangle \rangle, \ldots, \langle as_n, \langle P'_{G_n}, e'_n \rangle \rangle) \overset{def}{=} \langle AS^n, \langle P'_{G_1} \bowtie \ldots \bowtie P'_{G_n}, EN^{n'} \rangle \rangle$$

and **CheckLegal** is a function to check whether the interactions are legal in S, i.e., for each pair $\text{Send}_{(l_i,t_i)}^{\rightarrow G_j}(m_i, \delta_i)$ and $\text{Get}_{(l_j,t_j)}^{\leftarrow G_i}(m_j, \delta_j)$ in P_{G_i} and P_{G_j} respectively with $t_i = t_j$, if $m_i = m_j$ and $\delta_i = \delta_j$, then it returns **True**, else returns **False**. If no such pair exists, **CheckLegal** returns **True**.

3   Automatic Spray Painting of a Custom Car

Here we consider one smart spray painting factory for custom cars using Internet of Things techniques. The whole factory is 'alive' that every part (i.e., physical thing) of the system is able to sense the environment, communicate with each other and react in real time. Once a car is placed at the door of factory, it has been loaded with all its booking information, including the car number, the customer name, the timestamp of each event, the map and the detailed spray painting requirements (e.g., patterns, colors and paint material). The car moves automatically following the map. When starting approach the robots at location $Lappr$, it sends all necessary information (AP) to the robots. After receiving the information, the robots check the store of all paint material. They would find lack of some material with probability p_{fail}. Then the robots send message NE (which is 'do Not Enter') to forbid the car to enter the workstation. When the car receives the message at location $Lpass$, it stops progressively to location $Lstop$. Meanwhile the robots automatically refill the material, then send message ET (which is 'EnTer') to allow the car to enter. After receiving the message, the car continues to move towards the robots. When the automatic spray painting finishes, the robots send message OK to the car. Then the car moves to location $Lleav$ to end its procedure. We first establish two agent processes **Car** and **Robot**, with messages $\{AP, NE, ET, OK\}$, actions $\{Send, Get, Run, Stopping, Appr, Refill, Check\}$, states $\{Idle, Painting\}$, and locations $\{Lappr, Lpass, Lstop, Lleav\}$. We assume the message transmitting time is 2 unit time.

The agent process **Car** is defined as:

$$(\text{Send}^{\to R}_{(Lappr,t)}(AP,2) \parallel \text{Appr}_{(Lappr,t)}(Lpass,\delta_1)) \unrhd$$

$$\left(\begin{array}{l} \text{Get}^{\leftarrow R}_{(Lpass,t+\delta_1-2)}(ET,2) \to \text{Appr}_{(Lpass,t+\delta_1)}(L,\delta_2); \\ \qquad \text{Wait}^{\leftarrow R}_{(L,t+\delta_1+\delta_2)}(OK,\delta_3); \text{Run}_{(L,t+\delta_1+\delta_2+\delta_3)}(Lleave,\delta_4) \to \text{Stop} \\ \rotatebox{90}{$\parallel$} \\ \text{Get}^{\leftarrow R}_{(Lpass,t+\delta_1-2)}(NE,2) \to \text{Stopping}_{(Lpass,t+\delta_1)}(Lstop,\delta_5); \\ \qquad \text{Wait}^{\leftarrow R}_{(Lstop,t+\delta_1+\delta_5)}(ET,\delta_6); \text{Appr}_{(Lstop,t+\delta_1+\delta_5+\delta_6)}(L,\delta_7); \\ \qquad \text{Wait}^{\leftarrow R}_{(L,t+t_1)}(OK,\delta_8); \text{Run}_{(L,t+t_1+\delta_8)}(Lleave,\delta_9) \to \text{Stop} \end{array} \right)$$

where $t_1 = \delta_1 + \delta_5 + \delta_6 + \delta_7$.

The agent process **Robot** is defined as:

$$\text{Idle}_{(L,t_0)}(\infty) \unrhd$$

$$\text{Get}^{\leftarrow C}_{(L,t)}(AP,2) \to \text{Check}_{(L,t+2)}(L,\theta_1) \to$$

$$\left(\begin{array}{l} 0.8 : \{st = satisfied\} \\ \quad (\text{Send}^{\to C}_{(L,t+2+\theta_1)}(ET,2) \parallel \text{Wait}_{(L,t+2+\theta_1)}(\theta_2)) \unrhd_{\theta_2} \\ \qquad \text{Painting}_{(L,t+2+\theta_1+\theta_2)}(\theta_3); \text{Send}^{\to C}_{(L,t+t_2)}(OK,2); \\ \qquad \text{Idle}_{(L,t+t_2+2)}(\infty) \\ + \\ 0.2 : \{st = lack\} \\ \quad (\text{Send}^{\to C}_{(L,t+2+\theta_1)}(NE,2) \parallel \text{Refill}_{(L,t+2+\theta_1)}(L,\theta_4)); \\ \quad (\text{Send}^{\to C}_{(L,t+2+\theta_1+\theta_4)}(ET,2) \parallel \text{Wait}_{(L,t+2+\theta_1+\theta_4)}(\theta_5)) \unrhd_{\theta_5} \\ \qquad \text{Painting}_{(L,t+t_3)}(\theta_6); \text{Send}^{\to C}_{(L,t+t_3+\theta_6)}(OK,2); \\ \qquad \text{Idle}_{(L,t+t_3+\theta_6+2)}(\infty) \end{array} \right)$$

where variable st stands for the status of required material with initial value $satisfied$, and $t_2 = 2 + \theta_1 + \theta_2 + \theta_3$, $t_3 = 2 + \theta_1 + \theta_4 + \theta_5$.

The PSTeC model for the smart spray painting factory is specified as the system process: **Car** $\bowtie$ **Robot**, and we restrict that $t + \delta_1 - 2 = t + 2 + \theta_1, t + \delta_1 + \delta_2 + \delta_3 = t + t_2 + 2, t + \delta_1 + \delta_5 + \delta_6 = t + 2 + \theta_1 + \theta_4 + 2, t + t_1 + \delta_8 = t + t_3 + \theta_6 + 2$ for each pair of handshaking interactions.

4   Conclusion

In this paper, we have developed a modelling formalism, PSTeC, for specification of probabilistic real-time systems triggered by location and time. For this, we have extended the spatial-temporal consistency language STeC by adding probabilistic operations so that PSTeC, apart from location specifics, supports the specifation of nondeterministic, real-time and probabilistic aspects of behaviours. Considering concurrency between agents is far different from behaviours of one agent since sub agent processes in one system process have different traces of location and different message storages. We defined the syntax of PSTeC for system and agent separately, with some useful shorthands. Then we provided full details of the operational semantics, using the structured operational semantics style. After establishing the formalism of PSTeC, we refined the STeC model of a smart spray painting factory with additional probabilistic operations reflecting the existing probabilistic behaviours.

Recently, we have been working on a denotational semantics for PSTeC aiming at soundness as well as completeness. A tool to support building PSTeC models and doing verification is under development.

Acknowledgments. This work is supported by the National Basic Research Program of China (Grant No. 2011CB302802), the Innovation Group Project of the National Natural Science Foundation (Grant No. 61321064), the National Natural Science Foundation of China (Grant No. 61370100), the NSFC projects (Grant No. 61361136002 and No. 61202105) and Shanghai Knowledge Service Platform for Trustworthy Internet of Things (Grant No. ZF1213). Part of this work was done while the first author was visiting Saarland University, Germany. The authors thank Holger Hermanns (Saarland University, Germany) for his valuable contributions and discussions and helpful comments on the structure and contents of this paper. The authors would also like to thank the anonymous referees for their invaluable comments and suggestions.

References

1. Bohnenkamp, H., DArgenio, P.R., Hermanns, H., Katoen, J.: Modest: a compositional modeling formalism for hard and softly timed systems. IEEE Trans. Softw. Eng. **32**(10), 812–830 (2006)
2. Chen, Y.: STeC: a location-triggered specification language for real-timesystems. In: 2012 15th IEEE International Symposium on Object/Component/Service-Oriented Real-Time DistributedComputing Workshops (ISORCW), pp.1–6. IEEE (2012)

3. Chen, Y., Wu, H.: Semantics of sub-probabilistic programs. Front. Comput. Sci. China **2**(1), 29–38 (2008)
4. Chen, Y., Zhang, Y.: A hybrid clock system related to STeC language. In: 2014 IEEE EighthInternational Conference on Software Security and Reliability-Companion (SERE-C), pp. 199–203. IEEE (2014)
5. Dijkstra, E.W.: A Discipline of Programming, vol. 1. Prentice-Hall, Englewood Cliffs (1976)
6. Hahn, E.M., Hartmanns, A., Hermanns, H., Katoen, J.: A compositional modelling and analysis framework for stochastic hybrid systems. Formal Methods Syst. Des. **43**(2), 191–232 (2013)
7. Hahn, E.M., Hermanns, H., Wachter, B., Zhang, L.: INFAMY: an infinite-state markov model checker. In: Bouajjani, A., Maler, O. (eds.) CAV 2009. LNCS, vol. 5643, pp. 641–647. Springer, Heidelberg (2009)
8. He, K., Zhang, M., He, J., Chen, Y.: Probabilistic model checking of pipe protocol. In: 2015 International Symposium on Theoretical Aspects of Software Engineering (TASE), pp. 135–138. IEEE (2015)
9. Hermanns, H., Katoen, J.P., Meyer-Kayser, J., Siegle, M.: ETMCC: model checking performability properties of markov chains. In: Null, p. 673. IEEE (2003)
10. Jifeng, H., Seidel, K., McIver, A.: Probabilistic models for the guarded command language. Sci. Comput. Program. **28**(2), 171–192 (1997)
11. Katoen, J., Zapreev, I.S., Hahn, E.M., Hermanns, H., Jansen, D.N.: The ins and outs of the probabilistic model checker MRMC. Perform. Eval. **68**(2), 90–104 (2011)
12. Kwiatkowska, M., Norman, G., Parker, D.: PRISM 4.0: verification of probabilistic real-time systems. In: Gopalakrishnan, G., Qadeer, S. (eds.) CAV 2011. LNCS, vol. 6806, pp. 585–591. Springer, Heidelberg (2011)
13. Kwiatkowska, M., Norman, G., Segala, R., Sproston, J.: Automatic verification of real-time systems with discrete probability distributions. Theor. Comput. Sci. **282**(1), 101–150 (2002)
14. Kwiatkowska, M., Norman, G., Sproston, J., Wang, F.: Symbolic model checking for probabilistic timed automata. Inf. Comput. **205**(7), 1027–1077 (2007)
15. Plotkin, G.D.: A structural approach to operational semantics (1981)
16. Segala, R., Lynch, N.: Probabilistic simulations for probabilistic processes. In: Jonsson, B., Parrow, J. (eds.) CONCUR 1994. LNCS, vol. 836, pp. 481–496. Springer, Heidelberg (1994)
17. Shiryaev, A.N.: Probability. Graduate Texts in Mathematics, vol. 95 (1996)
18. Wu, H., Chen, Y., Zhang, M.: On denotational semantics of spatial-temporal consistency language-stec. In: 2013 International Symposium on Theoretical Aspects of Software Engineering (TASE), pp. 113–120. IEEE (2013)
19. Ying, M.: Reasoning about probabilistic sequential programs in a probabilistic logic. Acta Informatica **39**(5), 315–389 (2003)

Analysis of Hierarchical Semi-Markov Processes with Parallel Regions

Daniel Homm[✉] and Reinhard German

Department of Computer Science 7, University Erlangen-Nuremberg,
Martensstr. 3, 91058 Erlangen, Germany
{daniel.homm,reinhard.german}@fau.de

Abstract. We consider state charts with generally distributed state sojourn times and with parallel regions in composite states. This corresponds to semi-Markov processes (SMPs) with parallel regions consisting again of SMPs. The concept of parallel regions significantly extends the modeling power: it allows for the specification of non-memoryless activities that take place in parallel on many nested hierarchy levels. Parallel regions can be left either by final states or by exit states, corresponding to the maximum and the minimum of the sojourn times in the regions, respectively. Therefore, concurrent activities with synchronization and competition can easily be modeled. An SMP with parallel regions cannot simply be analyzed by flattening the state space. We propose an analysis based on a steady-state analysis of an embedded Markov chain (EMC) at the top level and by a transient analysis at the composite state level with a limited computational effort. An expression for the asymptotic complexity of the analysis is also provided. An example SMP containing all modeling features with parallel regions is illustrated. We carry out experiments on basis of this model and confirm the results by simulations.

Keywords: Markov regenerative process · Semi-Markov Process · concurrency

1 Introduction

A semi-Markov process (SMP) is a well-known stochastic process defined over a discrete state space: each state is associated with an independent and identically distributed (i.i.d.) random variable quantifying the sojourn time in the state and the possible transitions to other states are quantified by branching probabilities. A well-known analysis approach consists in defining an embedded Markov chain (EMC) at the instants of time when a state is left, solving this EMC and weighting this solution by the mean sojourn times in the states of the SMP. An SMP generalizes the model of Markov chains such that it allows for non-memoryless activities with arbitrary distributions instead of just the exponential or geometric distribution. However, as a structural restriction, concurrent activities cannot easily be modeled in an SMP. Nevertheless, SMPs can be used

© Springer International Publishing Switzerland 2016
A. Remke and B.R. Haverkort (Eds.): MMB & DFT 2016, LNCS 9629, pp. 92–106, 2016.
DOI: 10.1007/978-3-319-31559-1_9

in many contexts, e.g., [6] proposed this for stochastic Petri nets in computer performance modeling and [17,18] applied SMPs in statistical testing.

Several possibilities have been considered to relax this structural restriction. First, phase type distributions can be used, but they lead to a state space explosion and are not really feasible in case of several concurrent non-memoryless activities. A second approach is to extend the embedding and to allow a more complex behavior in between, leading to Markov regenerative processes, as applied in the analysis of the M/G/1 queue or in non-Markovian stochastic Petri nets [7]. In this approach the structural restriction can relatively easily be relaxed in such a way, that concurrently to non-memoryless activities other memoryless ones are allowed, leading however to higher analysis complexity. Going beyond and allowing concurrent non-memoryless activities is possible in principle by using the method of supplementary variables [7] or by using the theory of Generalized Semi-Markov-Processes [11], but this leads to much more involved partial differential or Volterra integral state equations.

In another work [15] the SMP model has been extended in the context of stochastic Petri nets by allowing simultaneous starting of non-memoryless activities. The analysis of this model is possible based on the minimum of the length of these activities. The approach presented here can be considered as a generalization of this. Bradley et al. have also worked on stochastic Petri nets with underlying SMPs, [2] presents a combination with stochastic model checking and [1] distributed algorithms for quantiles and distributions. However, the work has not extended the structural restriction. The concept of phase type distributions has also been extended by Buchholz and Telek to more general matrix exponential distributions and rational arrival processes with an analysis still based on Markov chains [4]. Carnevali, Vicario and coworkers have developped a further approach to analyze non-Markovian stochastic Petri nets by extending theory for the verification of reactive systems, allowing for a combined real-time and quantitative analysis [3,19]. In their approach a stochastic-class-graph is constructed with discrete states, clock regions and probability distributions. For the analysis it is necessary that all possible cycles in the model go through a regeneration such that Markov renewal theory can be applied. The approach allows well for concurrent non-memoryless activities but the structural restriction is not easy to understand and many known modeling examples do not fall into this class [19].

In this work we suggest hierarchical SMPs with parallel regions. They allow for a significantly extended modeling power not feasible with the other approaches: non-memoryless activities can take place in parallel on many nested hierarchy levels. States can be refined such that they are composed of nested sub-states, possibly leading to several hierarchy levels. They may contain a single or multiple parallel regions which are left either by final or by exit states. A composite state is left, if the regions either all have reached their final states or if at least one of the regions has reached its exit state. Final and exit states must not be mixed on the same hierarchy level inside a state, but they can be nested arbitrarily on different hierarchy levels. The steady-state analysis can be based on embedding by using the time instants when states at the top level are left to define an EMC. To obtain the solution of the actual process, the mean sojourn times in all states are required. For composite states with a single region, this is possible by solving a linear system (in case of acyclic structures even simpler calculations can be possible). For composite states with multiple parallel regions it is first necessary to perform a transient analysis of the regions to compute the distribution of their sojourn times. Based on that, the distribution of the sojourn time in the composite state can be obtained by the maximum in case of final states and by the minimum in case of exit states. This can be performed recursively over all hierarchy levels and allows for computing the steady-state probabilities on all levels.

The computations of the distributions can be done numerically by using a discretization scheme, in case of acyclic structures and small state spaces also symbolic solutions are possible which we will use for illustration purposes. Note that the discretization leads just to a linear increase of the computational costs. The proposed analysis method can be automated, takes full advantage of the hierarchical structure of the model and reduces the effort since a generation of a flattened state space is not necessary. We derive an expression for the asymptotic complexity of the analysis and show that the computational costs are much less compared with any method which would be based on the construction of a flattened state space.

The approach is based on previous work of the authors: in [10] the model and analysis were suggested for discrete-time Markov chain (DTMCs) with two hierarchy levels and final states, in [9] they have been extended to SMPs with two hierarchy levels and final states. Both papers concentrate on the application to usage models in statistical testing of complex embedded systems. The contribution of this paper is a generalization of the model and its analysis to arbitrarily many hierarchical levels both with final and exit states, we also provide a consolidated version of the theory.

The model structure of an SMP with parallel regions and the respective notation are elaborated in Sect. 2. The analysis is explained in detail in Sect. 3. It is followed by an example that makes use of all model features, analysis results are also provided in Sect. 4. Finally, the asymptotic computational effort is investigated in Sect. 5.

2   Definition of the Model and Introduction of Notation

The definition of an SMP with parallel regions is split into multiple parts for a better understanding. The first relates to the model structure, the second to the notation that is used to refer to elements within the model, and the latter is concerned with quantities that are of interest for the analysis.

2.1   Semi-Markov Processes with Parallel Regions

An SMP with parallel regions is comparable to a state machine with simple and composite states [8]:

- On the top level the model consists of a state machine with simple and composite states. Additionally, there is one initial pseudostate. Each simple state is associated with i.i.d. sojourn times. Transitions connect states and are associated with probabilities. The probabilities at outgoing transitions of a state sum up to 1.
- Composite states either have one single region or multiple parallel regions which all contain a state machine as defined above, giving rise to a recursive definition starting at the top level, with substates at the intermediate levels and only simple states at the bottom level.
- A region has an end pseudostate (also called absorbing state) which is either a final or an exit pseudostate. All regions on the level directly below a composite state must have the same type of end pseudostate.
- In case the regions on the level directly below a composite state have final states, it is left, when all these regions have reached their final state.
- In case the regions on the level directly below a composite state have exit states, it is left, when at least one of these regions has reached its exit state.
- There are no further synchronizations between regions.

2.2   Notation to Refer to States, Regions, and Substates

The possibility of nesting composite states demands for a notation that is able to consider the hierarchy induced by them and that provides an unambiguous identification of states, regions, and substates.

- Let c denote the context of a state. It is a list of pairs (i, j), where i relates to a composite state and j to a region in that state.
- All states with context c constitute the set S_c, a state with context c is written as $s_{c,i} \in S_c$.
- The j-th region within a composite state $s_{c,i}$ is referred to as $s_{c,i,j} = s_{c'}$ with $c' = (c, (i, j))$. For simplicity we omit nested brackets, i.e., $(c, (i, j))$ denotes a list c where (i, j) is appended. The amount of regions within composite state $s_{c,i}$ is denoted by $r_{c,i} \geq 1$.
- The absorbing state of a region s_c takes the index $s_{c,e}$ with $e = |S_c|$.
- The length of the context is given by $l = |c|$, it denotes the hierarchy level.
- The context can be omitted, if $c = \emptyset$. This is in general the case for states at top level. The length of an empty context is 0.

This notation can be applied recursively on nested composite states. Context information can thus be hidden by the context c. This preserves readability: For example, lets consider the substate named *state8* depicted in Fig. 1. Without context, it is referred to as $s_{2,1,1,1,1,1,2}$. This notation is almost unreadable. With context set to $c = ((2,1), (1,1), (1,1))$, we can simply refer to it by $s_{c,2}$. This notation also allows to refer to states on higher hierarchy levels.

2.3   Notation for Further Quantities

The analysis of an SMP with parallel regions requires the specification of further quantities that are related to composite states, their regions, and their substates.

They are defined based on the structural definitions from Sect. 2.1 and the notation introduced in Sect. 2.2. For all these quantities, it is assumed that $|c| > 0$.

- Let the random variable $X_{c,i}$ be the mean sojourn time in state $s_{c,i}$ without taking any state transitions according to exit states besides a possible exit in $s_{c,i}$ itself into account and let $F_{c,i}(t)$ be its distribution and $\mathbf{F}_c(t)$ the corresponding vector valid for region s_c.
- Let the random variable X_c be the mean sojourn time in region s_c without taking any state transitions according to exit states besides a possible exit in s_c itself into account and let $F_c(t)$ be its distribution.
- Let $\delta_{c,i,j}$ be the branching probability of going to state $s_{c,j}$ after leaving state $s_{c,i}$, $\mathbf{\Delta}_c$ is the corresponding matrix, valid for region s_c.
- Let $v_{c,i}(t)$ be the transient probability in state $s_{c,i}$ after entering region s_c at $t = 0$ without taking possible exits besides a possible exit in $s_{c,i}$ itself into account, $\mathbf{v}_c(t)$ is the corresponding vector, valid for region s_c.
- Let $V_{c,i,j}(t)$ be the conditional transient probability in state $s_{c,j}$ after entering region s_c in state $s_{c,i}$ at $t = 0$ without taking possible exits besides a possible exit in $s_{c,j}$ itself into account, $\mathbf{V}_c(t)$ is the corresponding matrix, valid for region s_c.
- Let $\pi_{c,i}$ be the steady-state probability in state $s_{c,i}$, $\boldsymbol{\pi}_c$ is the corresponding vector, valid for region s_c.
- Let $\sigma_{c,i}$ be the mean sojourn time in state $s_{c,i}$ after entering region s_c, $\boldsymbol{\sigma}_c$ is the corresponding vector, valid for region s_c.

Furthermore, the following notation will be used: A bar above a vector or matrix denotes a restriction to the non-absorbing states, i.e., in a vector the last element is removed and in a matrix the last column and last row are removed. $\overline{F}(t) = 1 - F(t)$ denotes the complement of the distribution. Applied to the vector $\overline{\mathbf{F}}_c(t)$ it means both element-wise complement of the distribution and restriction to non-absorbing states. $\mathbf{f}_c(t)$ is the vector of corresponding densities, also restricted to non-absorbing states. Finally, $diag(\mathbf{f}_c)(t)$ and $diag(\overline{\mathbf{F}}_c)(t)$ denote diagonal matrices in which the vector is put on the diagonal and all other elements are set to zero. $\mathbf{I}$ denotes the identity matrix of suitable dimension (all elements on the diagonal equal to one, all others equal to zero) and $\mathbf{e}$ is a vector of ones of suitable dimension.

3   Analysis

The analysis is based on the construction of an EMC. The EMC is embedded at time points when a state on the top level is left. The required mean sojourn times in the simple states can be obtained easily, however, the mean sojourn times of the composite states are more challenging and must be computed based on transient analysis. The analysis can thus be organized in the following steps:

1. For all composite states at top level the sojourn time distributions must be computed. To do this, one must go recursively from bottom to top and

must do a transient analysis and then compute the maximum in case of final states and the minimum in case of exit states. Exits that may occur in parallel regions on the same and on higher hierarchy levels are not taken into account.

2. Based on the computed sojourn time distributions one must go again from bottom to top in each composite state and compute the mean sojourn times in each state. Now the exits in parallel regions on the same and on higher levels are taken into account. To do this, integrations must be performed. The mean sojourn times in final states can then also be computed easily by subtraction.

3. Now the EMC on top level can be solved.

4. The steady state probabilities of substates can then be computed easily by multiplying the steady-state probability of the higher level with the fraction of mean sojourn time spent in the substate.

In the following we will explain the single steps in more detail.

3.1 Analysis if All Sojourn Time Distributions Are Known

We consider a region s_c with states $s_{c,i}$ for which all sojourn time distributions $F_{c,i}(t)$ are known. We differentiate between three important cases:

1. All sojourn times are exponentially distributed. In this case the stochastic process is a continuous-time Markov chain (CTMC) and can be described by a generator matrix $\mathbf{Q}_c(t)$ and the transient solution is given by

$$\overline{\mathbf{v}}_c(t) = \overline{\mathbf{v}}_c(0)e^{\overline{\mathbf{Q}}_c(t)} \tag{1}$$

2. All sojourn times are geometrically distributed. In this case the stochastic process is a DTMC and can be described by a stochastic matrix $\mathbf{P}_c(t)$ and the transient solution is given by

$$\overline{\mathbf{v}}_c(t) = \overline{\mathbf{v}}_c(0)\overline{\mathbf{\Delta}}_c(t)^{\lfloor t/\tau \rfloor} \tag{2}$$

3. In other cases the stochastic process is an SMP. Its dynamics are described by the following two equations coming from Markov renewal theory. The conditional transient probabilities are given by:

$$\overline{\mathbf{V}}_c(t) = \overline{\mathbf{E}}_c(t) + \mathbf{K}'_c(t) * \overline{\mathbf{V}}_c(t) \tag{3}$$

with local kernel $\overline{\mathbf{E}}_c(t) = diag(\overline{\mathbf{F}}_c(t))$ and global kernel $\overline{\mathbf{K}}(t)$ defined by $\overline{\mathbf{K}}'_c(t) = diag(\overline{\mathbf{f}}_c(t))\overline{\mathbf{\Delta}}_c$, $*$ stands for the convolution which has to be applied on the elements of this vector-matrix product. The unconditional transient probabilities are then obtained by:

$$\overline{\mathbf{v}}_c(t) = \overline{\mathbf{v}}_c(0)\overline{\mathbf{V}}_c(t) \tag{4}$$

Note that in all cases it is possible to derive a closed form solution if the topology is acyclic and the state space is small enough. It is, however, numerically not feasible in case of larger state spaces because of cancellation errors [12].

From the transient solution the distribution of the sojourn time in the region is given by summing up the probabilities on non-absorbing states:

$$F_c(t) = 1 - \overline{\mathbf{v}}_c(t)\mathbf{e} \tag{5}$$

Remark: If the composite state is at top level and contains just a single region, then the transient computations can be avoided and instead just linear systems have to be solved to compute the mean sojourn times directly. This special case is treated in the beginning of Sect. 3.3.

3.2   Computation of Sojourn Time Distributions for Composite States

If the composite state $s_{c,i}$ contains multiple regions $s_{c,i,j}$ which have

1. final states, then its sojourn time is given by the maximum over the sojourn times of its regions. The distribution $F_{c,i}(t)$ is hence given by

$$F_{c,i}(t) = \prod_{j=1}^{r_{c,i}} F_{c,i,j}(t) \tag{6}$$

2. exit states, then its sojourn time is given by the minimum over the sojourn times of its regions. The distribution $F_{c,i}(t)$ is hence given by

$$F_{c,i}(t) = 1 - \prod_{j=1}^{r_{c,i}} \overline{F}_{c,i,j}(t) \tag{7}$$

3.3   Computation of Mean Sojourn Times in Composite States

If the composite state is at top level and contains just a single region, the mean sojourn times can be computed by a system of linear equations. In case of CTMCs and DTMCs this can be derived from integrating the transient state equations for $\overline{\mathbf{v}}_c(t)$ from 0 to infinity [5].

1. The linear system in case of a CTMC is given by

$$-\overline{\mathbf{v}}_c(0) = \overline{\boldsymbol{\sigma}}_c\overline{\mathbf{Q}}_c \tag{8}$$

2. The linear system in case of a DTMC is given by

$$-\overline{\mathbf{v}}_c(0) = \overline{\boldsymbol{\sigma}}_c(\overline{\boldsymbol{\Delta}}_c - \mathbf{I}) \tag{9}$$

3. In case of an SMP the integration of the given transient state equations would lead to a linear system with a matrix of unknowns, the method of supplementary variables as described in Chap. 11 of [7] allows to derive a linear system with just a vector of unknowns first for a so-called embedded CTMC:

$$\overline{\mathbf{v}}_c(0) = \overline{\sigma}_c^*(\overline{\mathbf{\Delta}}_c - \mathbf{I}). \tag{10}$$

This can be converted easily to the mean sojourn times of the SMP by multiplying each sojourn time in the embedded CTMC with the mean sojourn time in each state in isolation:

$$\overline{\sigma}_c = \overline{\sigma}_c^* diag \left(\int_0^\infty \overline{\mathbf{F}}_c(t)dt \right) \tag{11}$$

Remark: In case of acyclic structures it is possible to compute the mean sojourn times even without solving a linear system, this simple case is not elaborated here and at least for small state spaces it will not lead to significant savings of the computational costs.

In all other cases, the transient analysis of the regions as specified in Sect. 3.2 has to be used. Afterwards, the exits have to be taken into account. The mean sojourn time $\sigma_{c,i}$ for a substate $s_{c,i}$ is given by the integral over its transient probability $v_{c,i}(t)$ taking exits in parallel regions on the same and on higher hierarchy levels into account.

$$\sigma_{c,i} = \int_0^\infty v_{c,i}(t) \cdot \overline{F}_c^{exit}(t)dt \tag{12}$$

The quantity $\overline{F}_c^{exit}(t)$ represents the product of complementary distributions from regions on this and on higher hierarchy levels that are executed in parallel and have an exit pseudostate. It is defined recursively by utilizing the context: if the regions in a surrounding composite state have exit pseudostates, their complementary distributions are taken into account. However, region s_c itself needs not to be taken into account, since its exits are already represented by the transient probabilities. This leads to a recursive definition, starting at a given context and going upwards:

$$\overline{F}_{(c,(i,j))}^{exit}(t) = \begin{cases} \prod_{l=1,l \neq j}^{r_{c,i}} \overline{F}_{(c,(i,l))}(t) \overline{F}_c^{exit}(t), & \text{if } s_{c,i} \text{ has exit pseudostates} \\ \overline{F}_c^{exit}(t), & \text{if } s_{c,i} \text{ has final pseudostates} \end{cases} \tag{13}$$

The recursion ends at the top level: $F_c^{exit}(t) = 1$ if $c = \emptyset$. The mean sojourn time σ_i in a composite state at top level is computed as integral from 0 to infinity over the complement of its sojourn time distribution.

$$\sigma_i = \int_0^\infty \overline{F}_i(t)dt \tag{14}$$

In case of regions, the same mean sojourn time is spent in them as in the directly surrounding composite state. Thus, we can set $\sigma_{(c,(i,j))} = \sigma_{c,i}$. In case of final states, the mean sojourn time $\sigma_{(c,(i,j)),e}$ in the final state of each region can be computed by subtracting the mean sojourn time spent in non-absorbing states from the mean sojourn time $\sigma_{c,i}$ of the surrounding composite state $s_{c,i}$.

$$\sigma_{(c,(i,j)),e} = \sigma_{c,i} - \overline{\sigma}_{(c,(i,j))}e \tag{15}$$

In case of exit states no time is left in them and we can simply set $\sigma_{c,e} = 0$.

3.4 Solution of the EMC

Let $\mathbf{P}$ be the stochastic matrix of the SMP with the branching probabilities of going from top level state to top level state. Let $\mathbf{u}$ denote the vector of steady-state probabilities of the EMC, it is given by the system of linear equations $\mathbf{u} = \mathbf{uP}$ subject to $\mathbf{ue} = 1$. The solution has to be weighted by the mean sojourn times in the top level states. The mean sojourn times are given by matrix $\mathbf{C}$, with $c_{i,j} = E[X_i] = \sigma_i$, if $i = j$, and otherwise $c_{i,j} = 0$.

The mean sojourn time for simple states is derived easily by $E[X_i] = \int_0^\infty \overline{F}_i(t)dt$. For composite states, the mean sojourn time is derived according to the analysis stated in Sect. 3.3. Once matrix C is complete, the final solution of the steady-state probabilities of the EMC is obtained by calculating

$$\pi = \frac{\mathbf{uC}}{\mathbf{uCe}}. \tag{16}$$

3.5 Computation of Substate Probabilities

The steady-state probability of a substate in a region can be obtained by multiplying the steady-state probability of the surrounding composite state with the fraction of mean sojourn times in the substate and the surrounding composite state.

$$\pi_{(c,(i,j)),k} = \pi_{c,i} \frac{\sigma_{(c,(i,j)),k}}{\sigma_{c,i}} \tag{17}$$

From the known solution at the top level, this calculation can be performed recursively on all hierarchy levels down to the bottom level.

4 An Illustrative Example

An exemplary SMP with parallel regions is shown in Fig. 1. States are numbered consecutively, starting at 1 at the top level and within each region. We also provide short names in italics for a simple reference. It contains all features: simple states, composite states with exit and final pseudostates, and nested composite states. Transitions are labeled with their branching probabilities which have all been set to one. We used the following sojourn time distributions for simple states, corresponding to the numbering in the short names:

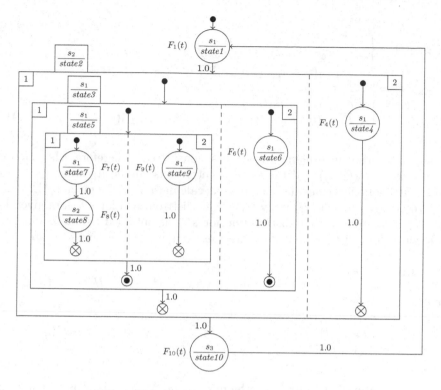

Fig. 1. Exemplary SMP with parallel regions.

- $F_1(t) = H(t - \phi)$, a unit step function with offset ϕ.
- $F_4(t) = H(t - \rho)$, a unit step function with offset ρ.
- $F_6(t) = 1 - e^{-\mu t}$, an exponential distribution with rate μ.
- $F_7(t) = 1 - e^{-\lambda t}$, an exponential distribution with rate λ.
- $F_8(t) = 1 - e^{-\omega t}$, an exponential distribution with rate ω.
- $F_9(t) = H(t - \tau)$, a unit step function with offset τ.
- $F_{10}(t) = H(t - \epsilon)$, a unit step function with offset ϵ.

We applied the analysis of this paper to the SMP from Fig. 1. Solving the EMC, i.e., solving the respective system of linear equations $\mathbf{u} = \mathbf{uP}$ subject to $\mathbf{ue} = 1$ yields $u = (1/3, 1/3, 1/3)$. The solution has to be weighted by the mean sojourn times in the top level states. The mean sojourn time tor $state1$ is $\sigma_1 = \int_0^\infty \overline{F}_1(t)dt = \phi$ and for $state10$ it is $\sigma_{10} = \int_0^\infty \overline{F}_{10}(t)dt = \epsilon$. Calculating the mean sojourn time for composite state $state2$ is challenging: it starts at the lowest hierarchy level by calculating the sojourn time distribution for composite state $s_{c,1}$ with name $state5$ and context $c = ((2,1),(1,1))$. First, the transient probabilities are calculated for each substate. Afterwards, the minimum is calculated over the sojourn time distributions of the regions according to Eq. (7) since $s_{c,1}$ contains exit pseudostates. The functions are given by Eq. (18).

$$v_{c,1,1,1}(t) = e^{-\lambda \cdot t}$$

$$v_{c,1,1,2}(t) = \begin{cases} \lambda \cdot t \cdot e^{-\lambda \cdot t} & \text{, if } \omega = \lambda \\ \frac{\lambda}{\lambda - \omega} \cdot (e^{-\omega \cdot t} - e^{-\lambda \cdot t}) & \text{, if } \omega \neq \lambda \end{cases}$$

$$F_{c,1,1}(t) = 1 - v_{c,1,1,1}(t) - v_{c,1,1,2}(t) = 1 - e^{-\lambda \cdot t} - v_{c,1,1,2}(t)$$

$$v_{c,1,2,1}(t) = 1 - H(t - \tau)$$

$$F_{c,1,2}(t) = 1 - v_{c,1,2,1}(t) = H(t - \tau)$$

$$F_{c,1}(t) = 1 - \overline{F}_{c,1,1}(t) \cdot \overline{F}_{c,1,2}(t) = 1 - (e^{-\lambda \cdot t} + v_{c,1,1,2}(t)) \cdot (1 - H(t - \tau))$$

$$\tag{18}$$

Subsequently, the next hierarchy level is considered. Therefore, the context changes to $c' = ((2,1))$ and the state of interest is composite state $s_{c',1}$ with name $state3$ and new context. The previous calculation results given by Eq. (18) are directly used in this hierarchy level. The distributions for $s_{c',1}$ are given by Eq. (19). The sojourn time distribution for $s_{c',1}$ is obtained as maximum over the sojourn time distributions for its regions, due to the final pseudostates.

$$v_{c',1,1,1}(t) = \overline{F}_{c,1}(t) = (e^{-\lambda \cdot t} + v_{c,1,1,2}(t)) \cdot (1 - H(t - \tau))$$

$$F_{c',1,1}(t) = 1 - v_{c',1,1,1}(t) = 1 - (e^{-\lambda \cdot t} + v_{c,1,1,2}(t)) \cdot (1 - H(t - \tau))$$

$$v_{c',1,2,1}(t) = e^{-\mu \cdot t}$$

$$F_{c',1,2}(t) = 1 - v_{c',1,2,1}(t) = 1 - e^{-\mu \cdot t}$$

$$F_{c',1}(t) = F_{c',1,1}(t) \cdot F_{c',1,2}(t) = (1 - (e^{-\lambda \cdot t} + v_{c,1,1,2}(t)) \cdot (1 - H(t - \tau)))$$
$$\cdot (1 - e^{-\mu \cdot t})$$

$$\tag{19}$$

Again, the context is updated and the next hierarchy level is considered. Since this is the top level, the context is empty. Therefore, we omit it in the following. The state of interest is composite state s_2. The calculation of its sojourn time distribution is comparable to that for composite state $s_{c,1}$, since it also utilizes exit pseudostates. The respective functions are given by Eq. (20).

$$v_{2,1,1}(t) = \overline{F}_{c',1}(t) = 1 - ((1 - (e^{-\lambda \cdot t} + v_{c,1,1,2}(t)) \cdot (1 - H(t - \tau)))$$
$$\cdot (1 - e^{-\mu \cdot t}))$$

$$F_{2,1}(t) = 1 - v_{2,1,1}(t) = (1 - (e^{-\lambda \cdot t} + v_{c,1,1,2}(t)) \cdot (1 - H(t - \tau)))$$
$$\cdot (1 - e^{-\mu \cdot t})$$

$$v_{2,2,1}(t) = 1 - H(t - \rho)$$

$$F_{2,2}(t) = 1 - v_{2,2,1}(t) = H(t - \rho)$$

$$F_2(t) = 1 - \overline{F}_{2,1}(t) \cdot \overline{F}_{2,2}(t) = 1 - (1 - (1 - (e^{-\lambda \cdot t} + v_{c,1,1,2}(t))$$
$$\cdot (1 - H(t - \tau))) \cdot (1 - e^{-\mu \cdot t})) \cdot (1 - H(t - \rho))$$

$$\tag{20}$$

Once all sojourn time distributions are known, the mean sojourn times can be calculated for each state at each hierarchy level. The mean sojourn times for each composite and substate are given in Eq. (21). The contexts are defined as above as $c = ((2,1),(1,1))$ and $c' = ((2,1))$. Exits are considered according to Sect. 3.3. Simple states from the top level are not listed, their mean sojourn time can directly be derived from the corresponding annotated sojourn time distribution. The mean sojourn time for all exit pseudostates is equal to 0. In contrast to exit pseudostates, the process spends time in final pseudostates. The mean sojourn times σ_{final1} and σ_{final2} relate to the final pseudostates in the first and the second region of composite state $s_{2,1,1}$. They are calculated according to Eq. (15). Finally, the steady-state probabilities are calculated for each state according to Eqs. (16) and (17).

$$
\begin{aligned}
\sigma_{c,1,1,1} &= \sigma_{state7} = \int_0^\infty v_{c,1,1,1}(t) \cdot \overline{F}_{c,1,2}(t) \cdot \overline{F}_{2,2}(t) dt \\
\sigma_{c,1,1,2} &= \sigma_{state8} = \int_0^\infty v_{c,1,1,2}(t) \cdot \overline{F}_{c,1,2}(t) \cdot \overline{F}_{2,2}(t) dt \\
\sigma_{c,1,2,1} &= \sigma_{state9} = \int_0^\infty v_{c,1,2,1}(t) \cdot \overline{F}_{c,1,1}(t) \cdot \overline{F}_{2,2}(t) dt \\
\sigma_{c',1,1,1} &= \sigma_{state5} = \int_0^\infty v_{c',1,1,1} \cdot \overline{F}_{2,2}(t) dt \\
\sigma_{c',1,2,1} &= \sigma_{state6} = \int_0^\infty v_{c',1,2,1}(t) \cdot \overline{F}_{2,2}(t) dt \\
\sigma_{2,1,1} &= \sigma_{state3} = \int_0^\infty v_{2,1,1}(t) \cdot \overline{F}_{2,2}(t) dt \\
\sigma_{c',1,1,2} &= \sigma_{final1} = \sigma_{2,1,1} - \sigma_{c',1,1,1} \\
\sigma_{c',1,2,2} &= \sigma_{final2} = \sigma_{2,1,1} - \sigma_{c',1,2,1} \\
\sigma_{2,2,1} &= \sigma_{state4} = \int_0^\infty v_{2,2,1}(t) \cdot \overline{F}_{2,1}(t) dt \\
\sigma_2 &= \sigma_{state2} = \int_0^\infty \overline{F}_2(t) dt
\end{aligned}
\tag{21}
$$

For the given SMP we carried out 11 experiments with varying parameters for the distributions: $\rho \in \{1.0, 2.0, 3.0, 4.0, 5.0\}$, $\tau \in \{1.0, 2.0, 3.0, 4.0\}$, and $\mu, \lambda, \omega \in \{0.5, 1.0\}$. For the sojourn time distributions $F_1(t)$ and $F_{10}(t)$ at top level, the parameters have been set to $\phi = \epsilon = 1.0$. In each experiment, we calculated the steady-state probabilities. We also measured the steady-state probabilities by means of a simulation. Therefore, we specified a simulation model for the SMP with parallel regions from Fig. 1 and set the parameters of the distributions accordingly. The simulation model was specified with Papyrus [14] and SimTAny [16] (formerly known as Syntony) was used to automatically transform it into a simulation for OMNeT++ [13]. About 100,000 independent repetitions were carried out for each experiment. The measured results validate our calculation results. The difference between the measured and calculated steady-state probabilities is given in % in Fig. 2. The steady-state probabilities are named by the corresponding state in Fig. 1. π_{final1} and π_{final2} relate to the final state in the first and the second region of composite state $state3$. The difference between the measured and calculated values is below 1 % on average, which is quite low. The biggest difference between calculated and measured steady-state probabilities applies to states that are subject to the synchronization in the simulation. These are the states $state8$ and the two final states. The effect of the synchronization will be amplified, if the steady-state probability of the concerned state is very small. In case of $state9$, it has only a minor impact due to its high steady-state probability in almost all experiments.

We also executed experiments with other types of distributions: We used the uniform distribution for $F_4(t)$ with $a = 1.0$ and $b \in \{1.0, 2.0, 3.0, 4.0, 5.0\}$, and the Weibull distribution for $F_7(t)$ with $\lambda = 1.0$ and $k \in \{1.0, 2.0, 3.0\}$. In this case, the impact of the synchronization mainly affects the difference for the first final state, which is at most 2.5 %. For all other states, the difference is quite stable and below 1.5 %.

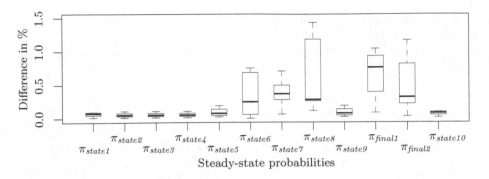

Fig. 2. Difference in % between the calculated and measured steady-state probabilities for all states in the example SMP with parallel regions.

5 Computational Effort

We consider the worst case in which the state space is as "nested" as possible and there are fully connected SMPs in each region. The (bottom) composite states at the deepest hierarchy level contain only simple states. Let n be the number of top-level states, r the number of regions in each (nested) composite state, l the number of hierarchy levels, and m the number of states in each region.

We want to estimate the order of continuous functions. They constitute a measure of both space and time complexity, since we have to discretize them in order to perform numerical operations.

Starting at a bottom composite state, the assumptions lead to $r \cdot m^2$ conditional transient probabilities for that state. Considering the next higher level, there is a composite state with r regions, each containing m bottom composite states. Taking the conditional transient probabilities of that state into account, the amount of functions rises to $r \cdot m(r \cdot m^2) + r \cdot m^2$. The procedure continues until the composite state at the top level is reached, leading to the sum $n \cdot \sum_{k=1}^{l} r^k \cdot m^{k+1}$ of continuous functions and the corresponding order $O(n \cdot r^l \cdot m^{l+1})$. The sojourn time distributions do not add to the asymptotic order. The required discretization of the continuous functions leads to a further linear increase in terms of the number of used discretization steps.

In case of the example we have $n = 3$, $l = 3$, $r = 2$, $m = 2$, leading to $n \cdot r^l \times m^{l+1} = 384$. Actually there are 9 transient probabilities and 9 sojourn time distributions to consider, significantly less than the worst case since the structure is not fully "nested".

If there would be an analysis that could be applied on the flattened state space, its computational effort would depend on the size of this space (if multidimensional supplementary variable spaces or phase type distributions would be used, the complexity would be even increased by the possible concurrent non-memoryless activities). A composite state with r regions each with m states has m^r states. This is continued on each hierarchy level, leading to an order of

$O(n \cdot m^{r^l})$ states in its flattened state space. It is obvious that the suggested hierarchical approach of this paper leads to a significant reduction.

We have also implemented a prototype based on equidistant discretization and Romberg integration, it required about 500 ms to calculate the steady-state probabilities for the example. Further results for larger state spaces will be investigated in future work.

6 Conclusion

In this paper, we introduced SMPs with parallel regions. They boost the modeling power significantly and are easy to understand, since they are similar to state machines with simple and composite states. Parallel and non-memoryless activities are modeled within separate regions of a composite state. The model allows to nest composite states, which leads to multiple different hierarchy levels. A hierarchy level either is left once all parallel activities on the same level are finished, or as soon as the first concurrent activity on the same or higher level exits. We also introduced an analysis that takes advantage of the model structure. Since flattening the state space is not possible here, we apply Markov renewal theory: First a steady-state analysis is performed on an EMC at the top level. Second, a transient analysis is recursively carried out at the composite state level. Finally, exit points are taken into account and mean sojourn times and steady-state probabilities are calculated for each simple state, composite state, and substate.

The concepts outlined in this paper have been applied to an exemplary SMP with parallel regions that makes use of all features. Multiple experiments have been carried out on that model by applying the analysis, each time with different parameters for the sojourn time distributions. We focused on the calculation of steady-state probabilities for each state in that model. We also implemented a simulation for each experiment and used it to measure the steady-state probabilities. The measured values confirm our calculation results.

Finally, we considered the computational effort of the analysis, showing a clear benefit of the suggested solution method based on computing minimum and maximum on the model structure. It is lower than the effort that would be required by any method which would be based on the construction of a flattened state space.

References

1. Bradley, J.T., Dingle, N.J., Harrison, P.G., Knottenbelt, W.J.: Distributed computation of transient state distributions and passage time quantiles in large semi-Markov models. Future Gener. Comput. Syst. **22**(7), 828–837 (2006)
2. Bradley, J., Dingle, N., Harrison, P., Knottenbelt, W.: Performance queries on semi-Markov stochastic Petri nets with an extended continuous stochastic logic. In: Proceedings of the 10th International Workshop on Petri Nets and Performance Models (PNPM 2003), Urbana, IL, USA, pp. 62–71 (2003)

3. Bucci, G., Carnevali, L., Ridi, L., Vicario, E.: Oris: a tool for modeling, verification and evaluation of real-time systems. Int. J. Softw. Tools Technol. Transf. **12**(5), 391–403 (2010)
4. Buchholz, P., Telek, M.: Rational automata networks: a non-Markovian modeling approach. INFORMS J. Comput. **25**(1), 87–101 (2013)
5. Ciardo, G., Blakemore, A., Chimento, P.F., Muppala, J.K., Trivedi, K.S.: Automated generation and analysis of Markov reward models using stochastic reward nets. In: Linear Algebra, Markov Chains, and Queueing Models. The IMA Volumes in Mathematics and its Applications, vol. 48, pp. 145–191. Springer, New York (1993)
6. Dugan, B.J., Trivedi, S.K., Geist, R., Nicola, V.: Extended stochastic petri nets: Applications and analysis. Technical report, Durham, NC, USA (1984)
7. German, R.: Performance Analysis of Communication Systems. Wiley, United Kingdom (2000)
8. Harel, D.: Statecharts: a visual formalism for complex systems. Sci. Comput. Prog. **8**(3), 231–274 (1987)
9. Homm, D., Eckert, J., German, R.: Combining time and concurrency in model-based statistical testing of embedded real-time systems. In: Bianculli, D., Calinescu, R., Rumpe, B. (eds.) SEFM 2015. LNCS, vol. 9509, pp. 22–31. Springer, Heidelberg (2015). doi:10.1007/978-3-662-49224-6_3
10. Homm, D., Eckert, J., German, R.: Concurrent streams in Markov chain usage models for statistical testing of complex systems. In: Proceedings of the 30th ACM Symposium on Applied Computing (SAC 2015), Salamanca, Spain (2015)
11. Lindemann, C.: Performance Modelling with Deterministic and Stochastic Petri Nets. Wiley, New York (1998)
12. Marie, R.A., Reibman, A.L., Trivedi, K.S.: Transient analysis of acyclic Markov chains. Perform. Eval. **7**(3), 175–194 (1987)
13. OMNeT++: An object-oriented modular discrete event network simulation framework. http://www.omnetpp.org. Accessed 26 October 2015
14. Papyrus: Graphical editing tool for UML 2. http://www.eclipse.org/papyrus. Accessed 26 October 2015
15. Puliafito, A., Scarpa, M., Trivedi, K.: Petri nets with k simultaneously enabled generally distributed timed transitions. Perform. Eval. **32**(1), 1–34 (1998)
16. Schneider, V., German, R.: Integration of test-driven agile simulation approach in service-oriented tool environment. In: Proceedings of the 46th Annual Simulation Symposium (ANSS 2013), San Diego, CA, USA, pp. 11: 1–11: 7 (2013)
17. Siegl, S., Dulz, W., German, R., Kiffe, G.: Model-driven testing based on Markov chain usage models in the automotive domain. In: Proceedings of the 12th European Workshop on Dependable Computing (EWDC 2009), Toulouse, France (2009)
18. Siegl, S., German, R.: Model-driven testing with timed usage models in the automotive domain. In: Proceedings of the 20th International Symposium on Software Reliability Engineering (ISSRE 2009), Mysuru, India (2009)
19. Vicario, E., Sassoli, L., Carnevali, L.: Using stochastic state classes in quantitative evaluation of dense-time reactive systems. IEEE Trans. Softw. Eng. **35**(5), 703–719 (2009)

Combining Mobility Models with Arrival Processes

Jan Kriege[✉]

TU Dortmund, Dortmund, Germany
jan.kriege@tu-dortmund.de

Abstract. The realistic modeling of mobile networks makes it necessary to find adequate models to mimic the movement of mobile nodes. In the past various such mobility models have been proposed, that either create synthetic movement patterns or are based on real-world observations. These models usually assume a constant number of mobility nodes for the simulation. Although in real-world scenarios new nodes will arrive and other nodes will leave the simulation area, only little attention has been paid to modeling these arrivals and departures of nodes.

In this paper we present an approach to easily extend mobility models to support the generation of arrivals and departures. For three standard mobility models the effect of this extension on the performance measures of a simple mobile network is shown.

Keywords: Mobility models · Scenario generation · Arrival processes · ARTA processes

1 Introduction

The adequate and realistic modeling of the traffic load is a crucial step when building stochastic models of computer and communication networks. For wired networks it is well known that packet interarrival times are correlated and that neglecting this correlation might have significant impact on performance measures [16]. With the increased availability of mobile devices performance evaluation of wireless networks has become more important. For a realistic load modeling the user mobility has to be considered additionally in wireless networks. To mimic movement patterns of users (or mobile nodes) in a wireless scenario mobility models are used. Mobility models basically consist of some rules that define how the nodes of a wireless network move. On an abstract level the mobility of a node consists of a spatial component, that defines to what destination a node is moving, and a temporal component, that defines when and at what speed the node is moving. It is well known, that unrealistic mobility models may lead to wrong assumptions on the performance of the system that is analyzed [21].

In the past various mobility models have been proposed and the overview we can give here is by far not complete. These models can be divided according

© Springer International Publishing Switzerland 2016
A. Remke and B.R. Haverkort (Eds.): MMB & DFT 2016, LNCS 9629, pp. 107–121, 2016.
DOI: 10.1007/978-3-319-31559-1_10

to different criteria [3]. The most distinctive criteria are probably whether the mobile model synthetically creates movements or is based on real-world observations and whether it treats movements of single nodes or groups of nodes.

An overview of models creating synthetic movements can be found in [10]. Those models are easy to implement, can be easily integrated into simulation models and do not need additional information and are therefore widely used. Classical examples are the Random Waypoint, Random Direction and Random Walk models, where a direction or destination and the speed of a node is randomly determined. While these models are memoryless, i.e. they do not use information from the past to determine the next destination or speed, the Gauss-Markov model [17] chooses these values depending on previous values. The QoS-RWP model [19] is based on the Random Waypoint model, but divides the nodes into two classes. One class moves according to the Random Waypoint model, while the second class is stationary unless their quality of service drops beyond a given threshold. Aside from these very general models, approaches like the City Section model [10], that aims at representing the topology of streets, exist for special applications.

More recent approaches use real world-observations as basis for the mobility models, because the synthetically generated movements might differ from real patterns and require an idealized, free simulation area [22], which could lead to wrong assumptions for performance measures [18].

For example the model from [14] considers buildings and obstacles by using Voronoi-diagrams. [22] constructs a list of trips from real data that consist of visited access points and in combination with a map realistic routes can be obtained for the mobile nodes. In [15] a matrix of transition probabilities for different locations and the distributions for pause times and speed values are estimated from real-world observations.

A different approach was chosen in [12] where a network of queues corresponding to the different access points was used to model the wireless network on a more abstract level.

In contrast, little attention has been paid at modeling of arrivals and departures of users in wireless scenarios. Usually the number of mobile nodes is set to a fixed value at the beginning of a simulation and does not change during simulation, because no nodes leave or enter the area. For short simulations these assumptions might be justified, though as pointed out in [21] the common short simulation times are not sufficient for modeling the mobility in WiFi networks. However, for longer simulation runs it is very likely that the number of nodes varies. Typical scenarios are an airport terminal or a shopping mall where there should be a large throughput of mobile nodes. These considerations clearly motivate that mobility models should also be able to account for a varying number of nodes. However, this has hardly been treated in the literature, yet. [4] used queueing networks to model a wireless network and considered external arrival rates. In [2] the arrivals of participants of a conference were analyzed and modeled as a Markov-Modulated-Poisson Process (MMPP) but not combined with a mobility model. As the authors state, a MMPP is sufficient for modeling the arrivals at a conference with phases of many arrivals (start of a session) and few arrivals (during a session), but is probably not adequate for other scenarios with more complicated arrival patterns.

In this paper we propose a general approach to enhance mobility models to account for arrivals and departures of nodes resulting in a varying number of nodes during the simulation of the model. Since the arrivals and departures are likely to exhibit correlation we propose a combination of mobility models with stochastic processes. The effect of incorporating these arrival patterns into the mobility models is systematically assessed by measuring the traffic load generated by the models in a wireless network scenario.

The paper is structured as follows. In Sect. 2 we briefly introduce the mobility models and stochastic processes used in our experimental analysis. Section 3 describes our approach to combine mobility models with arrivals and departures. In Sect. 4 we experimentally evaluate the effect of the added arrival patterns. The paper ends with the conclusions in Sect. 5.

2   Background and Notations

As already mentioned in Sect. 1 there exist various mobility models for different applications and requirements, though they usually assume a fixed number of nodes. In the following we will introduce three basic mobility models in more detail that are later used for our experiments. Additionally we present the theoretical background on ARTA processes that we will use to generate arrivals and departures.

2.1   Random Walk Mobility Model

In the Random Walk mobility model nodes change their location by randomly choosing the direction and the speed to travel. The model is parametrized by the bounds for the speed $[v_{min}, v_{max}]$ and either a time interval t or a distance d. Each movement then either takes t time units or covers the distance d. The direction is chosen from $[0, 2\pi]$. At the end of a movement a new speed and direction are randomly determined. Nodes that reach the border of the simulation area are reflected.

The Random Walk model is memoryless, since no information about past locations or speeds is used when determining the next speed and direction values. This might lead to unrealistic movements. Nevertheless the Random Walk is a widely used mobility model [10].

2.2   Random Waypoint Mobility Model

Nodes following the Random Waypoint model switch between pause periods and movements, i.e. they stay at a location for a randomly determined time and then randomly choose a speed between $[v_{min}, v_{max}]$ and a random destination in the simulation area. Having reached the destination the node pauses again and so on [10].

2.3 Random Direction Mobility Model

The Random Direction model [10] is similar to the Random Walk as the node also randomly chooses a speed from $[v_{min}, v_{max}]$ and a direction between 0 and 180 degrees. But in contrast to the Random Walk the node always moves to the border of the simulation area. Here the node pauses for a randomly determined time and after that chooses a new direction and a new speed.

The Random Direction model has the advantage to overcome so called density waves, i.e. a clustering of nodes in one part of the simulation area, that for example the Random Waypoint model suffers from [20].

2.4 Scenario Generation

As mentioned above a mobility model describes the behavior of a single node or a group of nodes by some formal definition. One common way to use mobility models in a simulation is to generate a mobility scenario. A mobility scenario contains the movement patterns of nodes that follow the definition from a mobility model, i.e. the scenario contains realizations of the mobility model. Scenario generators like BonnMotion [1] can create scenarios from a large list of mobility models that can then be loaded by simulation tools like OMNeT++ [13] to be used in a larger simulation model.

Without loss of generality we identify nodes by a number $i \in \mathbb{N}_{>0}$. We assume in the following that a scenario consists of waypoints that define at what time t a node i is at location (x, y), i.e. a waypoint is a tuple (i, t, x, y). The possible values for a location (x, y) are restricted by the size of the simulation area $\mathcal{C}$, i.e. we require $(x, y) \in \mathcal{C}$.

Then $\mathcal{S}^{(i)} = ((i, t_{i,1}, x_{i,1}, y_{i,1}), (i, t_{i,2}, x_{i,2}, y_{i,2}), \cdots, (i, t_{i,l}, x_{i,l}, y_{i,l}))$ contains all waypoints of a single node until the end of the simulation. The first waypoint, i.e. the initial location is usually chosen randomly. Further waypoints are always necessary when a node changes direction or speed, either explicitly by selecting a new destination, direction or speed randomly or implicitly when bouncing off the boundaries of the simulation area as for the Random Walk model. This implies for two consecutive waypoints $(i, t_{i,1}, x_{i,1}, y_{i,1})$ and $(i, t_{i,2}, x_{i,2}, y_{i,2})$ that in the time interval $[t_{i,1}, t_{i,2}]$ node i moves with constant speed from $(x_{i,1}, y_{i,1})$ to $(x_{i,2}, y_{i,2})$. For pause times the locations of two consecutive waypoints are identical.

The complete scenario for n nodes is then given by $\mathcal{S} = \left(\mathcal{S}^{(1)}, \mathcal{S}^{(2)}, \cdots, \mathcal{S}^{(n)} \right)$.

2.5 Autoregressive-To-Anything Processes

Autoregressive-To-Anything (ARTA) Processes [11] combine an autoregressive process of order p, denoted $AR(p)$, with an arbitrary marginal distribution F_Y. The $AR(p)$ is given by [7]

$$Z_t = \alpha_1 Z_{t-1} + \alpha_2 Z_{t-2} + \ldots + \alpha_p Z_{t-p} + \epsilon_t$$

where the α_i are autoregressive coefficients and the values ϵ_t, denoted as inno-
vations, are normally distributed with zero mean and variance σ_ϵ^2. The ARTA
process is then defined as a sequence

$$Y_t = F_Y^{-1}[\Phi(Z_t)], t = 1, 2, \ldots$$

where F_Y is the marginal distribution, Φ is the standard normal cumulative distribution function and $\{Z_t; t = 1, 2, \ldots\}$ is a stationary Gaussian $AR(p)$ process
as described above.

ARTA processes can model correlated input processes with a wide variety
of shapes for the distribution. The approach works for any distribution F_Y for
which F_Y^{-1} can be computed, either by a closed-form expression or by numerical
methods. Since the autocorrelations of the background $AR(p)$ process and the
ARTA process are directly related and autoregressive processes are very flexible
in modeling autocorrelation, the ARTA process inherits this property from the
$AR(p)$ process. In addition, there are approaches available to construct ARTA
processes from measured observations from a real system [5,11].

3   Mobility Models with Arrivals and Departures

There are basically two possible approaches that can be used to extend mobility
models such that they account for arrivals and departures. Of course, one can
modify the definition of the mobility model itself to include the generation of new
nodes and the deletion of departing nodes at runtime. Though, depending on the
complexity of the mobility model this can be complicated and it has to be done
for every mobility model that should be supported. Alternatively, one can leave
the mobility model untouched and add arrivals and departures to the generated
scenarios. Since for arrival and departure generation only the scenario is used,
no knowledge on the mobility model that generated this scenario is required. We
will follow this idea that is sketched in Fig. 1. Our model consists of three parts:

Fig. 1. Scenario generation with arrivals and departures

The (unmodified) mobility model generates a scenario S as described in
Sect. 2. The *Arrival Generator* then adds additional nodes to the scenario resulting in a new scenario S_A and the *Departure Generator* modifies the scenario such
that nodes leave the simulation area. The approach in Fig. 1 is very modular, as
we have no real restrictions on the choice of the mobility model or the generators
for arrivals and departures. We have already introduced three mobility models in
Sect. 2 that we used later in our experiments. But of course the approach works
for the other models mentioned in Sect. 1 as well.

In the following we describe the two generators from Fig. 1 in more detail
and present an algorithm for scenario generation with arrivals and departures of
nodes.

3.1 Arrival and Departure Generators

The Arrival and the Departure Generator work in a similar way, i.e. they have to (randomly) determine the time of an arrival or departure, the location where the node enters or leaves the simulation area and in case of departures also which node should leave. Therefore, the generators basically consist of probability distributions and stochastic processes to draw those random numbers.

In addition they have to utilize a set of entry coordinates $\mathcal{C}_{entry}$ and exit coordinates $\mathcal{C}_{exit}$, respectively. Of course, we have that $\mathcal{C}_{entry} \subset \mathcal{C}$ and $\mathcal{C}_{exit} \subset \mathcal{C}$ and additionally $\mathcal{C}_{entry}$ and $\mathcal{C}_{exit}$ should only consist of points at the boundary of $\mathcal{C}$. $\mathcal{C}_{entry}$ and $\mathcal{C}_{exit}$ can either be a discrete number of coordinates $(x_i, y_i), i = 1, \cdots, k$ or a continuous region $\{(x, y)|(x, y) \in \mathcal{C}\}$. Of course, also combinations of these two definitions are possible.

We define two sets here, because the entry and exit coordinates are not necessarily identical. If we model a part of an airport terminal, e.g. the route to the gates is only an exit point but not an entry point. In other scenarios like an university campus we might of course have that $\mathcal{C}_{entry} = \mathcal{C}_{exit}$, though.

The choice of the probability distributions or stochastic processes for random number generation of course depends on the system we want to model. In the simplest form one could just use standard distributions, e.g. an exponential distribution for interarrival and interdeparture times and an uniform distribution for the selection of entry and exit coordinates.

If the arrivals or departures should exhibit autocorrelation a stochastic process is required. We already introduced ARTA processes in Sect. 2 that are suitable for this task and that we used for our experiments. An alternative to this are Markovian Arrival Processes [9] that are more prominent for models that should be analyzed numerically, but can also be used in simulation.

It is of course also possible to use more elaborate stochastic processes like Marked MAPs [8] or Vector ARTA processes [6] that can generate interevent time and entry/exit coordinates in one step and can additionally express correlation between those two values.

For the Departure Generator a further distribution for the selection of the nodes has to be specified. Possible candidates are a discrete uniform distribution or a geometric distribution, that could be used to make the selection of a node with a small number (i.e. a node that is in the system for a long time) more likely.

Assume, that we have n initial nodes in the scenario without arrivals and departures. Then, more formally, the arrival generator creates a sequence

$$\left((n + 1, t_{n+1}^{(entry)}, x_{n+1}^{(entry)}, y_{n+1}^{(entry)}), (n + 2, t_{n+2}^{(entry)}, x_{n+2}^{(entry)}, y_{n+2}^{(entry)}), \cdots \right)$$

where $(x_{n+i}^{(entry)}, y_{n+i}^{(entry)}) \in \mathcal{C}_{entry}$. The i-th tuple is the first waypoint of node $n + i$. The remaining waypoints are then determined by the mobility model $\mathcal{M}$, i.e. we obtain

$$\mathcal{S}^{(n+i)} = \left((n + i, t_{n+i}^{(entry)}, x_{n+i}^{(entry)}, y_{n+i}^{(entry)}), (n + i, t_{n+i,2}, x_{n+i,2}, y_{n+i,2}), \cdots \right).$$

In a similar way, the departure generator creates a sequence

$$\left((i_1, t_{i_1}^{(exit)}, x_{i_1}^{(exit)}, y_{i_1}^{(exit)}), (i_2, t_{i_2}^{(exit)}, x_{i_2}^{(exit)}, y_{i_2}^{(exit)}), \cdots \right)$$

of nodes i_j that should leave the simulation area at location $(x_{i_j}^{(exit)}, y_{i_j}^{(exit)}) \in \mathcal{C}_{exit}$ at time $t_{i_j}^{(exit)}$. Assume that there are n initial nodes in the scenario and the arrival generator created l additional nodes. Let $\mathcal{N} \subseteq \{1, 2, \cdots, n+l\}$ denote all the nodes that exist in the scenario at a departure time $t^{(exit)}$. Then of course, the node i_j that should leave the area may only be drawn from $\mathcal{N}$.

In the final step the departure generator has to modify $\mathcal{S}^{(i_j)}$, i.e. a new waypoint $(i_j, t^{(reroute)}, x^{(reroute)}, y^{(reroute)})$ has to be determined. All waypoints $(i_j, t, x, y) \in \mathcal{S}^{(i_j)}$ with $t > t^{(reroute)}$ are discarded and $(i_j, t^{(reroute)}, x^{(reroute)}, y^{(reroute)})$ and $(i_j, t^{(exit)}, x^{(exit)}, y^{(exit)})$ are added as new waypoints. We will explain in the next section, where the scenario generation is described, how this new waypoint can be determined.

3.2   Scenario Generation

The algorithm for a scenario generation that includes arrivals and departures is sketched in Fig. 2. As already mentioned, we are using a modular approach and consequently the algorithm consists of three parts: The creation of the scenario from the mobility model without arrivals and departures (line 1), extending the scenario with arrivals (lines 2–10) and the addition of departures (lines 11–12). As inputs the algorithm takes the mobility model $\mathcal{M}$, the size or coordinates of the simulation area $\mathcal{C}$, the simulation time and the number of nodes n that populate the area in the beginning. Further inputs are related to the arrivals and departures, i.e. we need a list of entry and exit coordinates, an arrival generator $\mathcal{A}$ and a departure generator $\mathcal{D}$, that are basically probability distributions or stochastic processes we can sample from. The *offset* indicates when arrival and departure generation should start, i.e. we simulate the initial n mobile nodes only for *offset* time units before arrivals and departures start.

First, the algorithm generates a scenario $\mathcal{S}$ that contains the movement patterns for the n initial nodes according to the mobility model $\mathcal{M}$ in line 1, i.e. it calls a subroutine for an existing mobility model like Random Waypoint or Random Direction.

In the second step arrivals are added. We sample the next arrival time $t_c(arrival)$ from the arrival generator (line 5) and determine the entry coordinates from $\mathcal{C}_{entry}$ (line 6). In the algorithm the arrival time and the entry coordinates are determined independent of each other. Once the entry point and the arrival time are known we use the mobility model $\mathcal{M}$ to generate the movement patterns for the new node (line 7). Thus, the movements of the initial nodes and the generated nodes basically differ in the generation of the first waypoint. While the initial nodes start at $t = 0$ at some random point of the simulation area, nodes created by the arrival generator start at an entry point at some time during the simulation. After that they behave similar according to

Input: Mobility Model $\mathcal{M}$, Coordinates of simulation area $\mathcal{C}$;
Input: Arrival Generator $\mathcal{A}$, Entry coordinates $\mathcal{C}_{entry}$;
Input: Departure Generator $\mathcal{D}$, Exit coordinates $\mathcal{C}_{exit}$;
Input: simtime, offset, n
Output: Mobility scenario $\mathcal{S}_{AD}$;
  1: generate $\mathcal{S} = \left(\mathcal{S}^{(1)}, \mathcal{S}^{(2)}, \cdots, \mathcal{S}^{(n)}\right)$ from $\mathcal{M}$;
  2: t = offset;
  3: c = n+1;
  4: **repeat**
  5:    draw t_{sample} according to $\mathcal{A}$; $t_c^{(entry)} = t + t_{sample}$;
  6:    draw $(x_c^{(entry)}, y_c^{(entry)})$ from $\mathcal{C}_{entry}$ according to $\mathcal{A}$;
  7:    generate $\mathcal{S}^{(c)} = \left((c, t_c^{(entry)}, x_c^{(entry)}, y_c^{(entry)}), \cdots\right)$ from $\mathcal{M}$;
  8:    $t = t_c^{(entry)}$; c = c+1;
  9:    $\mathcal{S} = \mathcal{S} \cup \mathcal{S}^{(c)}$;
10: **until** t > simtime
11: t = offset;
12: **repeat**
13:    draw t_{sample} according to $\mathcal{D}$; $t^{(exit)} = t + t_{sample}$;
14:    draw $(x^{(exit)}, y^{(exit)})$ from $\mathcal{C}_{exit}$ according to $\mathcal{D}$;
15:    determine nodes $\mathcal{N}$ that are available at time t_{exit};
16:    draw i from $\mathcal{N}$;
17:    compute $(t^{(reroute)}, x^{(reroute)}, y^{(reroute)})$ from $\mathcal{S}^{(i)}$;
18:    $\mathcal{S}'^{(i)} = ((i, t_{i1}, x_{i1}, y_{i1}), \cdots, (i, t_{ij}, x_{ij}, y_{ij}),$
        $(i, t^{(reroute)}, x^{(reroute)}, y^{(reroute)}, (i, t^{(exit)}, x^{(exit)}, y^{(exit)}))$;
19:    $\mathcal{S} = \mathcal{S} \setminus \mathcal{S}^{(i)} \cup \mathcal{S}'^{(i)}$;
20:    $t = t^{(exit)}$;
21: **until** t > simtime
22: $\mathcal{S}_{AD} = \mathcal{S}$;

Fig. 2. Algorithm for scenario generation

mobility model $\mathcal{M}$. Finally, the movement patterns of the newly generated node is added to the scenario and the time is increased.

The last part of the scenario generation consists of the computation of departures. The first steps are similar to the arrival generation, i.e. we draw the departure time $t^{(exit)}$ and the exit coordinates (lines 13 and 14). In addition to this information we also have to determine which node should leave the simulation area (lines 15 and 16). Note, that our scenario $\mathcal{S}$ contains the movement of all nodes and some of them did probably not exist at time $t^{(exit)}$. Hence, we collect in $\mathcal{N}$ all nodes that inhabit the simulation area at $t^{(exit)}$. Recall, that we used an *offset* for the beginning of the arrival and departure generation. It is advisable to use an offset here as well, i.e. only nodes that have existed for at least *offset* time units in the model at time $t^{(exit)}$ are collected in $\mathcal{N}$. The reasons for this offset will become obvious later when we describe how the node is routed to the exit point.

From $\mathcal{N}$ we randomly determine one node for departure. In lines 17 and 18 new waypoints for this node are computed, i.e. we identify a time $t^{(reroute)}$ and a corresponding location $(x^{(reroute)}, y^{(reroute)})$ where the existing movements of the node are interrupted and from where it is rerouted to the exit point. We will explain below how this is done exactly. Finally, the old waypoints for the departing node are deleted from the scenario and replaced by new waypoints including the departure.

In accordance with Fig. 1 line 1 of the algorithm describes the scenario generation by the mobility model, lines 2–10 constitute the arrival generator and lines 11–21 describe the departure generator.

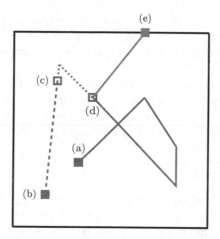

Fig. 3. Rerouting for departure (Color figure online)

Figure 3 depicts how the rerouting of mobile nodes for departure works. The blue lines starting at (a) and ending at (b) are the original movement patterns as generated from the mobility model. (e) is the exit point where the node is supposed to depart at time $t^{(exit)}$. First we compute the location of the node at time $t^{(exit)}$ according to the original movement pattern. This location is labeled with (c) in Fig. 3. The remaining part of the original movement pattern, i.e. the dashed line between (c) and (b) is discarded. Starting from (c) we process the node's movement backwards until we have found a location $(x^{(reroute)}, y^{(reroute)})$ and the corresponding time $t^{(reroute)}$, such that the node can cover the distance between $(x^{(reroute)}, y^{(reroute)})$ and the exit point in time $t^{(exit)} - t^{(reroute)}$ with an appropriate speed, i.e. a speed that is for example drawn from the speed range for that mobility model or corresponds to the node's mean speed. This location is labeled (d) in Fig. 3. The movements between the locations (d) and (c) are also discarded and the node gets new waypoints for the locations (d) and (e).

From Fig. 3 it becomes obvious why the *offset* introduced in the algorithm in Fig. 2 is helpful. If a departure is due at the very beginning of the lifetime of a node it might not be possible to find a suitable location to reroute the node, since it has hardly moved yet. The *offset* ensures that all nodes applicable for departure have existing movement patterns at the time of the departure.

Of course, the rerouting introduces some overhead when generating the scenario, because parts of the already generated movement patterns are discarded again. However, it has the important advantage that it can be used for any mobility model, since it works only on the generated movement patterns and no knowledge about the mobility model or changes to the mobility model are required.

4   Experimental Evaluation

To systematically assess the effect of arrivals and departures on the performance of a wireless network we combined mobility models with different arrival and departure generators with varying rates and correlation for the creation and deletion of nodes.

Although the approach presented in Sect. 3 is very general and not specific to certain mobility models, we conducted our experiments with three basic random mobility models that are well known and understood, in particular the Random Walk, Random Direction and Random Waypoint models.

4.1   Experiment Setup

Our experiments were performed using OMNeT++ [13] and the INET framework, that supports mobility scenarios in the form described in Sect. 2. The extension with arrivals and departures required slight modifications of the standard modules from OMNeT++ to allow for nodes to become active (i.e. arrive) or inactive (i.e. leave) during the simulation run.

For the experiments we used a simple quadratic simulation area of $100 \times 100\,\mathrm{m}^2$. There are four access points that cover the area as shown in Fig. 4. We added nine entry and exit points ($\mathcal{C}_{entry} = \mathcal{C}_{exit}$) evenly to the border of the area and generated various mobility scenarios using the algorithm from Fig. 2 for Random Walk, Random Direction and Random Waypoint models that differed in the number of initial nodes, the rate of arrivals and departures or the correlation of arrivals and departures. In all models we assumed that the mean arrival rate and the mean departure rate are equal to keep the mean number of nodes equal to the initial number of nodes. The speed of the mobile nodes lies within the interval $v_{min} = 3\,\mathrm{km/h}$ and $v_{max} = 8\,\mathrm{km/h}$. If the model supports pause times they are between 0 and 30 s. As *offset* we used 100 s, i.e. the model is simulated for 100 s before arrival and departure generation starts. In addition we required that a node has to exist for at least 100 s before it may be selected for departure. Each scenario was simulated for 180 min.

At randomly chosen times the mobile nodes generate traffic. To keep the model simple and allow for a better control of the generated data volume, we modeled traffic generation at an abstract level without including all the network layers. The access points are basically servers with a buffer size of 50 that handle

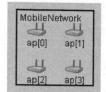

Fig. 4. Simulation area with access points

the traffic randomly generated by the nodes that are close to them, i.e. each node generates load for the access point that is closest to its current location. When a node is moving the nearest access point might of course change during the simulation. To be able to assess whether the different scenarios have an effect on the performance we measured the queue length distribution in the four access points.

4.2 Experimental Results

Before we present the results of the queue length distribution we visualize the effect of arrivals and departures using the spatial node distribution. The spatial node distribution shows the probability that nodes are at the different locations of the simulation area. Figure 5 shows the spatial node distribution for a Random Waypoint model with an initial number of $n = 30$ nodes with and without arrivals and departures. As we can see in Fig. 5(b) the probability that nodes are at the border of the simulation area where the entry and exit points are increases, while the distribution remains similar in other parts of the area. Figure 6 shows the number of nodes and the average number of nodes that are present in the simulation area for a Random Waypoint model with $n = 30$ and arrivals and departures for the first 6000 s. As we can see the number of nodes varies around $n = 30$ (while the average number of nodes remains almost constant), implying that there are periods with a higher load for the access points and periods with a lower load. The effect of these periods on the access points is evaluated in the following.

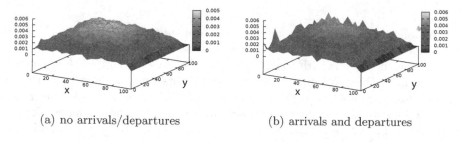

(a) no arrivals/departures   (b) arrivals and departures

Fig. 5. Spatial node distribution of random waypoint model

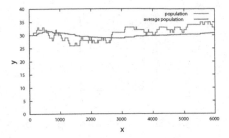

Fig. 6. Number of nodes present in the simulation area

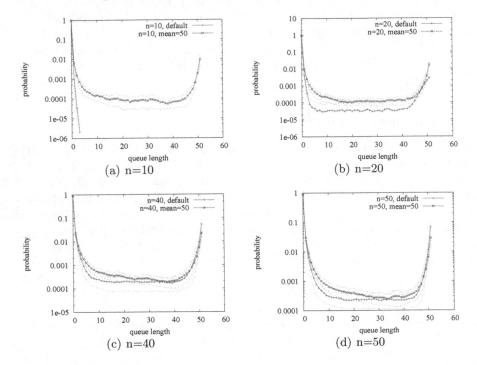

Fig. 7. Queue length distribution for different numbers of initial nodes and the Random Direction model (thin dashed lines denote the 90 % confidence intervals)

The following simulation results are all obtained from 30 replications of the simulation model. If applicable we also present 90 % confidence intervals for the results, though for plots with a larger number of curves we omitted them to keep the plots accessible. In a first series of experiments we compared the effect of arrival and departures for different numbers of initial nodes n. As a reference value we simulated the original default scenarios with a constant number of nodes and compared it with scenarios where arrivals and departures occur according to an exponential distribution with mean 50. The entry and exit nodes are drawn independently from an uniform distribution. Figure 7 shows the queue length

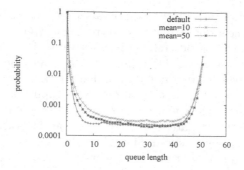

Fig. 8. Queue length distribution for different arrival rates for the Random Waypoint model and $n = 30$

distribution at the first access point for the Random Direction model for an increasing number of initial nodes. The results for the other access points and mobility models are similar. As we can see arrivals and departures have a large effect for the smaller node numbers but the effect diminishes if we increase the number of nodes (i.e. the difference in the mean values becomes smaller and the confidence intervals start to overlap). Obviously, this is because fluctuations in the node number caused by arrivals and departures have a larger influence if the initial number of nodes is relatively small compared to the size of the fluctuation, i.e. three additional nodes are easily noticeable if there are 10 nodes present but the effect disappears if there are 50 nodes.

For the next experiments we kept the initial number of nodes fixed and varied the arrival rate. Results for the Random Waypoint model are shown in Fig. 8. The plot shows the curves for the default model without arrivals and departures and for models where the arrivals and departures follow an exponential distribution with mean 10 and 50, respectively. As we can see, the queue length increases slightly with smaller mean values (i.e. larger rates).

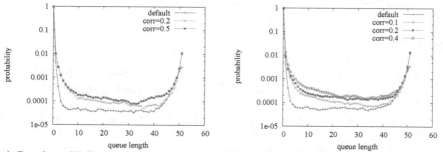

(a) Random Walk model, correlated arrivals

(b) Random Waypoint model, correlated arrivals and departures

Fig. 9. Queue length distribution for different levels of lag-1 autocorrelation for $n = 20$

As mentioned before, it is likely that arrivals and/or departures are correlated in some real world scenarios. We already introduced ARTA processes in Sect. 2 that can serve to model autocorrelated interarrival or interdeparture times. In the last experiments we evaluated the effect of autocorrelation on the mobile network. Figure 9(a) shows the results for a Random Walk model where the arrivals are generated according to an ARTA process with exponential distribution and different levels of autocorrelation, while the departures follow an exponential distribution and are uncorrelated. As we can see, an increased autocorrelation also results in a larger queue length. Similar results can be observed in Fig. 9(b) where both, arrivals and departures, are generated by identical ARTA processes and thus, are correlated.

The experimental results clearly indicate, that arrivals and departures can have a significant effect on the performance of a wireless network. We have also seen that this effect becomes larger if the variation in the number of nodes is relatively large compared to the mean number of nodes, which can be caused by a higher arrival rate or correlated arrivals.

5   Conclusions

We have presented an approach to combine mobility models with stochastic processes to account for the arrival and departure of nodes during simulation. The approach works on the generated scenarios and thus, can easily be combined with any mobility model. Arrivals and departures of mobility nodes occur in many real world scenarios (like airports, shopping centers, parts of an university campus) and our experimental study suggests, that modeling of arrivals and departures can have a significant effect on the performance results.

Of course, the results presented here can only serve as a first step towards more realistic mobility models. We only used completely synthetically generated mobility scenarios in our study. Mobility models based on real-world observations naturally qualify for an extension with arrival and departure generators since the observations already contain information about nodes that newly arrive or leave the area, but are subject to further research.

References

1. Aschenbruck, N., Ernst, R., Gerhards-Padilla, E., Schwamborn, M.: BonnMotion - a mobility scenario generation and analysis tool. In: Proceedings of the SIMUTools (2010)
2. Balachandran, A., Voelker, G., Bahl, P., Rangan, P.: Characterizing user behavior and network performance in a public wireless LAN. In: SIGMETRICS (2002)
3. Bettstetter, C.: Smooth is better than sharp: a random mobility model for simulation of wireless networks. In: Proceedings of the MSWIM (2002)
4. Bhatia, H., Lenin, R.B., Munjal, A., Ramaswamy, S., Srivastava, S.: A queuing-theoretic framework for modeling and analysis of mobility in WSNs. In: Proceedings of the PerMIS (2008)

5. Biller, B., Nelson, B.: Fitting time-series input processes for simulation. Oper. Res. **53**(3), 549–559 (2005)
6. Biller, B., Nelson, B.L.: Modeling and generating multivariate time-series input processes using a vector autoregressive technique. ACM Trans. Model. Comput. Simul. **13**(3), 211–237 (2003)
7. Box, G., Jenkins, G.: Time Series Analysis - Forecasting and Control. Holden-Day, San Francisco (1970)
8. Buchholz, P., Kemper, P., Kriege, J.: Multi-class markovian arrival processes and their parameter fitting. Perform. Eval. **67**(11), 1092–1106 (2010)
9. Buchholz, P., Kriege, J., Felko, I.: Input Modeling with Phase-Type Distributions and Markov Models - Theory and Applications. Springer, Heidelberg (2014)
10. Camp, T., Boleng, J., Davies, V.: A survey of mobility models for ad hoc network research. Wirel. Commun. Mob. Comput. **2**(5), 483–502 (2002)
11. Cario, M., Nelson, B.: Autoregressive to anything: time-series input processes for simulation. Oper. Res. Lett. **19**(2), 51–58 (1996)
12. Chen, Y., Kurose, J., Towsley, D.: A mixed queueing network model of mobility in a campus wireless network. In: Proceedings of the INFOCOM (2012)
13. Hornig, R., Varga, A.: An overview of the OMNeT++ simulation environment. In: Proceedings of the SIMUTools (2008)
14. Jardosh, A., Belding-Royer, E., Almeroth, K., Suri, S.: Towards realistic mobility models for mobile ad hoc networks. In: Proceedings of the MobiCom (2003)
15. Kim, M., Kotz, D., Kim, S.: Extracting a mobility model from real user traces. In: Proceedings of the INFOCOM (2006)
16. Leland, W.E., Taqqu, M.S., Willinger, W., Wilson, D.V.: On the self-similar nature of ethernet traffic (extended version). IEEE/ACM Trans. Netw. **2**(1), 1–15 (1994)
17. Liang, B., Haas, Z.: Predictive distance-based mobility management for PCS networks. In: Proceedings of the INFOCOM (1999)
18. Navidi, W., Camp, T.: Stationary distributions for random waypoint models. IEEE Trans. Mobile Comput. **3**(1), 99–108 (2004)
19. Resta, G., Santi, P.: The QoS-RWP mobility and user behavior model for public area wireless networks. In: Proceedings of the MSWiM (2006)
20. Royer, E., Melliar-Smith, P., Moser, L.: An analysis of the optimum node density for ad hoc mobile networks. In: Proceedings of the IEEE ICC (2001)
21. Tuduce, C., Gross, T.: A mobility model based on WLAN traces and its validation. In: Proceedings of the INFOCOM (2005)
22. Yoon, J., Noble, B., Liu, M., Kim, M.: Building realistic mobility models from coarse-grained traces. In: Proceedings of the MobiSys (2006)

Product Line Fault Tree Analysis by Means of Multi-valued Decision Diagrams

Michael Käßmeyer[1]([⊠]), Rüdiger Berndt[2], Peter Bazan[2],
and Reinhard German[2]

[1] Audi Electronics Venture GmbH, Gaimersheim, Germany
michael.kaessmeyer@audi.de
[2] Friedrich-Alexander-Universität Erlangen-Nürnberg, Erlangen, Germany
{ruediger.berndt,peter.bazan,reinhard.german}@fau.de

Abstract. The development of cyber-physical systems such as highly integrated, safety-relevant automotive functions is challenged by an increasing complexity resulting from both customizable products and numerous soft- and hardware variants. In order to reduce the time to market for scenarios like these, a systematic analysis of the dependencies between functions, as well as the functional and technical variance, is required (cf. ISO 26262). In this paper we introduce a new approach which allows for a compact representation and analysis of failure mechanisms of systems marked by numerous variants, also: Product Line Fault Tree (PLFTs), in a unified data structure based on Multi-valued Decision Diagram (MDDs). Therefore, instead of analyzing the Fault Tree (FT) of each variant separately, the proposed method enables one to analyze the FT in a single step. Summing up, this article introduces a systematic modeling concept to analyze fault propagation in variant-rich systems.

Keywords: Fault tree · Multi-valued decision diagrams · Safety engineering · Reliability · Dependability analysis · Variant management · Product line engineering · Minimal cut set

1 Introduction

Automotive functions of this day and age interact with most diverse digital networks, for example to realize new in-vehicle services, to increase road safety, to encourage an efficient control of the growing traffic volume, or to enable autonomous driving. Such Cyber-Physical System (CPSs) usually operate with respect to different and only partially predictable contexts and comprise a high number of embedded systems. This is why automotive functions are marked by variance and high complexity, in turn functional safety is of considerable importance.

In the last decade, model-based development has been established in the automotive sector to manage the increasing complexity which is mainly induced by highly-integrated Electronic Control Unit (ECUs) and the growing number of variant-rich functions [1]. In this context, an automotive safety standard is

© Springer International Publishing Switzerland 2016
A. Remke and B.R. Haverkort (Eds.): MMB & DFT 2016, LNCS 9629, pp. 122–136, 2016.
DOI: 10.1007/978-3-319-31559-1_11

given by the ISO 26262 [2] postulating normative requirements to ensure functional safety within electrical and electronic vehicle systems. These include a hazard and risk analysis, a safety analysis, as well as verification and validation of the resulting safety mechanisms, just to name a few. Consequently, the overall safety assessment is labor-intensive and time-consuming, also because available software tools that ought to support traceability or semi-automated consistency and completeness checks often do not meet specific user expectations.

All things considered, the development of a completely secure system incorporating all required safety mechanisms is hardly possible with state-of-the-art safety assessment methods such as Fault Tree Analysis (FTA). This is because on the one hand, systems are marked by different versions as well as numerous variants, and on the other hand, due to the lack of appropriate methods and tools to compactly represent and efficiently analyze such systems.

Therefore, in this article a new method is established to compactly represent the FT of variant-rich systems, i.e. PLFT, within a single data structure: MDDs, also referred to as 150 % model. Based on such compact MDD-based FT representations, the proposed method allows us to generate an MDD representation of the Minimal Cut Set (MCSs) of the system including all variants. This data structure, accordingly, enables one to extract the MCS of specific variants. Moreover, for a given MCS, the variants where the corresponding MCS will cause the system to fail can be identified.

The remainder of this article is structured as follows: Sect. 2 will give an overview of automotive safety engineering and MDDs. Then, in Sect. 3, the modeling approach of variants in FTs is presented. Section 4 demonstrates how FTs with variants can be superposed and represented as MDD. In Sect. 5, it is shown how the MCSs of the PLFT can be compactly encoded by an MDD. Finally, in Sect. 6, we summarize this article and suggest future research.

2   Related Work

2.1   Fault Tree Analysis

FTA is a method to identify potential hazards causing the violation of a system's safety goals (e.g., unintended acceleration of the car). It is used in the field of safety and reliability engineering to identify the causes which let a system fail [3,4]. Usually, this technique is applied considering different architectures, designs and abstraction levels (cf., function, component, system) to derive safety mechanisms (e.g., fault detection and reaction, redundancy, etc.) and thus to alleviate the identified problem spots.

The starting point for an FTA is the definition of an undesired event, also: Top Level Event (TLE). In the next step, this event is resolved into Basic Event (BEs), like failure of a certain hardware device, whose combined occurrence will trigger the TLE. By doing so, relations among basic events—which are, among others, induced by the system's architecture—are reflected by logical gates (AND or OR) [3,5]—see Fig. 1. In other words, the FT represents a Boolean Function encoding the fault propagation which will lead to the (undesired) TLE.

The benefits of constructing a FT within a defined boundary of the system, is given by the identification of all different mechanisms that will trigger the TLE. Moreover, during the development of the FT, an overall understanding of the system's basic errors and their interrelations is obtained. The main purposes of FTA are: (1) identify critical events, (2) identify critical paths of events that propagate to the top event, (3) identify potential system weaknesses, and (4) identify safety mechanisms to be integrated in the system. relationships between the top event and the primary events are described (Cut Set (CSs)).

The qualitative analysis of FTs is based on the CS and the MCS. The CS is a set of basic events whose occurrence will cause the system to fail. The MCS is a CS where no proper subset is a CS. The TLE will therefore only occur, if all basic events in a MCS happen at the same time [5,6].

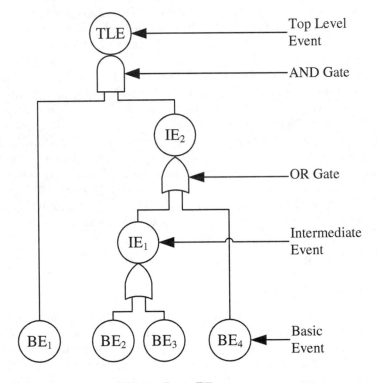

Fig. 1. Basic FT structure

Next, the related work on the overlapping areas of FTA and Product Line Engineering (PLE) are introduced. The Software Fault Tree Analysis (SFTA) is an extension of the FTA for safety-critical systems, it has proved to be an essential method for software/safety engineers during the design phase of safety-critical software products [7,8].

Dehlinger proposed how to attach commonality and variability attributes to the PLFT and managed it as a core asset [9]. Lu's work [10] extends Dehlinger's work and is another way to obtain the same result for product lines. The so-called Fault Contribution Tree (FCT) is a variability tree for the product line where nodes are features instead of events (or conditions) [11]. Feng's work [12] is another extension of Dehlinger's contribution constructing a software fault tree in a different manner: the method begins considering commonality and variability analysis as well as the product line architecture to obtain the so-called Extended Commonality and Variability Analysis (XCA). After that, the SFTA is carried out based on the XCA and the Software Failure Modes and Effects Analysis (SFMEA). Noda [13] proposes a method assuming the fault of features from the feature diagram. A feature is selected and turned into the root node of the FT, then this structure is analyzed to identify all paths to the root node. Based on that, countermeasures are identified—like adding optional features to the diagram.

In [14], the authors carry over product lines to the Component Fault Tree (CFT) approach. By doing so, the product line is steadily maintained over time and information on variability is considered w.r.t. FTAs. This method, for example, considers a component ("Ventilation System") to be reused from a previous Gas Turbine PL (SGT 500) within another Gas Turbine PL (SGT 400), the component is analyzed whether it is marked by the same software behavior, functions and structure. In the end, if the component is fully compatible with required characteristics, it is suited for the new product line [15, 16].

In contrast to these articles and the corresponding modeling approaches, this paper will rather focus on algorithms and data structures to efficiently analyze fault propagation of variant-rich automotive functions using MDDs.

2.2   Multi-valued Decision Diagrams

In [17], the authors introduce a graph-based structure (similar to Binary Decision Diagram (BDDs) [18, 19]) to represent and manipulate discrete functions which they refer to as MDD (also: function graph). The advantages of BDDs are the simple structure and the possibility of variable bit-wise interleaving. Compared to BDDs—specifically tailored with respect to Boolean functions—MDD are used to represent multi-valued functions and getting along with fewer variables. Therefore, the determination of a favorable variable order can be more efficient.

DEFINITION: MULTI-VALUED FUNCTION. A function

$$f : X_1 \times \cdots \times X_k \to Y \tag{1}$$

is called multi-valued if the domains of all variables $X_1, \ldots X_k$ and the image of the function $I \subseteq Y$ are finite sets.

EXAMPLE: LEAST COMMON MULTIPLE. In number theory, the least common multiple (LCM) of two integers is the smallest natural number that is divisible by both numbers without remainder. Let the function

$$\text{LCM} : \mathbb{Z} \times \mathbb{Z} \to \mathbb{N} \tag{2}$$

and two variables $X_1 := \{1, 2, 3, 4\}$ and $X_2 := \{1, 2, 3\}$ be given.

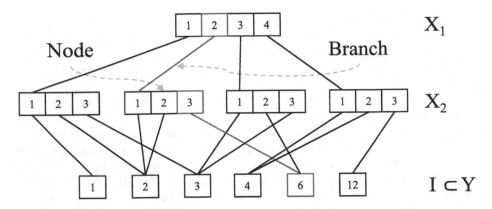

Fig. 2. MDD representation of the LCM of two integers (Color figure online)

Figure 2 shows an MDD encoding this example. MDDs are Directed Acyclic Graph (DAGs). The nodes of the first level represent X_1, the nodes of the second level X_2, and the nodes of the bottom level I. Since all branches always direct from a top to a lower node, they are depicted as non-oriented lines. The maximum number of outgoing branches and thus the maximum number of child nodes are determined by the cardinality of the corresponding domain. Each branch represents the allocation of a value. The red nodes and branches in Fig. 2, for example, represent $X_1 = 2$, $X_2 = 3$, and $Y = 6$.

An MDD is called ordered, if the variables occur in each path in the same order. It is called reduced, if no equivalent sub-graphs are contained. If an MDD fulfills both criteria it is called Reduced Ordered Multi-valued Decision Diagram (ROMDD)[1].

Most generally, decision diagrams are considered data structures to efficiently encode large sets. Therefore, they are supported by a rich body of research and used in many applications: among others for dependency and reliability analyses in safety critical systems, e.g., to encode the state space of the system or to include fault probabilities using edge-values [20,21].

3   Modeling Systems with Variants

Inspired by the related work, this section will describe two approaches on how to model variant-rich systems: while the first approach distinguishes variants by the absence of the system's components, the second approach suggests a concept where variants of the system are distinguished by different modules. Both approaches are illustrated by examples.

3.1   Structure-Preserving Fault Trees

In the following, the term variance refers to the components of the system and their presence or absence, respectively. Therefore, the structure of the fault

---

[1] For reasons of simplicity we henceforth write MDD instead of ROMDD.

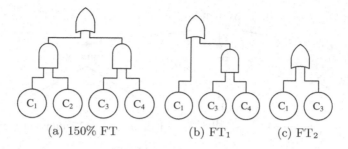

(a) 150% FT   (b) FT$_1$ (c) FT$_2$

Fig. 3. 150 % FT and the two available variants

propagation, i.e. the arrangement of the logical gates, remains untouched. Only components that are not part of a specific variant are removed from the structure (cf. [9]). Of course, unconnected gates need to be recursively removed from the FT. Let a system consisting of four components $\{C_1, C_2, C_3, C_4\}$ be given (Fig. 3a). Based on that, for example two variants can be derived:

- the first variant comprises $\{C_1, C_3, C_4\}$ (Fig. 3b),
- the second variant comprises $\{C_1, C_3\}$ (Fig. 3c).

Each of both FTs can be converted into the corresponding BDD representation as shown by Fig. 4a and b. In this notation solid lines correspond to the binary value 1 and dotted lines to the value 0—this value is omitted in most branches for simplicity. Constructing the BDDs representation of a FT is well known but will be shortly recapitulated at the beginning of Sect. 4.

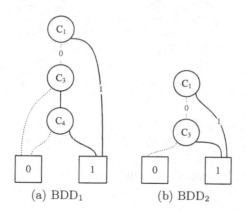

(a) BDD$_1$ (b) BDD$_2$

Fig. 4. BDD-based representations of FT$_1$ and FT$_2$

3.2   Modular Systems with Variants

This section describes another approach to model variant-rich FTs based on features and modules. Figure 5 depicts a feature model of a system consisting of

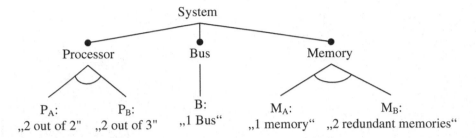

Fig. 5. Feature model

three modules: Processor (P), Bus (B), and Memory (M). There are two different variants of the processor module: P_A and P_B, and there are two variants of the memory module: M_A and M_B. In addition, the following constraint is used to restrict the configuration space:"if P_B is selected, then M_B must be selected". Next, for each available variation of the system's components a Sub Fault Tree (SFT) can be stated as illustrated by Fig. 6b to d.

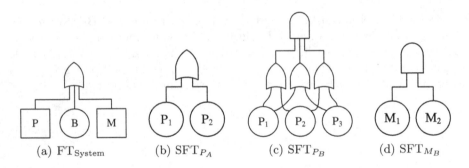

Fig. 6. Fault trees of the system, and of the modules' variations P_A, P_B, and M_B

Note that there is no variation of the bus module since it is considered mandatory in each configuration. The model of M_A, furthermore, is trivial because it only consists of one memory. The overall failure behavior of the system is shown in Fig. 6a, obviously the system will fail as soon as one of its modules will fail. The fault propagation within the modules themselves is reflected by the BDDs shown in Fig. 7a to c.

4   MDD-Based Representation of Variant-Rich FTs

The starting point to construct a BDD representation of a single FT is the TLE. Given that, a depth-first-search is carried out. By doing so, all gates and events are encoded by BDD nodes. Finally, each component of the FT is represented by variables (also: levels) of the BDD.

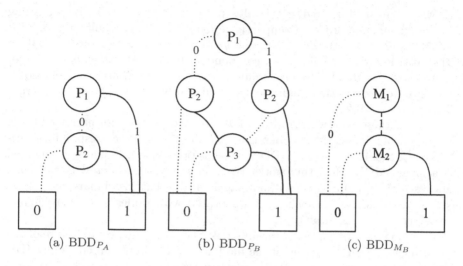

Fig. 7. BDD representations reflecting the fault propagation within the available variants of the modules

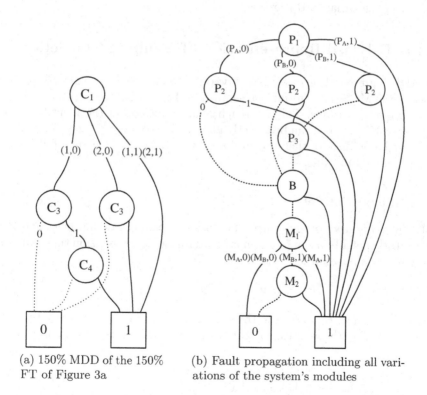

(a) 150% MDD of the 150% FT of Figure 3a

(b) Fault propagation including all variations of the system's modules

Fig. 8. MDD representations of fault trees with variants (Sects. 3.1 and 3.2)

However, instead of BDDs it is also possible to use MDDs for analyzing FTs. For example, in order to compactly represent Dynamic Fault Tree (DFTs) both BDDs [22] and MDDs [23] might be deployed. Furthermore, in [24] an MDD-based analysis of FTs whose components have three states is described. This approach is extended to any number of states in [25]. This idea can also be carried over to systems that might be distinguished by several phases or different fault conditions [20,26].

Following these ideas we introduce MDDs to incorporate information on both: the components behavior (i.e., operating or failure) and the corresponding variants. For example in Fig. 8 the BDD representations of Fig. 4a and b are merged into a single MDD. How this works is explained in more detail in Sect. 5.2. Branches with just 0 or 1 or without label means that just binary values are used. Now, the MDD's branches are annotated with tuples $(i, \{0, 1\})$ where i denotes the according variant.

Given modular systems with variants (see Sect. 3.2), the overall failure of the system, including all variations of the modules, can be represented as an MDD by joining the corresponding BDDs (see Fig. 8b). Here, the branches' annotations $(v, \{0, 1\})$ represent the variation v of the module and whether or not the according component has failed. Note, that this structure also reflects the trivial behavior of the variants M_A and B.

5   MDD-Based Representation of Minimal Cut Sets

The MDD representation of a FT with variants is the basis to construct an MDD encoding the MCSs. The formal presentation of the MCS are introduced for the derivation of algorithms. This approach is an extension of the identification of significant MCSs, which can be directly analyzed from a FT [27,28]. A significant MCS can be defined so that the probability of a failure does not fall below a specified minimum value.

5.1   Minimal Cut Sets

First, this section will briefly introduce basic terms and definitions. The BDD representation of a Boolean function is based on Boole's expansion theorem (also: Shannon decomposition):

$$F(v_1, ..., v_n) = v_i.F_{v_i=1} + \overline{v}_i.F_{v_i=0} \tag{3}$$

Here $F_{v_i=1}$ and $F_{v_i=0}$ denote the function F with argument v_i set to 1 or 0, respectively. This theorem can be carried over to the multi-valued case:

$$F : \{1, 2, \ldots, s\}^n \rightarrow \{0, 1\} \tag{4}$$

$$F(v_1, \ldots, v_n) = (v_i = 1).F_{v_i=1} + (v_i = 2).F_{v_i=2} + \ldots + (v_i = s).F_{v_i=s} \tag{5}$$

The assignment of values to F's variables can be written as *minterm*[2]. In the Boolean case, the *literal* v_i denotes the assignment $v_i = 1$ and the *literal* $\overline{v}_i$ denotes the assignment $v_i = 0$. Considering multi-valued functions, the literal $v_{i,j}$ corresponds to the variable assignment $v_i = j$. Obviously, minterms only contain one literal of each variable. A *conjunction term* is a set of literals which are exclusively connected by logical 'and' (also: conjunction). Accordingly minterms are special conjunction terms. Conjunction terms yielding $F = 1$ are called *implicants* of the function. Implicants that cannot be further reduced are called *prime terms*. According to [29] and based on a given set of literals L (also: 'literals of interest'), the set of MCSs of a function F is defined as the set of all prime terms given that all literals $l \notin L$ are removed. Let a static FT and the corresponding Boolean function F be given. According to [30] and based on the decomposition $F = v.F_1 + \overline{v}.F_0$, the MCSs can be derived as follows:

$$\mathrm{MCS}[F] = \mathrm{MCS}_1 \cup \mathrm{MCS}_0 \tag{6}$$

$$\mathrm{MCS}_0 = \mathrm{MCS}[F_0] \tag{7}$$

$$\mathrm{MCS}_1 = \{v.\pi | \pi \in \mathrm{MCS}[F_1 + F_0] \setminus \mathrm{MCS}_0\}. \tag{8}$$

5.2   Constructing the MDD Representation of the MCSs

This section introduces our approach to derive an MDD-based representation of the MCSs from the MDD-based representation of a PLFT.

Consider the example system of Sect. 3.1. By adding information on the variants at the branches, the corresponding BDD representations of Fig. 4a and b are transformed into equivalent MDDs, first (see Fig. 9a and b). Then the unification of those MDDs yields the 150 % MDD in Fig. 9c. However, when going from the top to the bottom, the variant is already determined by the branches of the root node (reflecting C_1). The construction process of the MDD-representation of the PLFT ensures that information on the variant is not further restricted while descending a path in the diagram. This is why information on variants can be removed on successive branches (see Fig. 9d).

Based on this structure and Shannon's decomposition, the MDD-representation of the MCSs can be recursively computed. The decomposition of C_1 yields three subtrees that are labeled by the bold numbers 1, 2, and 3 in Fig. 9d. While F_0 is represented by the union of the subtrees 1 and 2, F_1 is represented by the subtree 3. Furthermore, let us assume that the MCSs representations of F_0 and $F_1 + F_0$ have already been generated by recursive descent (see Fig. 10a and b).

Next, according to (7), MCS_0 is computed by adding the two 0-branches of C_1, reflecting that literal C_1 is not added to MCS_{F_0} (see Fig. 10c). According to (8), MCS_1 is computed by adding the two 1-branches of C_1. By doing so, literal

---

[2] A minterm is a product term in which each variable appears once. Boolean functions can be expressed as sum of minterms where each minterm corresponds to a row of the function's truth table. This final value of the function's output is 1.

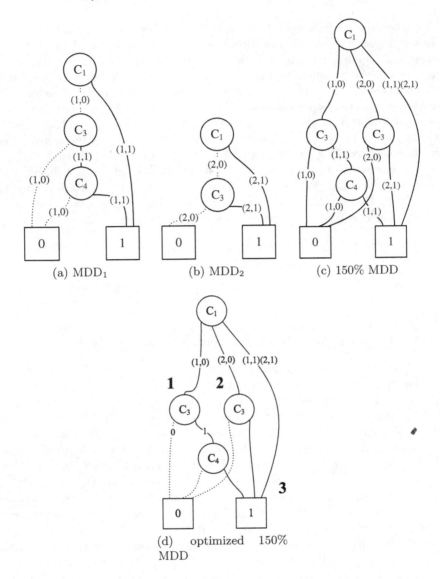

Fig. 9. First, two BDDs are transformed to MDDs and merged to a 150 % MDD in (a)–(c). Afterwards the redundant information has been removed from certain branches in (d).

C_1 is added to the set $MCS[F_1 + F_0] \setminus MCS_0$ (see Fig. 10d). Finally, following (6), the MCSs of the PLFT is computed by unifying MCS_1 and MCS_0 (cf. Fig. 10e). Note, that the MDDs in Fig. 10 omit the terminal node 0. This reduces both memory consumption and computational effort.

With the helo of MDD-based MCS representations several scenarios can be investigated in an efficient manner: for example the identification of the MCSs

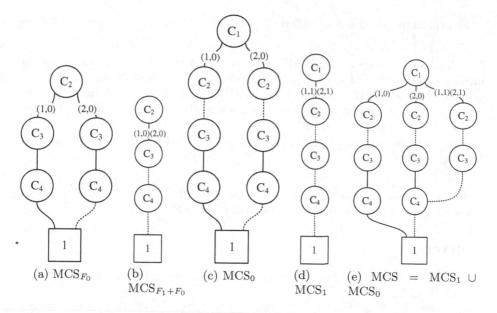

Fig. 10. Constructing the MDD-based representation of MCSs of PLFTs

w.r.t. specific variants; or vice versa, for given MCSs one might be interested in the affected variants. Such queries are based on intersect operations and MDD-based structures encoding the query (for example: a specific variant).

In order to determine the MCSs of the first variant (cf. Fig. 3b), the intersection operation will yield all paths $(1, *)$ of Fig. 10e which, in turn, represent the following set of minimal cut sets: $\{\{C_3, C_4\}, \{C_1\}\}$.

6   Conclusion and Future Work

The approach described in this article allows to efficiently analyze and compare the fault propagation of systems marked by variants, such as highly integrated, variant-rich and safety-relevant automotive functions. The underlying data structure is given by MDDs which are not only used to encode the fault propagation of all of the systems variants but also to represent the corresponding MCSs.

In the near future, we will evaluate the presented approach with real-world automotive systems. In more detail, we plan to derive an MDD representation from variant-rich fault trees, followed by the MCS analysis of a proper constructed MDD. Moreover, following basic analyze options will be evaluated:

- Searching of MCSs for each valid variant.
- Identification of all affected variants with a given MCS.
- Comparison of the MCSs of evolutions and variants of a safety-critical function, and analysis which cardinal number is equal or not.

– Identification of similar or differing safety mechanism in evolutions and variants of a function.

On this basis, we want to identify metrics to improve our approach, and to measure the impact of change requests affecting the product line of a given system. However, we plan to integrate the MDD analysis approach into a model-based safety and variant management framework (cf. [31,32]). Finally, in order to keep the approach practicable, we want to investigate the impact of diverse variable ordering methods (cf. [33–35]) upon the MDD-based representations of both, the PLFT and the MCSs.

Acknowledgment. Partially funded by the project SPES XT of the German Federal Ministry of Education and Research (grant no. 01IS12005C).

References

1. Ebert, C., Jones, C.: Embedded software: facts, figures and future. IEEE Comput. **42**(4), 42–52 (2009)
2. International Organization for Standardization: ISO/ IS 26262. - road vehicles - functional Safety (2011)
3. Vesely, W., Goldberg, F.F., Roberts, N., Haasl, D.F.: Fault tree handbook. In: No. NUREG-0492, Nuclear Regulatory Commission, Washington, DC (1981)
4. International Electrotechnical Commission: IEC 61025 fault tree analysis (1990)
5. Vesely, B.: Fault Tree Anaylsis (FTA): concepts and applications. In: NASA HQ (2002). http://www.hq.nasa.gov/office/codeq/risk/docs/ftacourse.pdf
6. Leveson, N.G., Diaz-Herrera, J.: Safeware: System Safety and Computer. Addison-Wesley (1995)
7. Hansen, K.M., Ravn, A.P., Stavridou, V.: From safety analysis to software requirements. IEEE Trans. Softw. Eng. **24**(7), 573–584 (1998)
8. Lutz, R., Woodhouse, R.M.: Requirements analsis using forward and backward search. Ann. Softw. Eng. **3**(1), 459–475 (1997)
9. Dehlinger, J., Lutz, R.: Software fault tree analysis for product lines. In: Proceedings of the 8th IEEE International Symposium on High Assurance Systems Engineering, pp. 12–21 (2004)
10. Lu, D., Lutz, R.: Fault contribution trees for product families. In: Proceedings of the 13th International Symposium in Software Reliability Engineering, pp. 231–242 (2002)
11. Lam, W.: A case study of requirements reuse through product families. Ann. Softw. Eng. **5**(1), 253–277 (1998)
12. Feng, Q., Lutz, R.: Bi-directional safety analysis of product lines. J. Syst. Softw. **78**(2), 111–127 (2005)
13. Noda, A., Nakanishi, T., Kitasuka, T., Fukuda, A.: Introducing fault tree analysis into product line software engineering for exception handling feature exploitation. In: Proceedings of the 25th Conference on IASTED International Multi-conference: Software Engineering, pp. 229–234 (2007)
14. Gómez, C., Liggesmeyer, P., Sutor, A.: Variability management of safety and reliability models: an intermediate model towards systematic reuse of component fault trees. In: Schoitsch, E. (ed.) SAFECOMP 2010. LNCS, vol. 6351, pp. 28–40. Springer, Heidelberg (2010)

15. Kaiser, B., Liggesmeyer, P., Mäckel, O.: A new component concept for fault trees. In: Proceedings of the 8th Workshop on Safety Critical Systems and Software, pp. 37–46 (2003)
16. Atkinson, C., Bayer, J., Muthig, D.: Component-based product line development: the KobrA approach. In: Software Product Lines, pp. 289–309 (2000)
17. Srinivasan, A., Ham, T., Malik, S., Brayton, R.: Algorithms for discrete function manipulation. In: ICCAD-90, International Conference on Computer-Aided Design, pp. 92–95, IEEE, November 1990
18. Lee, C.Y.: Representation of switching circuits by binary-decision programs. Bell Syst. Tech. J. **38**(4), 985–999 (1959)
19. Bryant, R.E.: Graph-based algorithms for boolean function manipulation. IEEE Trans. Comput. **35**, 677–691 (1986)
20. Mo, Y., Xing, L., Dugan, J.: MDD-based method for efficient analysis on phased-mission systems with multimode failures. IEEE Trans. Syst. Man Cybern.: Syst. **44**(6), 757–769 (2014)
21. Manikas, T., Thornton, M., Feinstein, D.: Using multiple-valued logic decision diagrams to model system threat probabilities. In: 41st IEEE International Symposium on Multiple-valued Logic, pp. 263–267, May 2011
22. Gulati, R., Bechta Dugan, J.:A modular approach for analyzing static and dynamic fault trees. In: 1997 Proceedings of the Annual Reliability and Maintainability Symposium, pp. 57–63, January 1997
23. Mo, Y.: A multiple-valued decision-diagram-based approach to solve dynamic fault trees. IEEE Trans. Reliab. **63**(1), 81–93 (2014)
24. Xing, L., Dugan, J.B.: Dependability analysis using multiple-valued decision diagrams. In: Proceedings of the 6th International Conference on Probabilistic Safety Assessment and Management (2002)
25. Xing, L., Dai, Y.: A new decision-diagram-based method for efficient analysis on multistate systems. IEEE Trans. Dependable Secure Comput. **6**(3), 161–174 (2009)
26. Mo, Y., Xing, L., Amari, S.: A multiple-valued decision diagram based method for efficient reliability analysis of non-repairable phased-mission systems. IEEE Trans. Reliab. **63**(1), 320–330 (2014)
27. Jung, W.S., Han, S.H., Ha, J.: A fast BDD algorithm for large coherent fault trees analysis. Reliab. Eng. Syst. Saf. **83**(3), 369–374 (2004)
28. Contini, S., Matuzas, V.: Analysis of large fault trees based on functional decomposition. Reliab. Eng. Syst. Saf. **96**(3), 383–390 (2011)
29. Rauzy, A.: Mathematical foundations of minimal cutsets. IEEE Trans. Reliab. **50**(4), 389–396 (2001)
30. Rauzy, A.: Binary decision diagrams for reliability studies. In: Misra, K. (ed.) Handbook of Performability Engineering, pp. 381–396. Springer, London (2008)
31. Schulze, M., Mauersberger, J., Beuche, D.: Functional safety and variability: can it be brought together?. In: Proceedings of the 17th International Software Product Line Conference, pp. 236–243. ACM (2013)
32. Käßmeyer, M., Velasco Moncaday, D., Schurius, M.: Evaluation of a systematic approach in variant management for safety-critical systems development. In: Proceedings of the 12th International Conference on Embedded and Ubiquitous Computing. IEEE (2015)
33. Berndt, R., Bazan, P., Hielscher, K.S.: On the ordering of variables of multi-valued decision diagrams. In: MMB (ed.): Leistungs-, Zuverlässigkeits- und Verlässlichkeitsbewertung von Kommunikationsnetzen und Verteilten Systemen, Hamburg, pp. 89–98 (2011)

34. Berndt, R., Bazan, P., Hielscher, K.-S., German, R.: Construction methods for MDD-based state space representations of unstructured systems. In: Fischbach, K., Krieger, U.R. (eds.) Proceedings of the 17th International GI/ITG Conference on Measurement, Modelling and Evaluation of Computing Systems and Dependability and Fault-Tolerance. LNCS, vol. 8376, pp. 43–56. Springer, Switzerland (2014)
35. Schmiedle, F., Gunther, W., Drechsler, R.: Selection of efficient re-ordering heuristics for MDD construction. In: Proceedings of the 31st International Symposium on Multiple-valued Logic, pp. 299–304. IEEE (2001)

Resolving Contention for Networks-on-Chips: Combining Time-Triggered Application Scheduling with Dynamic Budgeting of Memory Bus Use

Kai Lampka[1](✉) and Adam Lackorzynski[2]

[1] Department of Information Technology, Uppsala University, Uppsala, Sweden
kai.lampka@it.uu.se
[2] Department of Computer Science, Technische Universität Dresden,
Dresden, Germany
adam@os.inf.tu-dresden.de

Abstract. One of the challenges for the design of integrated real-time systems deployed on modern multicore architectures is the finding of system configurations where all applications are guaranteed to complete their computations prior to their individual deadlines. Traditionally, timing feasability analysis, i.e., sche-dulability tests, take activation patterns and worst-case execution times (WCET) of applications as input. In the setting of mutlicore architectures with shared infrastructure, WCET are drastically overestimated as the number of accesses to a shared resource and their service times not only depend on the application itself, the service times experienced at the shared resource are significantly influenced by its use by applications executing on other cores. There are several ways to deal with the above phenomenon and give guarantees for the timing behaviour of a real-time system deployed on concurrent hardware. One either devise analysis techniques and accept the potential under-utilization of the hardware or one may employ specific protocols for coordinating the resource sharing. In this paper, we do both: (a) we combine time triggered, core-local scheduling of real-time applications with a dynamic budgeting scheme for controlling the access to the main memory bus. (b) We show how the obtained access budgets can be used at design time to ensure timing correctness at design-time. The scheme is implemented in a microkernel based operating system and we present experiments to investigate its performance.

1 Introduction

1.1 Motivation

Modern multicore processors work for the parallel execution of applications. This features integration of previously isolated systems on a single platform and thereby promises significant cost reductions. For example, a high-end car might have more than 100 Electronic Control Units (ECU), each contributing to a

© Springer International Publishing Switzerland 2016
A. Remke and B.R. Haverkort (Eds.): MMB & DFT 2016, LNCS 9629, pp. 137–152, 2016.
DOI: 10.1007/978-3-319-31559-1_12

dedicated function e.g., breaking system. With multicore technology, different functions could be integrated into a single processor-architecture and thereby significantly reducing the number of ECUs. As this lowers the costs of hardware, packaging, maintenance, as well as weight and fuel consumption in the context of transportation systems, multicore technology is highly attractive to industry. For putting this vision into practice, it is required that the cost/benefit ratio of the built systems outperforms the existing single-core solutions.

In electronics, costs can be significantly reduced, if existing software arte-facts can be re-used (legacy code) and non-customized hardware, i.e., so called commercial-off-the-shelf (COTS) technology, can be exploited.

COTS multicores are characterized by a high degree of sharing of the common infrastructure among the different cores. This includes the sharing of parts of the memory hierarchy, e.g., main memory and communication links. As the accesses to these resources are serialized, an individual resource access may only be served after a significant time of waiting. As the waiting time adds to the execution time of an application, resource sharing significantly influences the timing behaviour of applications. Tightly bounding the individual waiting times and thereby guaranteeing timing correctness of applications is, however, difficult to achieve. Not only is the number of competing access requests stemming from the co-runners[1] unknown at design time. In addition, the arrival times of access requests cannot be predicted with a great precision.

For illustrating the timing effect stemming from the sharing of the main memory bus we run an experiment on a Intel Xeon X5650 2.67 GHz 6-core CPU. On one core we run a single real-time application and on 4 cores we run applications which we consider as best-effort applications, where we use applications from the industrial EEMBC benchmark suite [3]. The measured run-time data is shown in Table 1 which can be explained as follows: at first we run all applications by themselves and measure their execution time. Then we measure the execution time of all benchmarks running on one core, and all other benchmarks co-running on another core. We then measure the cache miss rate which is an indicator for the number of memory accesses of the respective application. The rates are normed to the lowest bus access rate which is produced by application *canrdr*. Thereafter we measured the slowdown for all pairings. The worst case occurs for the pairing *pntrch* and *bitmnp*: the slowdown was measured to be 47.6 % here. Many of the benchmarks are represented in the *worst co-runner* column. Thus, not only the bus access rate determines the delays, they are also affected by the concrete address space in the main memory the application are mapped to. This is because, accesses to different memory banks are emitted to different bus lines and therefore are executed almost in parallel.

There are several ways to deal with the above phenomenon and give guarantees for the timing behaviour of a real-time system deployed on COTS multicore. One either devise conservative analysis techniques and accept the potential under-utilization of the hardware or one may employ specific protocols

---

[1] With co-runners we refer to the applications which are located at other cores and executing in parallel to the application under consideration.

Table 1. Normalized memory bus access numbers. Worst case slowdown is in percent of execution time when applications run alone. Worst case co-runner is the application running on the other 3 cores when the worst slowdown was measured

Application	Normed Number of Bus Accesses	Extension of Execution Time	Best-effort Co-runner
a2time	1.408	32.3%	aifftr
aifftr	1.767	20.9%	bitmnp
aifirf	1.123	23.1%	canrdr
aiifft	1.405	25.6%	ttsprk
basefp	1.202	30.7%	aifirf
bitmnp	1.454	36.5%	aifirf
cacheb	1.179	17.0%	matrix
canrdr	1	25.5%	rspeed
idctrn	1.422	27.2%	cacheb
iirflt	1.488	22.7%	aiifft
matrix	1.981	30.9%	a2time
pntrch	2.306	47.6%	bitmnp
puwmod	1.62	28.6%	idctrn
rspeed	1.387	25.1%	idctrn
tblook	1.46	26.7%	idctrn
ttsprk	1.384	35.5%	bitmnp

for coordinating the resource sharing. In the latter case, the proposed schemes need to enforce assumptions made at design time and thereby guarantee the timing correctness of the system. However, resource arbitration needs to be done adaptively to improve response times of applications and avoid any drastic under-utilization of hardware.

1.2 Own Contribution

Most of the traffic experienced in a Network-on-Chip (NoC) is directed to the main memory controller. The resulting contention about the use of the NoC can be handled in several ways. Approaches range from sophisticated analysis techniques [10], through augmented feasibility tests [1] up to the use of dedicated protocols for organizing the use of the NoC [6]. In this paper, we apply a more comprehensive strategy:

1. we introduce a dynamic budgeting scheme for coordinating access to a shared resource, e.g., the NoC and
2. we show how the scheme can be used for deciding timing correctness of a given system layout at design time.

In contrast to existing techniques, the paper specifically intends to improvement the response time of best-effort applications which use the NoC in parallel to the real-time applications. As the later are treated as first class citizens of a system, best effort applications commonly have to accept significant performance degradation. This is not acceptable, specifically when it comes to user-centric services.

1.3   Organization

Section 2 presents the relevant scientific work. Section 3 introduces the assumed system model and Sect. 4 presents the budgeting scheme for throttling memory accesses in the presence of time-triggered scheduling of core-local workloads. The implementation and empirical evaluation is presented in Sects. 5 and 6 concludes the paper.

2   Related Work

Time-triggered scheduling as advocated by Koepitz is the predominant scheme in industry for coordinating the execution of real-time applications on a processor. For conciseness, we do not give a survey on timed triggered scheduling, e.g., see [5] as a prominent example.

Resource servers are a well known technique for organizing access to a shared resource in a budgeted and thereby time-safe manner. The basic functionality is as follows: an access to the shared resource decreases the budget. The budget is replenished at fixed points in time, commonly periodically. Whenever the budget is depleted, the server is not eligible to access the memory, i.e., the execution of applications is suspended. This way, the interference time of applications is limited to the size of the budget and real-time guarantees can be derived accordingly. In the past, several variants of this basic scheme have been proposed, an overview on resource servers can be found in the textbook [2].

For controlling the access to the NoC and in particular to the main memory bus, has already been proposed in the literature.

[12] guarantees memory bus bandwidth for one hard real-time core. The applications which are running on the other cores are considered to be best-effort applications and their accesses to the memory bus are throttled. The budgets of these so called soft cores are replenished periodically, and is measured by cache misses in the last level cache (LLC). The number of cache misses is either measured every 1ms or every context switch, whichever comes first. Once the budget of cache misses at a core is depleted, all ready applications on that core are moved away from the ready-queue, until the next replenishment point.

[13] presents a budgeting scheme which utilizes a predicted budget for each period. The difference between predicted budget and the actually consumed one is handed over to a global budget. From this global budget, best-effort applications may reclaim additional memory accesses, namely if their own budget is prematurely depleted.

The above works are based on static analysis for determining the budgets of applications. The worst case path w.r.t. memory accesses of applications may be traversed rarely in practice. As a consequence, the budgets assigned to the best-effort applications, respectively the cores they are mapped to, are unnecessarily low. This, together with the lack of balancing accesses between real-time and best-effort applications, yields large response times for the best-effort applications. E.g., budget shifting among best-effort applications as proposed in [13] lowers the average response time of a specific best-effort application. But, it does not solve performance degradation of all best-effort applications as the overall budget of the best-effort budget is constant and may be arbitrarily pessimistic.

In this work we exploit the adaptive budgeting scheme of [4] for overcoming these shortcomings, and propose its combination with a time-triggered application scheduling at core-level.

3   Abstract System Model

3.1   Basic Definitions

We consider a typical multicore architecture and abstractly characterize its workload as follows:

Hard Real-Time Cores. There are M CPU-cores, G of which are exclusively executing hard real-time applications. These cores are denoted as hard real-time cores.

Soft Real-Time Cores. There are $M - G$ soft real-time cores which exclusively execute best-effort applications. In the following we denote these best-effort applications as soft real-time tasks.[2]

Hard Real-Time Applications. There are N sporadic real-time applications, denoted as hard real-time tasks and defined by the set $\{\tau_1, \tau_2, ..., \tau_N\}$. τ_k is a quadruple $(C_k^{nm}, P_k, D_k, Mem_k^{on}, Mem_k^{off})$, where

- C_k^{nm} is the worst-case execution time (WCET) for the task, assuming that no cache miss, i.e., no memory access, occurred.
- P_k is the minimum inter-arrival time or period of the task.
- $D_k \leq P_k$ is the task's relative deadline.
- Mem_k^{on} is the maximum number of memory accesses issued by any execution of the task.
- Mem_k^{off} is the maximum number of memory accesses issued by all co-runners during the execution of τ_k.

Static Task to Core Mapping. Each task τ_k is mapped to a specific core out of the G hard real-time cores.

Time-Triggered Scheduling of Applications at Core-Level. The execution of tasks at the hard real-time cores follows a periodically repeating time-triggered schedule which we describe below, Sect. 4.1.

Scheduling at Soft Real-Time Cores. For the scheduling of the best-effort applications on the soft real-time cores, we do not make any assumption.

---

[2] The partitioning into hard and soft real-time cores simplifies the signalling overhead and simplifies the description of the scheme. If necessary, it could be dropped, but this would require maintenance of a budget also on the side of hard real-time cores.

3.2 Worst Case Execution Time When Sharing the Main Memory Bus

Hard and soft cores share the main memory, where the memory controller decides on the service order of incoming memory access requests. The worst case execution time (WCET) of a hard real-time task τ_k can be bounded as follows:

$$WCET(\tau_k) \leq C_k^{nm} + (Mem_k^{on} + Mem_k^{off}) \times TMEM^{nrh}$$

where $TMEM^{nrh}$ refers to the maximum access time for serving an isolated memory access provided that the item is not cached at its bank. Note, $TMEM^{nrh}$ needs to include also the time for looking up entries along the cache hierarchy. For data-centric tasks, i.e., for tasks which excessively access the main memory, $Mem_k^{on} \ll Mem_k^{off}$ hold and the above bounding of the WCET appears to be not too pessimistic.

In case of computation-centric tasks, i.e., tasks with sparse main memory access patterns the above bound may become extremely pessimistic as $TMEM^{nrh}$ is a very coarse over-estimation for a single cache access. In the following we assume that the WCET of any task is set to the above bound.

3.3 Worst Case Response Time When Sharing the Main Memory

The worst case response time (WCRT) R_k is the time between activation and completion of a task. It bounds the lifetime of all possible task invocations and can be computed from the following recurrence relation:

$$WCRT(\tau_k) = \sum_{\tau_k \in Preempt(\tau_k)} \lceil \frac{WCRT(\tau_k))}{P_l} \rceil \times WCET(\tau_k)$$

where $Preempt(\tau_k)$ refers to the set of tasks which may potentially preempt task τ_k which depends on the assumed scheduling scheme.

A system is denoted feasible if $\forall \tau_k : WCRT(\tau_k) \leq D_k$ holds.

4 Adaptively Budgeting Memory Accesses Under Time-Triggered Execution of Real-Time Tasks

4.1 Time-Triggered Execution of Tasks

Scheduling of hard real-time tasks is organized according to a standard time-triggered scheme, e.g., as defined in [5].

A time-triggered schedule at core i is a sequence of K_i time slots $s_{i,j}$, where $s_{i,j}^\Delta$ refers to the time length of each slot.

Let S_i be the sequence of slots of core i, each time-triggered core-local schedule is repeatedly executed with period $\Pi_i = \sum_{\forall s_{i,j} \in S_i} s_{i,j}^\Delta$. The hyperperiod of the time-triggered schedules executing on the hard real-time cores of G is the least common multiple of all periods ($\Pi = lcm(\Pi_1, \ldots \Pi_{|G|})$. In the following, we denote the hyperperiod of all hard real-time core schedules as **system cycle time** and the time $t \in [i\Pi, (i+1)\Pi]$ for any $i \in \mathbb{N}_0$ the j'th cycle γ_j with $j = i + 1$, i.e., we start indexing at one.

Let Ω_i be now the sequence of slots extended to the complete system cycle γ_j. This allows one to re-enumerate the slots executing on a core w.r.t. the system cycle, instead doing so for each core-local cycle. Let Ω be now the set of all extended sequences, $\Omega = \{\Omega_i | i \in G\}$. The re-enumeration of slots yields that $s_{i,j}$ **refers from now on to a unique slot appearing on** Ω.

Let $\tau(s_{i,j})$ be the tasks which are statically mapped to slot $s_{i,j}$ for execution. If a task is mapped to different slots or in case a task need to be partitioned over several slot to meet its timing requirements, we assume allocation of a sufficient number of new tasks, each added to the task set of the system. In this setting, we consider the overall system feasible if the following two condition hold

$$
\begin{aligned}
\forall s_{i,j} \in \Omega: & \\
(A) \quad & \forall \tau_k \in \tau(s_{i,j}): s_{i,j}^{\Delta} \leq D_i \\
(B) \quad & \sum_{\tau_k \in \tau(s_{i,j})} WCET(\tau_k) \leq s_{i,j}^{\Delta}
\end{aligned} \tag{1}
$$

Condition (A) states that each task of a slot must not be completed before the end of the slot. This is usefull as it follows to freely shift memory bus accesses among the tasks mapped to the same slot.

Condition (B) requires that the slot is large enough to accommodate all task executions under the worst case assumption, which is the maximum number of assumed interference from the task's off-core co-runners and the maximum number of preemptions suffering from the local co-runners. The off-core co-runners are the hard real-time task which execute in parallel on other cores, the local co-runners are the tasks which are assigned to the same slot ($\tau(s_{i,j}) \setminus \tau_k$).

For the execution order of hard real-time tasks within a slot, we do not make any assumption, solely that the scheduling scheme produces a feasible schedule such that condition (A) and (B) of Eq. (1) hold.

4.2 Feasibility Checks with Budgets

For each slot $s_{i,j}$ we define a local and an external budget

$$
B_{i,j}^{local} = \sum_{\forall \tau_k \in \tau(s_{i,j})} Mem_k^{on} \text{ and } B_{i,j}^{ext} = \sum_{\forall \tau_k \in \tau(s_{i,j})} Mem_k^{off} \tag{2}
$$

with the following meaning: the local budget $B_{i,j}^{local}$ is an upper bound on the memory bus accesses of all tasks executing in slot $s_{i,j}$. The external budget $B_{i,j}^{ext}$ is the upper bound of all memory access requests which we can be tolerate by the tasks executing in $s_{i,j}$.

Theorem 1. *A system maintains its feasibility if the off-core interference for all tasks $\tau(slots_{i,j})$ is bounded by $B_{i,j}^{ext}$ and the local memory bus accesses of all tasks of $\tau(slots_{i,j})$ is bounded by $B_{i,j}^{local}$.*

The validity of the above theorem needs to be shown w.r.t. the individual tasks mapped to slot $s_{i,j}$ and feasibility needs to be maintained, even if a single task τ_k is exposed to the complete interference and would issue even more than M_k^{local} memory bus accesses. What matters is the sum of memory bus accesses, local and external.

Proof. We re-write Eq. (1).B as follows:

$$
s_{i,j}^{\Delta} \geq \sum_{\tau_k \in \tau(s_{i,j})} WCET(\tau_k)
$$
$$
= \sum_{\forall \tau_k \in \tau(s_{i,j})} C_k^{nm} + TMEM^{nrh} \times (B_{i,j}^{ext} + B_{i,j}^{local}) \tag{3}
$$

The number of local memory bus accesses and external memory interferences is constant for the slot. Therefore, a shifting of individual accesses cannot increase the execution times of all tasks together. The delay is bounded for the slot by $TMEM^{nrh} \times (B_{i,j}^{ext} + B_{i,j}^{local})$ no matter where it is placed. System feasibility is ensured as all slot-related tasks complete within the slot and all slot-related tasks meet their deadlines due to the pre-assumed validity of condition (A) of Eq. (1).

In case a task's relative deadline is not larger than the slot execution time, i.e., Condition (A) of Eq. (1) is violated, it is required that

$$
\forall s_{i,j} \in \Omega : \forall \tau_k \in s_{i,j} :
$$
$$
\sum_{\tau_x \in Preempt(\tau_k)} \lceil \frac{WCRT(\tau_k))}{P_x} \rceil
$$
$$
\times (C_k^{nm} + TMEM^{nrh} \times (Mem_k^{on} + B_{i,j}^{ext})) \leq D_k \tag{4}
$$

holds. This way, we guarantee that the budgets of memory bus accesses can be freely shifted among the tasks mapped to a single slot.

Let $CoR(s_{i,j})$ be the set of slots which are co-active w.r.t. slot $s_{i,j}$. $CoR(s_{i,j})$ is a sequence of slots of the kind $CoR(s_{i,j}) = (s_{1,.}, \ldots s_{i-1,.}, \ldots s_{i+1,.}, \ldots s_{|\tau|,.})$, ß where $s_{k,.}$ refers to some co-running slot from core k.

Please note, there is a single set of co-active slots per slot $s_{i,j}$ only. This results from the fact that we introduced a global numbering for the slots.

For each core $x \neq i$ we have at least one slot $s_{x,y}$ and at most K_x slots. With respect to core i, there are no slots of the kind $s_{i,.}$ contained in $CoR(s_{i,j})$.

From the set $CoR(s_{i,j})$ we compute a bound on the budget of memory bus accesses stemming from off-core co-runners of $s_{i,j}$ as follows:

$$
B^{cor}(s_{i,j}) = \sum_{\forall s_{k,x} \in CoR(s_{i,j})} B_{k,x}^{local} \tag{5}
$$

with $B_{k,x}^{local}$ as the maximum on memory bus accesses of all tasks of $\tau(s_{k,x})$.

Theorem 2. *The core-local time-triggered schedules maintain their feasibility under main memory contention if the following condition holds:*

$$
\forall s_{i,j} \in \Omega : B^{cor}(s_{i,j}) \leq B_{i,j}^{ext}. \tag{6}
$$

where $B_{i,j}^{ext}$ is the assumed bound on the number of interfering main memory bus accesses which can be tolerated by the tasks executing in slot $s_{i,j}$ (cf. Eq. (2)).

Proof. This directly arises by replacing $B_{i,j}^{ext}$ in Eq. (3) with $B^{cor}(s_{i,j})$.

The above equation immediately gives one the number of memory bus accesses which can be tolerated from the cores executing the best-effort applications in addition to the memory bus accesses from the hard real-time cores.

$$\forall s_{i,j} \in \Omega : B^{eff}(s_{i,j}) \le B_{i,j}^{ext} - B^{cor}(s_{i,j}) \tag{7}$$

such that the system maintains feasibility.

One may note that the above definitions and requirements introduce some pessimism: the budgets are based on the sum of cache misses. Upon execution, the assumed worst case might actually not appear or at least not for all tasks executing while slot $s_{i,j}$ is active. This is even more true, as slots may only overlap in parts, yielding that only some of their tasks actually execute in parallel. Thus, the definition of $B_{i,j}^{cor}$ in Eq. (5) might be too pessimistic, but it provides a safe upper bound to be checked against the allowable off-core memory bus accesses.

4.3   Enforcing Budgets at Run-Time

Main Idea. While executing a slot $s_{i,j}$, we need to guard that all the cores running best-effort applications do not issue more than $B^{eff}(s_{i,j})$ accesses to the main memory in total. As there is one slot active per hard real-time core, we need to ensure the bounding not only for one slot, but for all active ones. This boils down to only distribute the minimum budget of the currently active slots over the best effort cores.

In case the budget enforcing slot terminates, i.e., the one with the smallest number of memory bus accesses, we need to decrease the remaining active budgets accordingly. This, one has to do, as a budget must be guarded for its whole lifetime, not only during the time it is the decisive one, i.e., the one bounding the number of memory accesses.

Below we detail on the algorithms to implement this basic functionality, as well as the mechanism to donate budgets in a timely safe manner. For simplicity, we ignore the distribution of budgets and donations over multiple cores executing a best-effort workload. For the presented algorithms, the distribution could be arranged transparently, through a dedicated administering core.

Scheduling of the Hard-Real-Time Workloads. On a hard real-time core we execute exclusively hard real-time tasks in a time triggered fashion, where a set of tasks is put together to execute within a slot $s_{i,j}$. With respect to the scheduling of tasks within the respective slot, we do not make any assumption, except that feasibility of the scheme has been shown on beforehand, e.g., by verifying Eq. (1) A and B.

Algorithm 1. Budget handling: hard real-time core

1: *Input: task set of* $s_{i,j}$
2: **procedure** STARTSLOT(τ_j^i)
3:    $setTimer(X, s_{i,j}^{\Delta})$)
4:    signalActivate(type($s_{i,j}$))
5:    resetPMC()
6:    Schedule(getTaskSet($s_{i,j}$), $s_{i,j}^{\Delta}$)
7:    **if** readTimer(X) > δ **then**
8:       **if** readPMC() > ϵ **then**
9:          signalDonate(type($s_{i,j}$), $B_{i,j}^{eff} - PMC()$)
10:      **end if**
11:      signalDeactivate(type($s_{i,j}$))
12:   **end if**
13: **end procedure**

Main Idea to Algorithm 1. Before executing the slot-specific tasks, we signal activation of a budget to the cores executing the best effort workload. In case the tasks are completed early enough, we signal a deactivation of the budget or even execute a donation of memory bus accesses.

Implementation Details to Algorithm 1. For putting the requested functionality in operation the algortihm proceeds as follows: in line 3, we set a timer X to track the consumed computation time. The timer is set to the maximum value and gives a signal once it as been decremented to 0. Time tracking is done to ensure, that explicit invalidation of budgets only occur, if a threshold value δ is exceeded (line 7 and 11). We do not need to signal the ending of a slot in general, as each slot is of a predefined, fixed length. Hence, budget invalidation on the side of the best -effort cores upon slot termination is done implicitly, namely, once a new budget is activated from the same core or the budget exceeded its lifetime.

For simplification, Algorithm 1 uses typed signals, such that for each slot $s_{i,j}$ a respective signal type is used. Consequently, when sending the signal for activating the budget referring to the newly activated slot $s_{i,j}$ (line 4), the best-effort cores can retrieve the respective budget $B^{eff}(s_{i,j})$ from a predefined list of Budgets.

In line 6 we call the core-local scheduler to execute all tasks associated with the active slot $s_{i,j}$ during the time window $s_{i,j}^{\Delta}$. Upon return from the scheduling and execution of tasks, Algorithm 1 tests if the residual slot time, i.e., remaining clock ticks, shown by X justify an explicit cancellation of the budget or a donation of memory bus access from the hard real-time core under consideration to the cores executing the best-effort workload. Both activities are guarded by a threshold value to justify the additional overhead (line 7 and 8). Function readPMC($LLC - register$) reports the number of cache misses which have occurred since the last reset of the respective register which happens just before the slot-local task set is executed (line 5). The register for monitoring the memory fetches is commonly denoted as last-level cache counter (LLC). It belongs

---

Algorithm 2. Enforcing budgets for best-effort workloads

1: *Requires: timer X, budget B, set of budgets Budget*
2: *Input: signal e mapping to a slot and action*
3: **procedure** BSCHEDULER(signal *e*)
4:     $PREEMPTION = OFF$
5:     **if** action(*e*) ∈ {*depleted, expired*} **then**
6:         delay(*X*)
7:     **end if**
8:     update(*Budgets, B.b^{eff}* − readPMC(), *B.t − T*)
9:     **if** action(*e*) == *activate* **then**
10:         insert(*Budgets*, slot(*e*))
11:     **else if** action(*e*) == *deactivate* **then**
12:         remove(*Budgets*, slot(*e*)))
13:     **else if** action(*e*) == *donated* **then**
14:         *C* = peek(*Budgets*, slot(*e*))
15:         updateDonation(*Budgets, B.d, C.t*)
16:     **end if**
17:     **while** *B* = peek(*Budgets*)) ≠ ∅ ∧ *B.t* ≤ 0 **do**
18:         remove(*Budgets, B*)
19:     **end while**
20:     **if** *B* == ∅ **then**
21:         stopTimer(*T*)
22:     **else**
23:         setPMC(*B.b^{eff}*)
24:         setTimer(*B.t*)
25:     **end if**
26:     $PREEMPTION = ON$
27: **end procedure**

---

to the class of core-local performance monitor counters (PMC). Like timers, a PMC can be set to a value, decrements upon the associated event, here last-level cache miss and issues a respective signal once the register hits the 0.

Budget donation takes place in line 9, it is directed towards the cores executing the best-effort workload. Budget donation between hard real-time tasks is pointless, as we assume that their parameters are conservative estimates.

Budget Enforcement for Best-Effort Workloads. With any best-effort core, we do not execute any hard real-time task. Consequently, execution of applications can be suspended there without corrupting a system's feasibility. The required functionality for guarding the number of memory bus accesses such that timing correctness of the hard real-time tasks is ensured, is provided by Algorithm 2.

Main Idea to Algorithm 2. Input signals are typed such that they refer to an action and a specific budget. A budget is a tuple (b^{eff}, t, d), where b^{eff} refers to the size of the budget, i.e., allowable cache misses, t refers to its lifetime and d

is used for making donations from the owner of the budget, which is a slot on a specific core. At runtime, the minimum budgets from the set of active budgets bounds the number of allowable cache misses and does so until it has reached its lifetime, or a smaller budget becomes active. In the following we denote this budget as decisive budget. Once a decisive budget is replaced, the active budgets in the queue needed to be updated, i.e., their lifetimes and budget sizes need to be decremented by the number of clock ticks and cache misses which have occurred during the presence of the decisive budget. An active budget might be the decisive one for several periods.

Details to Algorithm 2. We assume that there is a queue *Budgets* of active budgets, with at most one active budget per hard real-time core.

Within the queue, the active budgets are ordered by increasing budget sizes. The following functions are used to access items of the queue: function `replace` and `remove`, which work as expected. Function `update`($Budgets, a, b$) decreases all budgets of the queue by value a and decreases their lifetimes by value b. This is needed once the decisive budget has reached its lifetime or is replaced by a newly activated budget. Function `peek` gives the head of the queue, i.e., the active budget with the smallest number of cache misses. The functions does not remove the item from the queue.

The algorithm itself works as follows: upon depletion of the decisive budget or at the end of its lifetime the core suspend execution for the remaining lifetime, which in case of the "*end of lifetime*" situation is 0 (line 5).

In case the decisive budget has reached the end of its life time or a new budget to be activated has arrived, we update all active budgets w.r.t. the number of cache misses and the expired time occurred during the current budget has been made the decisive one.

In case of a premature deactivation, the decisive budget is removed from the budget queue and the next active budget is fetched. This can either be the same, but updated budget, a new one, where budgets with invalid lifetime are discarded, or it is an empty budget (line 17–19).

In case of an empty budget all active budget have been prematurely invalidated and the core has a non-restricted allowance to the main memory.

In case a valid budget is fetched from the queue, the LLC-register and the lifetime clock counter are set accordingly (line 23 and 24).

Budget donation is considered before actually fetching a budget from the queue. Function `updateDonation`($Budgets, a, b$) adds value a to each budget, here parameter $B.b^{eff}$ and does so for those budgets which have a residual lifetime below b.

5   Implementation and Evaluation

5.1   Virtual Machine Monitor: Coordinating the Acces to a Shared Resource

Operating systems (OS) provide services to run applications concurrently on a system and make hardware devices available to them. Deploying applications which need to fulfill very different constraints in a single system requires an OS that provides real-time and virtualization capabilities. In this paper we added our budgeting techniques into the L4Re system [8]. This is a 3rd-generation, open source and capability-based operating system which provides virtualization features to host other legacy systems, for example, applications that come from a deeply embedded setup [7,11].

5.2   Hardware Performance Counters

Modern processors have a performance monitor counter (PMC) unit that allows to count hardware-related events in the CPU core, such as memory bus accesses and instruction counts. Upon an overflow of an event register, the core can generate an interrupt.

Using the performance counters it is possible to count the number of memory bus accesses. If the number of memory bus accesses reaches a certain threshold, the hypervisor may suspend the execution of soft real-time applications.

5.3   Flexible OS Support for Resource Budgets

A central task of an operating system is to multiplex between different resources. The most prominent resource is time, however, other resources can be considered as well, for example, the aforementioned performance counter events.

To enhance our operating system with performance counter support we built upon the scheduling context (SC) mechanism introduced in [9]. SCs are an operating system mechanism that are the base for scheduling in the system. An SC contains scheduling parameters required for the OS to schedule OS threads. Each OS thread has at least one SC (SC-0), however, it can have multiple SC. This allows, for example, to give an OS thread an additional small budget with a higher priority to perform low-latency work. This is especially useful for virtual machines that handle guest threads internally and are only visible to the hypervisor as a single thread: a virtual CPU (vCPU). SCs can be arbitrarily selected by the guest, as long as budget is available in the selected SC. When an SC runs out of budget, the host system will select SC-0 of the thread. If SC-0 is also out of budget, the thread is suspended and scheduling is performed. The host system also requires that SCs are created and configured with scheduling parameters. Especially configuration is supervised by separate policy components that restrict client's settings. This prevents that a client, such as virtual machines, can monopolize the CPU.

For this work, we extended the SC mechanism to also consider performance counters. Besides a time budget, a SC also has a budget of performance counter events. Whenever this budget is used up, the SC is dropped and the thread-/vCPU continues running on its SC-0. If SC-0 is out of budget, the thread is suspended. This allows us to give individual OS threads separate budgets for accessing the main memory bus.

5.4   Using Performance Counters

Initially, we were using an Intel Core-i7-4770 CPU to perform experiments, how-ever, it turned out that this type of CPU is not suitable for memory bus access accounting. Using the last-level-cache miss performance counter and reading the counter while using the full memory bus bandwidth delivered usable counter val-ues. But when inserting delays, with the goal to not fully use up all memory bus bandwidth, the respective last-level-cache-miss counter shows significantly less events although the same amount of memory is accessed. This is likely because of the hardware memory prefetcher where memory accesses are not counted, as they are no cache misses. Disabling the prefetcher via the Model Specific Regis-ter (MSR) IA32_MISC_ENABLE yields a general protection fault. Using non-cached memory is no choice either because these accesses do not cause cache-relevant events, such as misses. Other counters available either showed the same behavior (significantly different values for with and without delay loops), or did not count at all.

For that reason we switched architectures to a TI OMAP5 platform. The OMAP5432-EVM has two ARM Cortex-A15 cores, clocked at 800 MHz. The A15's performance counter offers a BUS_ACCESS counter which is a perfect fit for our needs.

5.5   Memory Bus Usage

First, we confirm our assumption that the memory bus bandwidth impairs per-formance in applications when running in parallel on multiple cores. For that, we're using a self-made memory-intensive benchmark that we execute on one core alone and twice on each core. We based our evaluation on an arbitrarily crafted piece of memory-intensive code for the following: today's real-time applications, e.g., as collected in the EEMBC [3] benchmark suite, have considerably small memory footprints which allows one to completely load them into the core-local cache and thereby nullifying most of the traffic to the main memory.

The results produced by our synthetic data-intensive application are pre-sented in Table 2. They indicate that our benchmark does a good job using up the available memory bandwidth on the used platform. With a non-greedy memory-access pattern, i.e. a delay loop between the memory accesses, the par-allel run shows that the memory bus is not fully used for a single benchmark run but still the two cores influence each other.

Considering real-time tasks, this means that a real-time task running alone on a core is influenced in its execution behavior by other tasks running on other cores.

5.6   Limiting Memory Access

To restrict best-effort tasks in their memory bus use, we use our newly developed budgeting mechanism. We continue to use the benchmark used in the previous section. An undisturbed run of the greedy benchmark runs for 8.7 s as shown

Table 2. Results for an artificial data-centric benchmark running on one and on two cores.

	(A) Greedy memory use			(B) RT Non-Greedy use	
Core Usage	CPU0	CPU1		CPU0	CPU1
1	8762ms	-		14678ms	-
2	15228ms	15551ms		18583ms	12855ms

in Table 2-A. Let us now assume the real-time task represented by the benchmark shall have a randomly chosen WCET of 10 s. As seen in Table 2 a task running on a different core can influence the benchmark to run for more than 10 s. Our goal is now to restrict the best-effort task in its execution so that the real-time task has sufficient memory bus bandwidth available to finish within its WCET budget of 10 s.

Experimentation shows that we need to configure the best-effort task with a budget of 27300 performance counter ticks per 10ms period to allow the real-time task to always finish within its WCET (a largest measured run-time is 9.993 s in this configuration). In this case the best-effort task runs for 45.4 s which is significantly longer than when running standalone (8.7 s). When we lift the budget of the best-effort task after the real-time task has finished its work, the runtime of the best-effort task reduces to 17.1 s.

The same principle can be applied for the non-greedy run (Table 2-B) where the real-time task adds delays in the memory bus access, unlike the best-effort task. Assuming a WCET of 16 s for the real-time task, we need set the allowed budget for the best-effort task to 33000 ticks per 10 ms. The budget is higher as in the greedy run as the real-time task uses the memory bus less. With this configuration, the best-effort task runs for 43.6 s, and with lifting the best-effort tasks budget after the real-time task has finished, for 21.8 s. Concluding, the experiments show that our budgeting approach using performance counter events is effective and allows to limit the execution of disturbing tasks.

6   Conclusions

Parallel execution of real-time workloads on non-customized multicore platforms is hampered by mutual interferences of applications which result from the sharing of general resources like communication buses and memory. The sharing of resources can inject unexpected delays into the worst-case response time of applications and thereby corrupt the timing correctness of a system. The challenge inherent to such integrated systems is to build them in a way that compute-capacity is not wasted, strict and non-strict timing constraints are met. This paper combines a time-triggered execution policy for processing real-time workloads with dynamic budgeting of resource accesses. With this, we aim at ruling out unexpected execution delays occurring with the joint access of parallel applications to the shared main memory. Contrary to existing work, the presented scheme not only takes advantage of the core-local execution policy. We also propose mechanisms which make the scheme more reactive and thereby help to increase the performance of best-effort applications running in parallel to the hard real-time applications. In addition to the formalized side conditions and algorithms for guaranteeing timing correctness, we also presented an implementation of the scheme which we integrated as a new scheduling capability into a contemporary micro-kernel.

References

1. Alhammad, A., Pellizzoni, R.: Schedulability analysis of global memory predictable scheduling. In: 2014 International Conference on Embedded Software, EMSOFT 2014, NewDelhi, India, 12-17 October 2014, pp. 20:1–20:10 (2014)
2. Buttazzo, G.C.: Hard Real-time Computing Systems: Predictable Scheduling Algorithms And Applications. Real-Time Systems Series. Springer, Santa Clara (2011)
3. EEMBC. http://www.eembc.org/
4. Flodin, J., Lampka, K., Yi, W.: Dynamic budgeting for settling DRAM contention of co-running hard and soft real-time tasks. In: Proceedings of the 9th IEEE International Symposium on Industrial Embedded Systems, SIES 2014, pp. 151–159 (2014)
5. Fohler, G.: Joint scheduling of distributed complex periodic and hard aperiodic tasks in statically scheduled systems. In: Proceedings of the 16th IEEE Real-Time Systems Symposium, pp. 152–161 (1995)
6. Giannopoulou, G., Stoimenov, N., Huang, P., Thiele, L., de Dinechin, B.D.: Mixed-criticality scheduling on cluster-based manycores with shared communication and storage resources. Real Time Syst. **51**, 1–51 (2015)
7. Wang, A., Schild, H., Lackorzynski, A.: Faithful virtualization on a real-time operating system. In: 11th Real-Time Linux Workshopp (2009)
8. Lackorzynski, A., Warg, A.: Taming subsystems: capabilities as universal resource access control in l4. In: Proceedings of the 2nd Workshop on Isolation and Integration in Embedded Systems, IIES 2009, pp. 25–30, ACM, New York (2009)
9. Lackorzyński, A., Warg, A., Völp, M., Härtig, H.: Flattening hierarchical scheduling. In: Proceedings EMSOFT 2012, pp. 93–102. ACM, New York (2012)
10. Lampka, K., et al.: A formal approach to the WCRT analysis of multicore systems with memory contention under phase-structured task sets. Real Time Syst. **50**(5–6), 736–773 (2014)
11. Peter, M., Schild, H., Lackorzynski, A., Warg, A., Virtual machines jailed: virtualization in systems with small trusted computing bases. In: Proceedings of VDTS, pp. 18–23. ACM, New York (2009)
12. Yun, H., Yao, G., Pellizzoni, R., Caccamo, M., Sha, L.: Memory access control in multiprocessor for real-time systems with mixed criticality. In: 2012 24th Euromicro Conference on Real-Time Systems (ECRTS), pp. 299–308 (2012)
13. Yun, H., Yao, G., Pellizzoni, R., Caccamo, M., Sha, L.: Memguard: memory bandwidth reservation system for efficient performance isolation in multi-core platforms. In: Real-Time and Embedded Technology and Applications Symposium (RTAS) 2013, pp. 55–64 (2013)

The Weak Convergence of TCP Bandwidth Sharing

Wolfram Lautenschlaeger[✉]

Bell Labs, Nokia, Stuttgart, Germany
Wolfram.Lautenschlaeger@nokia.com

Abstract. TCP is the dominating transmission protocol in the Internet since decades. It proved its flexibility to adapt to unknown and changing network conditions. A distinguished TCP feature is the comparably fair resource sharing. Unfortunately, this abstract fairness is frequently misinterpreted as convergence towards equal sharing rates. In this paper we show in theory as well as in experiment that TCP rate convergence does not exist. Instead, the individual TCP flow rate is persistently fluctuating over a range close to one order of magnitude. The fluctuations are not short term but correlated over long intervals, such that the carried data volume converges rather slowly. The weak convergence does not negate fairness in general. Nevertheless, a particular transmission operation could deviate considerably.

Keywords: TCP · Congestion · Resource sharing · Fairness · Convergence

1 Introduction

The Transmission Control Protocol (TCP) is used for reliable data transmission over packet switched networks. The TCP transmitter splits the data into segments, encapsulates them into IP packets, and sends them to the receiver. The receiver reassembles the data from the incoming segments. Lost packets are detected by means of sequence numbers. The receiver signals back to the transmitter the successful reception of data by acknowledgement packets (ACK). Duplicate and selective acknowledgements (SACK) are used to signal packet loss. The transmitter in turn retransmits the previously lost packets. Packet transmission and the acknowledgement back take some time, in particular for forwarding, propagation, queuing, and processing in both directions, which is altogether called the Round Trip Time (*RTT*).

TCP restricts its own transmission rate for congestion control. This is done by a congestion window (*cwnd*) that at any time limits the amount of data that has been sent out, but that has not been acknowledged yet (the so called data in flight). This way the transmission rate is limited to *cwnd* divided by *RTT* (i.e. packets/s). Since the transmitter typically does not know the available transmission capacity along the path, it continuously probes for more bandwidth by gradually increasing the *cwnd*. In contrast, as soon as packet loss is signaling congestion, the *cwnd* is shrunk, typically by half. The succession of slow increases and abrupt decreases (sawtooth oscillation) eventually stabilizes the transmission rate at the limit of the available transmission capacity [1].

© Springer International Publishing Switzerland 2016
A. Remke and B.R. Haverkort (Eds.): MMB & DFT 2016, LNCS 9629, pp. 153–167, 2016.
DOI: 10.1007/978-3-319-31559-1_13

If several TCP flows share the same limited transmission resource, then each of them tries to get more of the shared resource at the cost of the others. Under the assumption of similar conditions, it is natural to expect convergence of flow rates, eventually leading to equal sharing. A first proof of rate convergence was given in [2]. The convergence speed was analyzed in [3], yielding a 98% convergence towards fair sharing rate within seven sawtooth cycles. The convergence time into an ε-environment of the fair sharing rate was frequently used for characterization of different TCP flavors [4, 10].

Unfortunately, and in opposite to what the mentioned papers suggest, something like a monotonic TCP rate convergence towards the fair sharing rate does not exist. In this paper we show that the rate of a TCP flow walks randomly around its fair sharing rate. It deviates down to 1/3 and up to the 3 fold of that rate, altogether within a 1:10 span of possible flow rates. The rate variations are not short term, so that no significant averaging can be observed up to the minutes range, and it takes hours to get stable average values. Why the theories on TCP rate convergence missed that effect? The problem is typically linked to a premature average assumption in the course of modelling the bandwidth sharing process, which finally proves only convergence of an expectation value of the flow rate. However, the expectation value tells little about the actual rate, its distribution, and its realization over time. What remains undisputed with this paper is the equal *cumulative* rate sharing over infinite time, in contrast to other potential assumptions like e.g. "winner takes all".

The paper is structured as follows: After the introduction we elaborate in Sect. 2 the theoretical TCP flow rate distribution at random packet loss. In Sect. 3 we reproduce the distribution in an experiment with real network equipment. Then we show that bandwidth sharing creates quite similar distributions like at purely random loss. Furthermore we investigate the temporal aspects and show that rate deviations are not short term, but much larger than the round trip time. In Sect. 4 we illustrate the consequences of the weak convergence for streaming applications and for the flow completion times of typical short lived flows. We further discuss the implications for Active Queue Management (AQM) and the related experimental work. Section 5 summarizes the findings.

2 TCP Bandwidth Theory

2.1 Basic TCP Equations

TCP operation in congestion avoidance mode as explained in the introduction follows a number of well-known formulas that we recall here for reference:

With the maximum segment size *MSS* (roughly the packet size) in bits and the round trip time *RTT*, the bit rate b of a congestion window *cwnd* limited TCP flow is

$$b = \frac{MSS \cdot cwnd}{RTT} \tag{1}$$

For TCP Reno [17] the gradual additive increase of *cwnd* during congestion avoidance per *RTT* is

$$cwnd \leftarrow cwnd + 1 \tag{2}$$

In reality it is *cwnd* ← *cwnd* + 1/*cwnd* per received acknowledgement. (Here, the arrow sign ← represents an assignment operation.) Since *cwnd* segments are in flight, *cwnd* acknowledgements return during one RTT, which yields Eq. 2. We will see later that the real increase is slower due to the delayed acknowledgments. Other TCP flavors like Cubic have variable and partially larger growth rates.

The abrupt multiplicative *cwnd* reduction due to loss detected follows

$$cwnd \leftarrow \frac{cwnd}{2} \tag{3}$$

Here also variations are possible, e.g. Cubic does a smaller reduction according to *cwnd* ← 0.7·*cwnd*.

The steady state performance of a TCP flow at certain packet loss probability P_{loss} has been multiply derived [5–7]. Taking into account the delayed acknowledgment ratio $a = 2$ (cf. Sect. 2.3) we get for the expected *cwnd*:

$$E[cwnd] = \sqrt{\frac{3}{2a}} \frac{1}{\sqrt{P_{loss}}} \tag{4}$$

Together with Eq. 1 the expected flow bit rate *b* is

$$E[b] = \sqrt{\frac{3}{2a}} \frac{MSS}{\sqrt{P_{loss}}RTT} \tag{5}$$

Equation 5 can be reverted: Bandwidth sharing with certain flow bit rate *b* must result in a corresponding packet loss ratio P_{loss}.

The behavior of TCP Cubic is slightly different. We recall here the formula from the original Cubic paper [10]:

$$E[cwnd_{cubic}] = 1.17 \cdot \left(\frac{RTT}{P_{loss}}\right)^{\frac{3}{4}} \tag{6}$$

where *RTT* is given in seconds.

2.2   Origin of Packet Loss

Packets are almost exclusively lost due to buffer overflow in intermediate nodes. Other sources of packet loss like bit errors or link degradation are out of scope of TCP for different reasons: Wireline links operate at bit error rates below 10^{-12}, thus causing CRC errors on packet level by orders of magnitude below typical TCP loss rates.

Wireless links use link layer handshake protocols for packet delivery to hide the drastic loss rates from higher layers. TCP sees only throughput and delay degradations that in turn might induce buffer overflow and retransmission time outs, but no packet drops.

Buffer overflow occurs due to deterministic queue filling by TCP sources, due to stochastic reasons (typically modelled by M/D/1 queues or some kind of burstiness), or, in practice, due to a combination of both. In the simplest case, one TCP flow crossing one bottleneck link, the process is fully deterministic: If the link is already loaded at 100%, any further *cwnd* increase grows the queue before the link until it overflows the available buffer space. Finally, at overflow, one packet is dropped, TCP reduces its *cwnd* by half, and the queue size goes down, accordingly. It looks like the *cwnd* is oscillating between a maximum and half that value. Simple TCP theories are built on that assumption. Nevertheless, it is not the *cwnd* maximum, but the queue size that triggers the loss. It is just that both go synchronized in the single flow case.

If two (or more) TCP flows cross the same bottleneck, the initial picture looks similar: The cumulative increase of *cwnd* in both sources grows the queue. But then, at overflow, one or two packets are dropped. It is not assured that both flows catch a loss. First of all it could be only one drop. Second, if two packets are dropped, they could belong to one and the same flow, leaving the other one untouched. For the queue it does not matter. It is sufficient that one source reduces its *cwnd* to get away from the buffer limit. In either way, it is not the rule that both flows reduce their *cwnd* at the same time. The two flows, even if started synchronous, move apart from each other. One continues to grow its *cwnd*, while the other one resumes its *cwnd* growth at only half that level. That inequality is going to be resolved at next drop cycle, right? Unfortunately not. The *cwnd* size does not matter for the drop; only the queue matters, which is identical for both flows. Admittedly, the flow with the larger *cwnd* sends more packets than the other flow. This increases its probability to catch a drop, if one occurs. In the long run this results in the (weak) convergence. But at the moment it is not unlikely that the flow with the smaller *cwnd* catches once more the drop, and shrinks its *cwnd* further, while the larger flow continues to grow.

A detailed mathematical analysis of the bandwidth sharing process can be found in [7]. As one of the results, with a tail drop queue, approximately half of the competing flows are affected by a single buffer overflow event. For this paper it does not really matter how many packets are dropped at once and why. The only required plausible insight is that, once drops occur, not all but only a random subset of flows is affected. This is the main difference to the misleading convergence analysis of [2, 3].

2.3   Flow Rate at Random Packet Loss

In this section we investigate the probability distribution of TCP flow rates at random drop, irrespective of a particular bandwidth sharing assumption. We presume that every packet of a TCP flow is dropped at probability P_{loss} with no regard of preceding losses, which results in a Poisson loss process. In context of bandwidth sharing the assumption of a Poisson loss process *per flow* is not arbitrary. A proof in [13] (Sect. 7.7.1) indicates that for an increasing set of concurrent flows the loss process *per flow* converges towards independence of losses, no matter what loss distribution holds for the whole aggregate.

We analyze TCP Reno with Delayed Acknowledgements [14] but without Appropriate Byte Counting (ABC) [15]. Delayed ACK means the receiver sends less than one ACK per received segment for efficiency reasons, typically one ACK per two segments. ABC was intended to compensate the delayed ACK effect on the *cwnd* handling. However, in the Linux kernel the ABC feature was switched off by default since years and recently it has been removed completely [16]. We account for the uncompensated effect of delayed ACK by the acknowledgement ratio a = 2 (segments per ACK).

The expected flow bit rate is given by Eq. 5. The probability distribution of the flow bit rate can be obtained by investigating the evolution of the congestion window *cwnd* as a continuous Markov chain. (We stick here to a method from [8].) Figure 1 shows a fragment of the Markov chain, where the state nodes correspond to the actual *cwnd* size, and transition arcs correspond to conditional transition rates between the states. An arrow from node i to node j, labeled by rate r_{ij}, indicates that, if *cwnd* is in state i, this state is left towards state j at rate r_{ij}. The absolute transition rate depends on the probability p_i to find *cwnd* in state i. Thus, the absolute rate from i to j is $p_i \cdot r_{ij}$. If we assume for a moment that in a given state the sum of arriving rates is larger than the sum of departing rates, obviously its probability would go up. Since probabilities are static by definition, we need to find the equilibrium, where for all nodes the sum of arriving rates equals the sum of departing rates. The equilibrium can be calculated as follows:

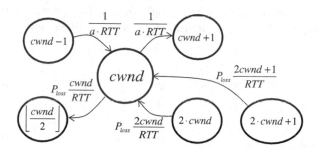

Fig. 1. Fragment of the congestion window state diagram

For the upper part of Fig. 1 holds: The *cwnd* is incremented by an amount of 1/*cwnd* for every arriving ACK. Since *cwnd* packets are in flight, after one *RTT* the total *cwnd* increment should be one per *RTT*. Due to the uncompensated delayed ACKs, however, only 1/*a* (i.e. half) of the 1/*cwnd* increments are executed. Hence, the rate of *cwnd* increments is 1/*a* per one *RTT*; the transition rate from *cwnd* to *cwnd*+1 is:

$$r_{cwnd \to cwnd+1} = \frac{1}{a \cdot RTT} \tag{7}$$

For the lower part of Fig. 1 holds: The actual packet rate is $r_{pack}=cwnd\,/\,RTT$. Packets are lost at probability P_{loss}. Correspondingly the packet loss *rate* (lost packets per second) is $r_{loss} = P_{loss} \cdot r_{pack}$. Thus the *cwnd* halving rate (transition rate from state *cwnd* to state *cwnd/2*) is:

$$r_{cwnd \to \frac{cwnd}{2}} = P_{loss} \frac{cwnd}{RTT} \tag{8}$$

In fact, this reflects that, even though the drop probability P_{loss} is equal for all flows, the hit *rate* of a particular flow depends on the amount of packets sent, so that larger flows are more likely affected than smaller ones.

The equilibrium equation of state i, where incoming and outgoing rates are equal, is

$$(1/a)p_{i-1} + 2iP_{loss} \cdot p_{2i} + (2i+1)P_{loss} \cdot p_{2i+1} = (P_{loss}i + 1/a)p_i \tag{9}$$

The state probabilities p_i of *cwnd* to be in state $i \in [1, cwnd_{max}]$ form a set of linear equations. In matrix notation the corresponding state probability vector $P_{cwnd} = (p_1, p_2, \cdots, p_{cwnd_{max}})^T$ fulfills following equilibrium equation:

$$P_{cwnd} = A \cdot P_{cwnd} \tag{10}$$

The extreme cases need special care: TCP limits *cwnd* to at least 2 since otherwise the loss detection by duplicate ACKs would not work anymore. As consequence, state 2 can be left only by increment, but not by *cwnd* halving. Furthermore state 2 can be reached not only from states 4 and 5 by halving, but additionally from state 3. At the other end, the maximum *cwnd* can be left only by halving, but not by increment.

With the shortcut $P=a \cdot P_{loss}$ the transition matrix A (with e.g. $cwnd_{max}=9$) looks as follows:

$$A = \begin{bmatrix} 0 & 0 & 0 & 0 & 0 & 0 & 0 & 0 & 0 \\ 1 & 0 & \frac{3P}{1} & \frac{4P}{1} & \frac{5P}{1} & 0 & 0 & 0 & 0 \\ 0 & \frac{1}{1+3P} & 0 & 0 & 0 & \frac{6P}{1+3P} & \frac{7P}{1+3P} & 0 & 0 \\ 0 & 0 & \frac{1}{1+4P} & 0 & 0 & 0 & 0 & \frac{8P}{1+4P} & \frac{9P}{1+4P} \\ 0 & 0 & 0 & \frac{1}{1+5P} & 0 & 0 & 0 & 0 & 0 \\ 0 & 0 & 0 & 0 & \frac{1}{1+6P} & 0 & 0 & 0 & 0 \\ 0 & 0 & 0 & 0 & 0 & \frac{1}{1+7P} & 0 & 0 & 0 \\ 0 & 0 & 0 & 0 & 0 & 0 & \frac{1}{1+8P} & 0 & 0 \\ 0 & 0 & 0 & 0 & 0 & 0 & 0 & \frac{1}{9P} & 0 \end{bmatrix} \tag{11}$$

Since Eq. 10 is a homogeneous system, we replace for a numeric solution one of the component equations by the normalizing condition $\Sigma\ p_i =1$. Then, the bit rate distribution is the *cwnd* state probability vector, scaled according to the TCP throughput Eq. 1.

In Fig. 2, the graph labeled "theory" shows the numerically evaluated bit rate probability density of a TCP flow. A similar result has been published already in [9].

The flow bit rate distribution has a substantial spreading. The 95% interval is ranging roughly from less than 40% up to more than 200% of the expected rate.

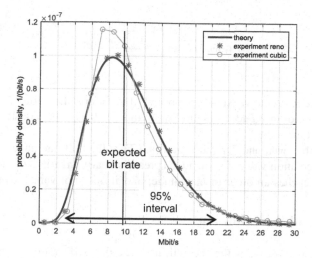

Fig. 2. Bit rate probability distribution of a TCP flow at random packet loss

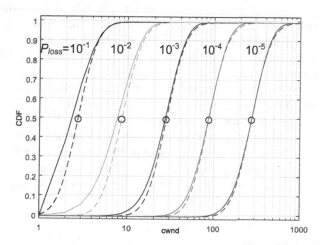

Fig. 3. Numerically calculated CDF of the congestion window *cwnd*; dashed lines are the log normal CDF of Eq. 12; markers show the *cwnd* expectation value of Eq. 4

Needless to say, that the equilibrium probability distribution is static. It holds whenever the process is inspected at any arbitrary point in time, and it does not change or converge. The spreading statement is quite strong. It holds for a wide range of loss probabilities. Figure 3 shows numerically calculated cumulative distribution functions (CDF) of the congestion window. The relative spreading is fairly constant over 5 decades of P_{loss}. For better understanding we complement the graphs with plots of the log normal distribution

$$F(cwnd) = \Phi\left(\frac{\ln\dfrac{cwnd}{\mathrm{E}[cwnd]}}{\sigma}\right), \tag{12}$$

where Φ is the cumulative standard normal distribution function, $\mathrm{E}[cwnd]$ – the expectation value of $cwnd$ according to Eq. 4, and $\sigma = 0.41$ – the constant logarithmic standard deviation.

Obviously the $cwnd$ and derived thereof the TCP flow bit rate have a stable spread around the expectation value. The relative spread is nearly invariant of the packet drop probability; it reaches an order of magnitude; and it does not vanish over time.

3 Experimental Evaluation

In this section we verify, if the theoretically calculated bit rate distribution can be observed in practice. We present an experiment with just one TCP flow in an uncongested network, but with artificial random packet drop, thus reproducing the scenario of the theoretical analysis. Then we compare the results with bandwidth sharing experiments with 2, 3, and 10 concurrent flows, but without artificial packet drop. Here we show that the bit rate spreading is comparable with the random drop case. Finally we investigate how long flow rate deviations persist and how fast deviating flow rates return towards their fair sharing value.

The experiments have been executed on a networking testbed of Linux servers and Ethernet switches. All connections are 10G Ethernet with all TCP offloading features disabled. TCP parameters, if not specially mentioned, are the defaults of Linux kernel 3.16. The conditions are chosen such that each flow has a bit rate expectation value of $\mathrm{E}[b]=10$ Mbit/s. This way we exclude bit rate dependent transmitter or receiver specific variations from our experiments. Round trip time, if not stated otherwise, was $RTT = 100$ ms. Duration of each run was 12 h. The total throughput of all bandwidth sharing experiments was above 99% of the link capacity.

3.1 Random Packet Loss

In this experiment we use a single TCP flow. The transmitted packets are randomly dropped by a specially adapted **iptables** rule. The rule draws for every arriving packet a uniformly distributed random number between 0 and 1. The packet is dropped if the random number is smaller than the requested drop probability. The 10G Ethernet network is loaded in average at 10 Mbit/s so that no queuing or congestion impact is to be expected. We performed the experiments with TCP Reno (the reference) and TCP Cubic as the current Linux default. To reach the 10Mbit/s target we used a drop probability according to Eq. 5 for TCP Reno, and for TCP Cubic according to Eq. 6 (i.e. $P_{reno}=1.1 \cdot 10^{-4}$, $P_{cubic}=3.4 \cdot 10^{-4}$). The flow rate distribution is captured by counting the carried bytes in one second intervals. The count values are then accumulated in the bins of a histogram. More than 43,000 count values per experiment (12 h) have been obtained to get a stable estimation of the distribution function.

Figure 2 of Sect. 2.3 shows besides the theoretical distribution a comparison with the experimental results. Obviously the TCP Reno experiment reproduces exactly the theoretically calculated flow rate distribution. Remaining deviations are so small that they easily can be attributed to the finite duration of the experiment. The experiment with TCP Cubic shows a small deviation. Nevertheless, the spreading of the distribution is similar to TCP Reno.

3.2   Bandwidth Sharing

In this experiment we used 2, 3, or 10 identical TCP flows that share a common bottleneck of 20, 30, or 100 Mbit/s, respectively, which results always in the same target rate of 10Mbit/s per flow. The bottleneck and the corresponding queue are created by the traffic control subsystem of an intermediate Linux server (the `tc qdisc` command). The buffer size for the bottleneck queue was chosen according to the bandwidth delay product rule (BDP). Figure 4 shows the flow rate distribution of the bandwidth sharing experiments, again in comparison to the theoretical distribution at random drop. The bit rate distribution has been measured for one arbitrarily picked flow out of the 2, 3, or 10 flows by the same histogram method as in Sect. 3.1.

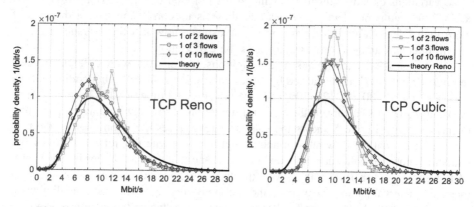

Fig. 4. Experimental probability distribution of bandwidth sharing TCP flow rates

The shape and spread of the curves is similar to the theoretical distribution. TCP Cubic shows a slightly more concentrated distribution around the expected bit rate of 10 Mbit/s. Nevertheless, in all cases the spread of flow rates is so large that deviations down to half of the expectation value and up to double that value are possible. Even after 12 h of continuous bandwidth sharing there is no sign of rate convergence. Table 1 summarizes the experimental flow rate distributions by their mean and the 5%, 50%, and 95% quantiles.

Table 1. Flow rate statistics

		Quantiles, Mbit/s			Mean, Mbit/s
		5%	50%	95%	
Reno	random drop (numeric)	4.7	10.0	19.0	10.7
	random drop (experiment)	4.9	10.0	18.7	10.7
	1 of 2 flows	5.0	10.0	15.0	10.0
	1 of 3 flows	4.7	9.6	16.0	9.9
	1 of 10 flows	4.5	8.9	16.6	9.5
Cubic	random drop (experiment)	5.0	9.4	20.0	10.6
	1 of 2 flows	6.5	10.0	13.6	10.0
	1 of 3 flows	6.3	9.8	14.6	10.0
	1 of 10 flows	6.1	9.8	16.0	10.3

3.3   Duration of Rate Variations

A frequently raised argument for a technical convergence is that the TCP flow rate might be highly unsteady or even bursty at time scales of one RTT or below, but that these variations quickly vanish if looking at the duration of typical TCP flows of few RTTs. The argument silently assumes that there is no correlation over a distance of more than a few RTTs. In this section we investigate how fast the average rate over certain interval duration converges towards the expectation rate.

We repeated all experiments of the previous sections but with different interval settings, i.e. we counted the carried bytes not only in intervals of 1 s but additionally in intervals of 4, 16, 30, 60, 120, 300, and 600 s over a total time of 12 h. From the series of count values we calculated the standard deviation of the flow rate at the particular interval settings. Figure 5 shows the results. It reproduces the impression of the previous sections that the flow rate variations slightly grow with the number of flows, but still stay below the value at purely random loss, and that they are larger in general for TCP Reno than for TCP Cubic. As expected, the standard deviation shrinks with increasing interval duration. However, the decline is very slow. It remains negligible up to 20 – 30 s intervals, and even for 10 min intervals the standard deviation stays in the range of 10% of the mean (10Mbit/s).

The graphs also justify our experimental approach for verification of the theory. In fact, the theory of Sect. 2, if applied to bit rate, is correct in a strong sense for intervals of one round trip, including the queuing delay, i.e. variable 100–200 ms, depending on the actual queue size. In contrast, the experimental data have been obtained as data volume carried over constant intervals of one second. In our case the graphs are comparably flat in the neighborhood of one second, so that the interval mismatch with the theory can be accepted.

In a further experiment we investigated the impact of the round trip time. Instead of $RTT = 100$ ms (the default RTT in this study), we used an RTT of only 10 ms and a corresponding bandwidth delay product (BDP) sized buffer. The results are shown in Fig. 6.

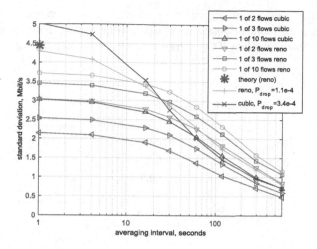

Fig. 5. Standard deviation of short term average rates at different interval durations; bandwidth sharing and random drop experiments

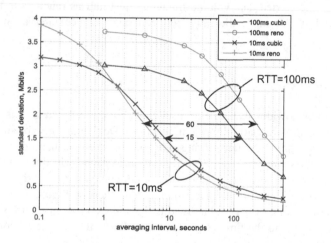

Fig. 6. Impact of the RTT on the convergence

As expected, the convergence slope shifts left, towards smaller intervals. The shift is much more pronounced for TCP Reno than for Cubic, so that the mutual order reverts. The shift for Reno is by a factor of 60, which can be weakly associated with the theoretical sawtooth interval that scales quadratic with the *RTT*, i.e. a shift of 100 could be expected. The shift for Cubic is much smaller, by a factor of 15, which is in line with Cubic's original intention to make TCP less *RTT* sensitive. Nevertheless, the reduction is even larger than what Cubic's performance Eq. 6 might suggest. We verified that by measuring the actual packet loss rates and comparing them with the theory. The values fit well for all experiments, except the 10 ms Cubic case. Here Cubic drops 5 times more packets than required according to Eq. 6. The reason for this mismatch is a fallback heuristic in the Cubic algorithm (a bit misleadingly named `tcp_friend-liness`): According to the original Cubic paper [10] it approximates, in addition to its own *cwnd*, the corresponding TCP Reno window and takes the larger of the two windows.

Table 2. RTT dependence of convergence

	RTT	P_{loss}		Sawtooth interval	50% convergence interval	Ratio
		Theory	Experiment			
reno	10 ms	3.8e-3	3.3e-3	0.37 s	4 s	11
	100 ms	3.8e-5	4.0e-5	29.5 s	220 s	7.5
cubic	10 ms	6.2e-4	2.8e-3	0.42 s	9.5 s	22
	100 ms	2.9e-4	2.5e-4	4.7 s	130 s	27

The experimental results are summarized in Table 2. The sawtooth interval is calculated from the experimental loss ratio. The 50% convergence interval is the duration where the carried data volume fluctuates just half as much as at the smallest intervals. The last column is the ratio between convergence interval and sawtooth interval.

4   Consequences

The bit rate of a bandwidth sharing TCP flow does not converge at all. Instead it walks randomly around its fair sharing expectation value. Deviations are not small; they go down to less than half of the fair sharing rate, and up to more than double that value. Deviations are not short term; they last thousands of round trip times; in our experiments many minutes. And the deviations do not attenuate over time; their spread stays the same after many hours of continuous bandwidth sharing. Figure 7 illustrates these facts for the last 10 min of a 12 h bandwidth sharing experiment with just two flows. (The link was loaded all the time at constant 20 Mbit/s; the two flows complemented each other at any time.)

The effect is relevant for streaming applications, like video streaming. These applications rely on a continuous arrival of new content. They need sufficient margins to cope with the rate variations or flatten the arrival by a playout buffer. Figure 5 gives an impression of how long a playout buffer needs to store to get a reasonable flattening effect.

The effect is also relevant for the flow completion time of finite TCP flows. In general it is assumed that a new flow entering a congested link with N-1 pre-established flows grabs a $1/N$ fraction of the link bandwidth and completes accordingly. However, the actual flow rate variates according to Fig. 4. If the variations persist longer than the flow duration, the actual flow completion time gets a similar spread, i.e. ranging from half the expected duration up to more than double that time.

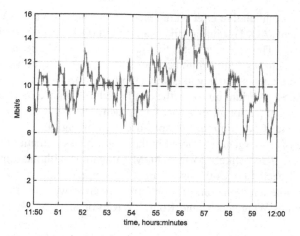

Fig. 7. Random walk: Last minutes after 12 h of continuous bandwidth sharing; one of two TCP Cubic flows at RTT=100 ms in 20Mbit/s link bandwidth

In the experiment of Fig. 8 we run 9 long lived TCP flows over a link of 100 Mbit/s. Then we launched repeatedly a 10th short lived flow with a data volume of 12 Mbyte. The expected rate is 10Mbit/s, the expected duration 10 s. The displayed four shots carry all the same data volume, but it takes between 7 and up to 17 s till completion. In a more exhaustive experiment with 2500 repetitions, 5% of the flows take less than 8 s, whereas another 5% take more than 22 s till completion.

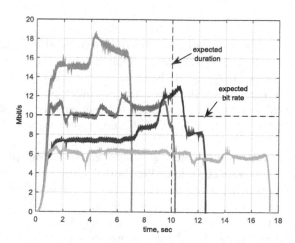

Fig. 8. Transmission of 12 Mbyte at expected fair sharing rate of 10Mbit/s; 4 independent shots in an otherwise identical set-up

The weak convergence bears more implications on TCP rate control. It seems to be impossible to directly control a TCP flow rate by applying random packet drop according to the well-known TCP bandwidth formula Eq. 5. The reaction is too fuzzy, and if relying on a cumulative effect, the response is much too slow. Existing Active Queue Management (AQM) solutions like Random Early Detection (RED) [11] always incorporate a queue. That queue is not acting just as an averaging device. Instead, in the first instance it establishes equilibrium between the congestion windows of all involved transmitters and the queueing delay, this way stabilizing the total rate. Only secondarily RED confines the equilibrium queue to the available buffer space by random dropping. Since the queue is unique for all flows, this approach stabilizes only the total rate of all flows. The particular flow continues to spread out as of Fig. 4.

Since the weak convergence is rooted in the arbitrary assignment of packet drops to the affected flows, it is unlikely to find AQM mitigation without some kind of *flow notion*. In normal packet nodes this is not the case, impractical, or at least undesirable due to the noticeable additional effort. For further reading we refer to the well-known queueing disciplines Weighted Round Robin (WRR) or Stochastic Fairness Queueing (SFQ) [12].

Special care is required in measurement experiments for characterization of novel TCP and queuing approaches. Metrics like the ε-convergence time of [4] are inherently undefined, since a flow that reached the ε environment of the expected rate is not guaranteed, not even likely, to stay in that ε environment. Experiments that claim such convergence anyway likely stopped prematurely at the first visit. In general, the experimental acquisition of per flow metrics requires extremely long observation times of hours or days, rather than seconds or minutes. Nonetheless, this must not be confused with global metrics, characterizing the combined effect of all involved flows like total rate, queue size, or drop ratio. These metrics usually converge much faster.

5 Summary

TCP is able to fill a network bottleneck at 100% of its transmission capacity. If multiple flows share the same bottleneck, then the available bandwidth is distributed between the flows in a comparably fair way: (1) None of the flows is able to monopolize the available bandwidth. (2) None of the flows starves. Under uniform conditions (same RTT, same TCP flavor) the rate expectation and the long term average are equal for all sharing flows. The carried data volume of the flows converges to equal values at infinity.

In this paper we investigate to which extent this "equal sharing" proposition can be applied to technically relevant conditions. We show that the actual rate of a particular flow does not converge at all. It deviates randomly down to one third and up to three fold of its expected rate. The random deviations do not attenuate over time, neither in theory nor in experiment. In our experiments they appear even after many hours of continuous bandwidth sharing. And the deviations are long lasting. Their correlation span is many times larger than the Round Trip Time or the TCP sawtooth interval. Accordingly, the carried data volume converges only slowly after thousands of RTT. The findings have been theoretically derived and subsequently verified by comprehensive series of bandwidth sharing experiments in a test bed of Ethernet servers and switches.

Acknowledgement. This work has been funded in part by the German Bundesministerium für Bildung und Forschung (Federal Ministry of Education and Research) in scope of project SASER under grant No. 16BP12200.

References

1. Jacobson, V.: Congestion avoidance and control. In: Proceedings of the SIGCOMM 1988 (1988)
2. Chiu, D.-M., Jain, R.: Analysis of the increase and decrease algorithms for congestion avoidance in computer networks. J. Comput. Netw. ISDN Syst. **17**(1), 1–14 (1989)
3. Podlesny, M., Gorinsky, S.: Multimodal Congestion Control for Low Stable-State Queuing. Technical Report WUCSE-2006–41, August 2006. http://openscholarship.wustl.edu/cse_research/192
4. Li, Y.-T., Leith, D., Shorten, R.N.: Experimental Evaluation of TCP Protocols for High-Speed Networks. IEEE/ACM Trans. Netw. **15**(5), 1109–1122 (2007)
5. Mathis, M., Semke, J., Mahdavi, J., Ott, T.: The macroscopic behavior of the TCP congestion avoidance algorithm. Comput. Commun. Rev. **27**(3), 67–82 (1997)
6. Padhye, J., Firoiu, V., Towsley, D., Kurose, J.: Modeling TCP throughput: A simple model and its empirical validation. In: Proceedings of the ACM SIGCOMM, 1998, pp. 303–314 (1998)
7. Lautenschlaeger, W.: A Deterministic TCP Bandwidth Sharing Model, April 2014. http://arxiv.org/abs/1404.4173
8. Handbook Teletraffic Engineering, ITU-D Study Group 2 Question 16/2 (2008)
9. Bogoiavlenskaia, O.: Markovian Model of Internetworking Flow Control, Kalashnikov Memorial Seminar, Petrozavodsk, Информационные процессы, 2.2 (2002)
10. Ha, Sangtae, Rhee, Injong, Lisong, Xu: CUBIC: a new TCP-friendly high-speed TCP variant. ACM SIGOPS Operating Syst. Rev. **42**(5), 64–74 (2008)
11. Floyd, S., Jacobsen, V.: Random early detection gateways for congestion avoidance. IEEE/ACM Trans. Netw. **1**(4), 397–413 (1993)
12. McKenney, P.E.: Stochastic fairness queueing. In: Proceedings of the INFOCOM 1990 (1990)
13. Briscoe, R.: Re-feedback: Freedom with Accountability for Causing Congestion in a Connectionless Internetwork, Diss. UC London (2009). http://www.bobbriscoe.net/projects/refb/refb_dis.pdf
14. Braden, R. (ed.) Requirements for Internet Hosts - Communication Layers, IETF, RFC 1122 (1989)
15. Allman, M.: TCP Congestion Control with Appropriate Byte Counting (ABC), IETF, RFC 3465 (2003)
16. Hemminger, S.: tcp: remove Appropriate Byte Count support (2013). https://github.com/torvalds/linux/commit/ca2eb5679f8ddffff60156af42595df44a315ef0
17. Allman, M., Paxson, V., Blanton, E.: TCP Congestion Control, IETF, RFC 5681 (2009)

Analysis of Mitigation Measures for Timing Attacks in Mobile-Cloud Offloading Systems

Tianhui Meng$^{(\boxtimes)}$ and Katinka Wolter

Department of Mathematics and Computer Science, Freie Universität Berlin,
Takustr. 9, 14195 Berlin, Germany
{tianhui.meng,katinka.wolter}@fu-berlin.de

Abstract. Mobile cloud offloading has been proposed to migrate complex computations from mobile devices to powerful servers. While this may be beneficial from the performance and energy perspective, it certainly exhibits new challenges in terms of security due to increased data transmission over networks with potentially unknown threats. Among possible security issues are timing attacks which are not prevented by traditional cryptographic security. Usually random delays are introduced in such systems as a popular countermeasure. Random delays are easily deployed even if the source code of the application is not at hand. While the benefits are obvious, a random delay introduces a penalty that should be minimized. The challenge is to select the distribution from which to draw the random delays and to set mean and variance in a suitable way such that the system security is maximized and the overhead is minimized. To tackle this problem, we have implemented a prototype that allows us to compare the impact of different random distributions on the expected success of timing attacks. Based on our model, the effect of random delay padding on the performance and security perspective of offloading systems is analyzed in terms of response time and optimal rekeying rate. We found that the variance of random delays is the primary influencing factor to the mitigation effect. Based on our approach, the system performance and security can be improved as follows. Starting from the mission time of a computing job one can select a desired padding policy. From this the optimal rekeying interval can be determined for the offloading system.

Keywords: Mobile cloud offloading · Security attributes · Random delays · Timing side-channels

1 Introduction

Mobile devices are now ubiquitous in the modern life, which are no longer used only for voice communication and short message service (SMS); instead, they are used for watching videos, gaming recording health data and social networking. While the last decades witness great advances in hardware technology, mobile devices still face the restriction of resources, such as battery life and network bandwidth.

© Springer International Publishing Switzerland 2016
A. Remke and B.R. Haverkort (Eds.): MMB & DFT 2016, LNCS 9629, pp. 168–182, 2016.
DOI: 10.1007/978-3-319-31559-1_14

"Mobile-cloud offloading" is a solution to augment these mobile systems' capabilities by migrating computation to more resourceful computers (i.e., servers). Mobile-cloud offloading is different from the traditional client-server architecture, where a thin client always migrates computation to a server [1]. In many scenarios, the limited power storage of mobile systems can be enhanced by mobile cloud offloading. One example is the working implementation of CDroid [2], with the focus on offloading mobile computation to software clones of real devices in the cloud, makes it enable to increase the gain of offloading of computation-intensive apps. Another example is context-aware computing infrastructure [3] – where multiple streams of data from different sources like GPS, maps, accelerometers and temperature sensors need to be analyzed together in order to obtain real-time information about a user's context.

However as more and more information on individuals and business are placed in the cloud, concerns are beginning to spring up about how safe an environment it is. Despite of all the hype surrounding the cloud, enterprise customers are still reluctant to deploy their business in the cloud [4]. Protecting user privacy and data secrecy from an adversary is a key to establish and maintain consumers' trust in the mobile platform, especially in mobile cloud computing. Metrics on which offloading decisions are based must include security aspects in addition to performance and energy-efficiency. Numerous works about security in mobile cloud offloading and cloud computing have been presented in recent years. Researchers in [5] present a mobile cloud computing platform which allows users to choose to run their applications either in the cloud (for high security guarantees), or on their local mobile device (for better user experience). [6] proposes to enable a secure and efficient cloud-assisted image sharing architecture for mobile devices. Indeed, security is such a big area covering large numbers of issues. In this work, we deal with the specific threat of timing attacks whose remote feasibility has been proved [7,8]. Remote timing attacks make a practical threat against web services as well as offloading systems [9].

Quantitative analyses of system dependability and reliability have received great attention for several decades [10]. However quantification of security has only recently attracted more attention, and some initial conceptual work has been published already decades ago, serious model-based evaluation of security mechanisms has been published only recently. Previous work on the security of computing and information systems has been mostly assessed from a level point of view. The authors in [11] make an effort to examine the security vulnerabilities of operating systems of routers within the cloud carrier by assessing the risk based on the National Vulnerability Database (NVD) and gives a quantifiable security metrics for cloud carrier, which is very useful in the Service Level Agreement (SLA) negotiation between a cloud consumer and a cloud provider.

To proceed to a quantitative analysis of the mitigation measure for timing side-channel attacks in mobile cloud offloading systems we have improved our hybrid CTMC (Continuous-time Markov chain) and queueing model. Our model is aimed to deal with a general mobile cloud offloading system with a master secret stored on the server side, where the attacking client can also get normal offloading service. In a timing attack to such a system, the attacker deduces information about a secret key from runtime measurements of successive requests. This process can be interrupted by changing the server secret frequently [12]. By solving the model, we propose security and performance metrics on which offloading decisions can be based. One of the popular countermeasures against timing attacks is to add random delays in every service response. While the benefits are obvious, a random delay introduces a penalty that should be minimised. The challenge is to select the distribution from which to draw the random delays and how to set mean and variance in a suitable way such that the system security is maximised while the overhead is minimised. To tackle this problem, we have implemented a prototype that allows us to compare the impact of different random distributions on the expected success of timing attacks. Afterwards, Weibull distributed delays with different parameter sets are added to the Cloud service side to mitigate timing attacks. Based on the proposed model, the effect of random delay padding on the performance and security perspective of offloading systems is analyzed in terms of response time and optimal rekeying rate. We found that the variance of random delays is the primary influencing factor to the mitigation effect. Meanwhile, using our approach one may improve system performance and security as follows. Starting from the mission time of a computing job one can select a desired padding policy, from which the optimal rekey interval can be determined for the offloading system.

The remainder of this paper is structured as follows. In Sect. 2, we summarize the system and attackers' behavior and the random delay countermeasure. Then we proposes a hybrid model for a generic offloading system. The system metrics on which the evaluation based are addressed in Sect. 3. Section 4 shows a series of experiments that have been performed to analyze the effectiveness of random delay countermeasure. Section 5 gives discussion of the experiment results and suggestions. Finally, the paper is concluded in Sect. 6.

2   System Overview and the Model

A mobile cloud offloading system is a common solution to enhance the capabilities of the mobile system by migrating computation to more resourceful computers (i.e., servers) [13]. To quantitatively analyze the performance and security attributes of such a system under the threat of timing attacks, we have to incorporate the actions of an attacker who is trying to capture sensitive information in conjunction with the protective actions taken by the system. Therefore, we have to develop a hybrid CTMC and queueing model that takes into account the behavior of both actors.

2.1   Behavior of System and Attackers

In the considered offloading system, a master key stored in the server is used for the RSA encryption and decryption operations of all user data. The keying scheme is that the server regularly changes the master key, which is called the rekeying process, with a rekeying rate. The system needs to process all user-files with both the new and the old master key. In this process, the system does not accept any other user commands. When user data is very large, this process will take long. Therefore, it is reasonable to recommend an optimal interval time for the master key replacement cycle, and select a suitable time, when there is a low amount of user access (e.g. at night).

Implementations of cryptographic algorithms often perform computations in non-constant time, due to performance optimization. If such operations involve secret parameters, these timing variations can leak some information and a careful statistical analysis could even lead to the total recovery of these secret keys. Timing attacks gain secret information from the server response time and rather than brute force attacks or theoretical weaknesses in the algorithms they are a real threat to mobile cloud offloading systems. However this threat is not covered by traditional notions of cryptographic security [14]. It was commonly believed that timing attacks can be directed only towards smart cards or affect inter-process locally, but more recent research reveals that remote timing attacks are also possible and should be taken into consideration [7,8]. In this remote timing attacks to our offloading system, an attacker continues to send normal requests to the server and the obtained offloading service will be properly performed by the server. In addition the attacker records each response time for a certain service and tries to find clues to the master secret of the server by statistical analysis of the timing measurements. If the attacker successfully breaks the secret information from the timing results, he may hack into the system, read and even modify other users' information without authorization. Systems that perform cryptographic operations with inconstant response time are exposed to such timing attacks, and no man-in-the-middle or other kind of attack is considered. It is worth mentioning that a timing attack also poses a threat to other types of systems.

2.2 Random Delays

Random delays are easily deployed even if the source code of the application is not at hand. Interposition of random delays in the cryptographic algorithm execution flow is a simple but rather effective countermeasure against side-channel and fault attacks. Random delays are widely used for protection of cryptographic implementations in embedded devices [15]. The first detailed analysis of the this kind of countermeasure is shown in [16] that the number of traces for a successful differential power analysis (DPA) attack grows quadratically or linearly with the standard deviation of the delay, while the researchers in [17] implement random delays on FPGA and obtain the optimal parameters for delay generators. To date, based on random delay insertion, an processor architecture resistant to side-channel attacks was proposed in [18] using a combination of randomized scheduling, randomized instruction insertion and randomized pipeline-delay. Researchers in [19] presents a design and hardware implementation of asynchronous AES with random noise injection for improved side-channel attack resistance.

In this paper, random delays are introduced in the offloading system to mitigate the timing information leakage.

2.3   The System Model

As compared to our previous work [20], in which the model only considered the security attributes of offloading systems, the proposed hybrid CTMC and queueing model in this work takes the performance properties of a generic offloading system into account (Fig. 1). When jobs are generated by a mobile device, they are either offloaded to the cloud or executed locally, expressed by the two queues, respectively. The parameters λ and λ' indicate the arrival rates for the two queues. A job dispatched to offload comes to the upper queue and is processed by the server with service rate μ, which also includes the data transmission time. For jobs dispatched to execute locally, the service rate is μ' which is assumed to be lower than μ.

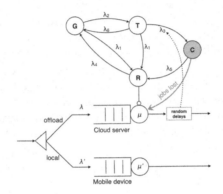

Fig. 1. State transition diagram for a generic offloading system (Color figure online)

The states and parameters of the CTMC state transition model are summarized here:

- G Good state in which the offloading system works properly.
- T Timing attack happening state.
- C Compromised state after the attacker knows the secret of the system.
- R Rekeying state in which system renews its master secret.
- λ_1 rate at which the system launches the rekeying process in state G and state T.
- λ_2 rate at which an attacker triggers a timing attack to the system.
- λ_3 rate at which a timing attack succeeds to break the system secret.
- λ_4 rate at which the system is brought back to the good state by the rekeying process.
- λ_5 rate at which the system launches the rekeying process in state C.

– λ_6 rate at which the attacker fails to conduct a successful timing attack or he successfully breaks the key, while fails at accessing the data.

The upper part of Fig. 1 shows a CTMC model representing the states of the system. After initialization, the system starts to operate properly in the good state G. The system is under the specific threat of timing attacks conducted by random attackers. We describe the events that trigger transitions among states in terms of transition rates. It is assumed that there is only one attacker in the system at one time. If an attack happens, the system is brought to the timing attack state T at rate λ_2. In this state the attacker tries to break the server encryption key by making time observations. So while the system is in state T, the attacker is not yet able to access confidential information.

It takes a certain time to perform the timing attack after which the attacker may know the encryption key and the system moves to the compromised state C at rate λ_3. Consequently λ_3^{-1} is the mean time a timing attack takes. There is a possibility indicated by the arc λ_6 that the attacker fails to conduct a successful timing attack due to connection failures or he successfully breaks the key, while fails at accessing user data. If the attacker succeeds to determine the encryption key through time measurements, confidential data will be disclosed which is assumed to incur a high cost. This can only happen if the system is in the compromised state C and we call the incident of entering the compromised state a security failure. In this state, all jobs dispatched to offload are not secure any more, therefore they must be repeated and do not contribute to the throughput. The jobs lost is represented by the red arc in Fig. 1.

Renewing the server encryption key can prevent or interrupt a timing attack. The arcs from other states to state R represent these operations in the server. The rekeying rate is the parameter one can tune as a system administrator. It indicates how often the system launches the rekeying process. The rate λ_1 is the rekeying rate when the system is in good state G or in the timing attack state T. We assume the offloading system has intrusion detection mechanisms running on it, that can find clues of compromised behavior, in which case the system will trigger the rekeying process more frequently. So in the compromised state C, we assume the rekeying process is triggered at a different rate, $\lambda_5 = n\lambda_1 (n > 1)$. The parameter n is called the coefficient of rekeying in the compromised state because it represent the relationship between the rekeying rate (or rekeying frequency) in good state and the rekeying rate in compromised state. All these three paths transfer the system to the rekeying state R from which it will finally return to the initial state G. The challenge is to find an optimal value for the rekeying interval. The rekeying should in the optimal case happen before or soon after the system enters the compromised state.

In the rekeying state the system refuses all user requests. So we put a inhibitor arc on the cloud server. All the jobs are dispatched to the local queue and some jobs will be lost in this state. As a result, the system throughput is degraded. The rekeying process will bring the system back to the initial state G at rate λ_4. Consequently, the mean time to perform the rekeying process is λ_4^{-1} and during this time the server refuses user requests.

When random delay padding is added after the cloud service, the attacker needs more samples to successfully guess the secret in the server. So it takes more time for him to conduct the timing attack. As a result, the rekeying rate λ_3 decreases as this mitigation method is taken.

3   Metrics

3.1   Security Metrics

After defining the model and its parameters, we must now establish the measures we want to investigate. We present security and performance metrics, respectively. The security measures are defined in this work as confidentiality and system (security) cost that are functions of the steady-state probabilities of the CTMC model. The steady-state probabilities π_i may be interpreted as the proportion of time that the CTMC spends in state i, where $i \in \{R, G, T, C\}$.

If a timing attack to the offloading system is successful, the attacker obtains the master key and can browse unauthorized files thereafter. The entered states denote the loss of confidentiality. Therefore, the steady-state confidentiality measure can be computed as

$$Confid = 1 - \pi_C. \tag{1}$$

We also define a system cost metric. In our scenario, the offloading system suffers from cost in two states, the compromised state C and the rekeying state R. The system loses sensitive information in the compromised state, and cost is also incurred when the system deploys a rekeying process. The rekeying cost and the data disclosure cost are both interpreted as the proportion of system life time, that is, the steady-state probability of the CTMC. We define a weight w and its complement $1 - w$ for the two kinds of cost. We use normalised weights for simplicity. So the system cost is defined as:

$$Cost = w\pi_R + (1 - w)\pi_C, \tag{2}$$

where $\pi_i, i \in \{R, C\}$ denotes the steady-state probability that the continuous-time Markov process is in state i. $0 \leq w \leq 1$ is the weighting parameter used to share relative importance between the loss of sensitive information and the effort needed to rekey regularly.

3.2   Performance Metrics

The performance metrics we are interested in describe the system in terms of its throughput, completion times, or response times, as defined e.g. in queueing theory or networking. In this paper we use the response time as the performance metric for the offloading system. By Little's Law, the response time (denoted $E[R]$) is defined as:

$$E[R] = \frac{E[N]}{\lambda}. \tag{3}$$

For the offloading queue, the response time equals the average number of jobs in the queueing station ($E[N]$) divided by arrival rate (λ).

4 Model Analysis

In this section, we derive and evaluate the security and performance attributes of the offloading system using methods for quantitative assessment of dependability, known as the dependability attributes, e.g. reliability, availability, and safety which have been well established quantitatively.

4.1 CTMC Steady-State Probability Computation

For the system security attributes, we have described the system's dynamic behavior by a CTMC model with the state space $X_s = \{R, G, T, C\}$ and the transitions between these states. In order to carry out the security quantification analysis, we need to determine the stationary distribution of the CTMC model.

The steady-state probabilities $\{\pi_i, i \in X_s\}$ of the CTMC can be computed by solving the system of linear equations [21]

$$\pi \mathbf{Q} = 0, \tag{4}$$

where $\pi = [\pi_R, \pi_G, \pi_T, \pi_C]$ and $\mathbf{Q}$ is the infinitesimal generator (or transition-rate matrix) which can be written as:

$$
\mathbf{Q} = \begin{array}{c} \\ R \\ G \\ T \\ C \end{array}
\overset{\displaystyle R \qquad G \qquad\quad T \qquad\quad C}{
\begin{pmatrix}
-\lambda_4 & \lambda_4 & 0 & 0 \\
\lambda_1 & -\lambda_1 - \lambda_2 & \lambda_2 & 0 \\
\lambda_1 & \lambda_6 & -\lambda_1 - \lambda_3 - \lambda_6 & \lambda_3 \\
\lambda_5 & 0 & 0 & -\lambda_5
\end{pmatrix}} \tag{5}
$$

In addition, we have the total probability relationship:

$$\sum_i \pi_i = 1 \quad i \in X_s. \tag{6}$$

The transition-rate matrix $\mathbf{Q}$ describes the dynamic behavior of the security model as shown in Fig. 1. The first step towards quantitatively evaluating security attributes is to find the steady-state probability vector π of the CTMC states by solving Eqs. 4 and 6. We can get solutions:

$$\pi_R = \frac{[(\lambda_1 + \lambda_2)(\lambda_1 + \lambda_3) + \lambda_1 \lambda_6]\lambda_5}{\phi}, \tag{7}$$

$$\pi_G = \frac{(\lambda_1 + \lambda_3 + \lambda_6)\lambda_4 \lambda_5}{\phi}, \quad \pi_T = \frac{\lambda_2 \lambda_4 \lambda_5}{\phi}, \quad \pi_C = \frac{\lambda_2 \lambda_3 \lambda_4}{\phi}.$$

For the sake of brevity, where:

$$\phi = (\lambda_1 + \lambda_4)(\lambda_1 + \lambda_3 + \lambda_6)\lambda_5 + [(\lambda_1 + \lambda_4)\lambda_5 + (\lambda_4 + \lambda_5)\lambda_3]\lambda_2.$$

Given the steady-state probabilities of CTMC model, the *Cost* measure can be computed:

$$Cost = w\frac{[(\lambda_1 + \lambda_2)(\lambda_1 + \lambda_3) + \lambda_1\lambda_6]\lambda_5}{\phi} + (1 - w)\frac{\lambda_2\lambda_3\lambda_4}{\phi}. \tag{8}$$

5   Evaluation

We performed a series of experiments to demonstrate the effectiveness of random delay countermeasure against remote timing attacks.

5.1   Experiment Setup

Our server and client applications are developed using the OMNeT++ simulation tool based on the INET 2.6 framework. The connection between two hosts are enabled by TCP protocol. All tests were run under Mac OS X 10.10 on a 2.6 GHz Intel Core i5 processor with 8 GB 1600 MHz DDR3 RAM.

A timing attack uses statistical analysis of how long it takes one application to do some calculation in order to learn about the secret it is operating on. The key idea of conducting a timing attack is to find the time difference. For simplifying the implementation, we mimic a timing attack by recording and analyzing the amount of time takes by the server application to compare two values bit by bit. Once the server finds one bit in the value received from the client is different from what restored in the server, it send back the result to the client immediately. Otherwise, the server continues to compare the next bit in the received value.

5.2   Convolution Method for Timing Attack Distribution

Firstly, we analyze the completion time distribution for timing attacks. As the implementation in [8], a complete remote timing attack can be viewed as a binary search for a system secret and it consists of several steps to recover the ith bit of the secret. The attacker repeats these steps to recover the secret bits one by one. After recovering the half-most significant bits of the system secret, he can use Coppersmith's algorithm [22] to retrieve the complete factorization. Then the system is successfully compromised by the attacker by timing attack. From the setup of [8], a typical attack takes approximately 2 h, and to get its distribution may take days. So we try to simplify this process by convolution method.

For each secret bit, the attacking behavior can be regarded as a single entity. And these entities are assumed to be independent and identically distributed (i.i.d.). When the distribution of the attack entity time is known, the cumulative distribution function (CDF) of one complete attack duration can be computed by interactively convolution method. It is needed 256 attack entities to factor a RSA-1024 bit key. To simplify the computational process, we propose Algorithm 1 by doing the convolution pairing.

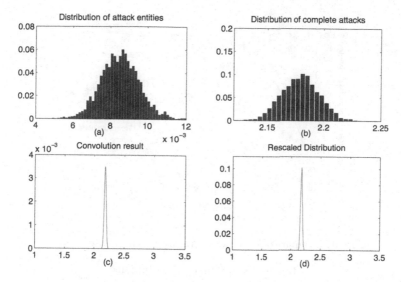

Fig. 2. Test and verify the convolution method. (a) The time distribution for an attack entity. (b) The time distribution of complete attacks which consists of 256 entities. (c) The result of interactively convolution method. (d) The rescaled distribution of complete attacks.

```
Algorithm 1.      for i=1:8
                      p = conv (p,p);
                  end
```

Then we can get the 256 attack entities distribution by 8 self-convolutions. The results are shown in Fig. 2. The mean of Fig. 2c is 2.181 h and the variance is 0.000264 respectively. For Fig. 2d, the mean is 2.179 h and the variance is 0.000267. We test and verify that the convolution method is adequate for our scenario. This method can radically decrease the computation time for the subsequent evaluation.

5.3 Comparison of Different Distributions

This experiment aims at comparing the impact of different random distributions to the limits of timing attacks against offloading systems. The parameters, the mean and the variance of different distributions are shown in Table 1. We set the mean of all random distribution as 0.1 ms while the variances are different for the brevity of parameters. For the Erlang distribution, it is difficult to get a large variance because the shape parameter has to be integer.

The attacking client sends two messages separately with a certain bit equals 0 and 1 to the server. Random delays are added after the server processes each message received from the client. Different numbers of timing samples are taken from the client measurement. When the client can distinguish the time difference

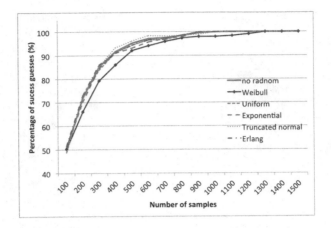

Fig. 3. Comparison of different random delay distributions

Table 1. Continuous distributions

	Mean	Variance	SCV
Weibull (0.05, 0.5)	0.1	0.05	5
Uniform (0, 0.2)	0.1	0.0033	0.33
Exponential (0.1)	0.1	0.01	1
Truncated normal (0.1, 0.1)	0.1	0.01	1
Erlang (5, 0.1)	0.1	0.002	0.2

of server application processing two different messages from statistical analysis of the samples, we call it a success attack. We use the percentage of success guesses to represent the moderating influence upon timing attacks exercised by random delay countermeasure.

The result is depicted in Fig. 3. It shows that the Weibull distributed delays can mitigate the timing attacks as the attacker needs more samples to guess the secret than no random delays are added. The results of the rest three random distributions are superposition of the result with no random added. The impact of the rest three distributions is negligible because the variances are small.

In the next subsection, we choose Weibull distribution because it is widely used in reliability engineering and failure analysis and it is easy to change the variance of Weibull distribution by tuning the parameters.

5.4 Comparison of Weibull Distributed Delays with Different Parameter-Sets

To compare the effect of the random delays countermeasure with Weibull distribution to mitigate timing attacks, we conduct this experiment by changing the shape parameter $k \in \{0.5, 0.45, 0.4, 0.37, 0.35, 0.34\}$ while keeping the scale parameter $\eta = 0.05$.

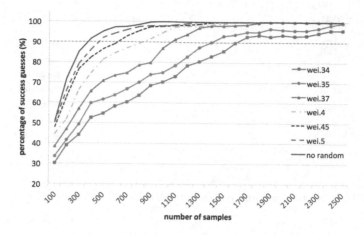

Fig. 4. Comparison of Weibull distributed delays with different parameter-sets

Table 2. Parameter-set of Weibull distribution and the metrics

	Mean	Variance	SCV	Number of samples	Optimal rekeying rate	Response time
No random				375	0.2996	7.7161
wei .5	0.1	0.0500	5	470	0.2705	7.8177
wei .45	0.1239	0.1043	6.7931	625	0.2372	7.8423
wei .4	0.1662	0.2725	9.865	830	0.2075	7.886
wei .37	0.2092	0.5642	12.8912	1070	0.1837	7.9305
wei .35	0.2515	0.9980	15.7774	1400	0.1614	7.9743
wei .34	0.2788	1.3682	17.6019	1610	0.1507	8.0027

Figure 4 shows the comparison of Weibull distributed delays with different parameter-sets. It is assumed that the attacker use error detection and correction strategy as described in [23], so 90 % success guesses is adequate for his attack. We record the numbers of samples on 90 percentage of success guesses and calculate the *Cost* measure using Eq. 8 to obtain the corresponding optimal rekeying rate as. The system cost metric changing with the rekeying rate λ_1 is shown in Fig. 5. We set the weighting parameter $w = 0.5$ to put equal importance to the loss of sensitive information cost and the effort needed to rekey regularly. As the administrator of an offloading system, one can set the optimal rekeying rate to gain the lowest system cost for a particular random padding. Meanwhile, the results and the properties of Weibull distributed delays are listed in Table 2. The SCV property is the squared coefficient of variation which is defined as the ratio of the variance and the square of the mean.

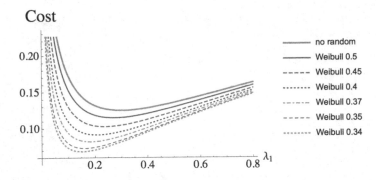

Fig. 5. System measure *cost* as a function of the rekeying rate λ_1

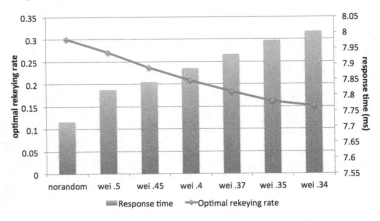

Fig. 6. Response time and optimal rekeying rate changes with different Weibull parameter sets

The results of this experiment show that the Weibull distribution random delays padding can efficiently mitigate the timing attacks and the system cost diminishes with decreasing shape parameter k of Weibull distribution.

6   Discussion

As depicted in Fig. 6, the growth of service response time is mainly due to the increasing mean of the Weibull distribution when we diminish the shape parameter k while keeping the scale parameter steady. So one should use low mean random padding to mitigate timing attacks.

The decrease of the optimal rekeying rate shows that the mitigating effect of random delay measure increases with the variance of Weibull distribution. We found that the variance of random delays is the primary influencing factor to the mitigation effect. Thus, when random delays are deployed in offloading systems, one should try to enlarge the variance of the random delay while keeping the mean as low as possible by tuning the parameters, i.e., distributions with an large coefficient of variation are recommended.

7   Conclusion

To add random delays into the process time is a popular strategy for defending against timing attacks. It can be easily deployed even the source code of the application is hard to get touch. While the benefits are obvious, a random delay introduces a penalty into the system. We have implemented a prototype that allows us to compare the impact of different random distributions on the expected success of timing attacks. Afterwards, Weibull distributed delays with different parameter sets are added to the Cloud service side to mitigate timing attacks. We found that the variance of random delays is the primary influencing factor to the mitigation effect. So, one should tune the parameters to enlarge the variance while keeping the mean as low as possible when random delays are deployed in offloading systems. Meanwhile, one may improve system performance and security using our results. Starting from the mission time of a computing job one can select a desired padding policy, from which the optimal rekey interval can be determined for the offloading system.

Extending the analysis to include a key refresh protocol and validating against implementation will be the future work. At the same time, the analysis will be extended to include fault models.

References

1. Kumar, K., Liu, J., Lu, Y.-H., Bhargava, B.: A survey of computation offloading for mobile systems. Mob. Netw. Appl. **18**(1), 129–140 (2013)
2. Barbera, M., Kosta, S., Mei, A., Perta, V., Stefa, J.: Mobile offloading in the wild: findings and lessons learned through a real-life experiment with a new cloud-aware system. In: INFOCOM, Proceedings of IEEE, pp. 2355–2363. IEEE (2014)
3. Hong, J.I., Landay, J.A.: An infrastructure approach to context-aware computing. Hum.-Comput. Interact. **16**(2), 287–303 (2001)
4. Subashini, S., Kavitha, V.: A survey on security issues in service delivery models of cloud computing. J. Netw. Comput. Appl. **34**(1), 1–11 (2011)
5. Hao, Z., Tang, Y., Zhang, Y., Novak, E., Carter, N., Li, Q.: SMOC: a secure mobile cloud computing platform. In: IEEE Conference on Computer Communications (INFOCOM), pp. 2668–2676. IEEE (2015)
6. Cui, H., Yuan, X., Wang, C.: Harnessing encrypted data in cloud for secure and efficient image sharing from mobile devices. In: IEEE Conference on Computer Communications (INFOCOM), pp. 2659–2667. IEEE (2015)
7. Brumley, B.B., Tuveri, N.: Remote timing attacks are still practical. In: Atluri, V., Diaz, C. (eds.) ESORICS 2011. LNCS, vol. 6879, pp. 355–371. Springer, Heidelberg (2011)
8. Brumley, D., Boneh, D.: Remote timing attacks are practical. Comput. Netw. **48**(5), 701–716 (2005)
9. Braun, B.A., Jana, S., Boneh, D.: Robust and efficient elimination of cache and timing side channels (2015). arXiv preprint arxiv:1506.00189
10. Nicol, D.M., Sanders, W.H., Trivedi, K.S.: Model-based evaluation: from dependability to security. IEEE Trans. Dependable Secure Comput. **1**(1), 48–65 (2004)

11. Lenkala, S.R., Shetty, S., Xiong, K.: Security risk assessment of cloud carrier. In: 13th IEEE/ACM International Symposium on Cluster, Cloud and Grid Computing (CCGrid), pp. 442–449. IEEE (2013)
12. Rebeiro, C., Mukhopadhyay, D., Bhattacharya, S.: An introduction to timing attacks. In: Timing Channels in Cryptography, pp. 1–11. Springer, Switzerland (2015)
13. Wu, H., Sun, Y., Wolter, K.: Analysis of the energy-response time tradeoff for delayed mobile cloud offloading. SIGMETRICS Perform. Eval. Rev. **43**, 33–35 (2015)
14. Köpf, B., Basin, D.: Automatically deriving information-theoretic bounds for adaptive side-channel attacks. J. Comput. Secur. **19**(1), 1–31 (2011)
15. Coron, J.-S., Kizhvatov, I.: An efficient method for random delay generation in embedded software. In: Clavier, C., Gaj, K. (eds.) CHES 2009. LNCS, vol. 5747, pp. 156–170. Springer, Heidelberg (2009)
16. Clavier, C., Coron, J.-S., Dabbous, N.: Differential power analysis in the presence of hardware countermeasures. In: Paar, C., Koç, Ç.K. (eds.) CHES 2000. LNCS, vol. 1965, pp. 252–263. Springer, Heidelberg (2000)
17. Lu, Y., O'Neill, M.P., McCanny, J.V.: FPGA implementation and analysis of random delay insertion countermeasure against DPA. In: International Conference on ICECE Technology, FPT 2008, pp. 201–208. IEEE (2008)
18. He, Z., Deng, X., Yang, B., Dai, K., Zou, X.: A SCA-resistant processor architecture based on random delay insertion. In: International Conference on Computing and Communications Technologies (ICCCT), pp. 278–281. IEEE (2015)
19. Kotipalli, S., Kim, Y.-B., Choi, M.: Asynchronous advanced encryption standard hardware with random noise injection for improved side-channel attack resistance. J. Electr. Comput. Eng. **2014**, 19 (2014)
20. Meng, T., Wang, Q., Wolter, K.: Model-based quantitative security analysis of mobile offloading systems under timing attacks. In: Remke, A., Manini, D., Gribaudo, M. (eds.) ASMTA 2015. LNCS, vol. 9081, pp. 143–157. Springer, Heidelberg (2015)
21. Stewart, W.J.: Probability, Markov Chains, Queues, and Simulation: The Mathematical Basis of Performance Modeling. Princeton University Press, Princeton (2009)
22. Coppersmith, D.: Small solutions to polynomial equations, and low exponent RSA vulnerabilities. J. Crypt. **10**(4), 233–260 (1997)
23. Chen, C., Wang, T., Tian, J.: Improving timing attack on RSA-CRT via error detection and correction strategy. Inf. Sci. **232**, 464–474 (2013)

Capabilities of Raspberry Pi 2 for Big Data and Video Streaming Applications in Data Centres

Nick J. Schot, Paul J.E. Velthuis, and Björn F. Postema$^{(\boxtimes)}$

Centre for Telematics and Information Technology,
University of Twente, Enschede, The Netherlands
{n.j.schot,p.j.e.velthuis}@student.utwente.nl, b.f.postema@utwente.nl
http://www.utwente.nl/ewi/dacs/

Abstract. Many new data centres have been built in recent years in order to keep up with the rising demand for server capacity. These data centres require a lot of electrical energy and cooling. Big data and video streaming are two heavily used applications in data centres. This paper experimentally investigates the possibilities and benefits of using cheap, low power and widely supported hardware in the form of a micro data centre with big data and video streaming as its main application area. For this purpose, multiple Raspberry Pi 2 Model B (RPi2)'s have been used in order to build a fully functional distributed Hadoop and video streaming setup that has acceptable performance and extends to new research opportunities. We experimentally validated the new setup to fit in a data centre environment by analysis of its performance, scalability, energy consumption, temperature and manageability. This paper proposes a high concurrency and low power setup in a small 1U form factor with an estimated number of 72 RPi2's as an interesting alternative to traditional rack servers.

Keywords: Micro data centre · Raspberry Pi 2 · Benchmarking · Hadoop · Big data · Video streaming · Cloud computing

1 Introduction

In data centres, the density of servers increased significantly in the past years [16]. New technologies emerge, e.g., blade servers, that not only decrease the physical appearance of what used to be an entire rack full of servers, but also decrease power consumption by implementing new technologies. ARM processors, another relatively new technology, might actually fit the increasing demand for modularity in data centres. Since Raspberry Pi's are fully functional servers, that have an ARM processor, a relatively powerful graphical chip onboard and

B.F. Postema—The work in this paper has been supported by the Dutch national STW project Cooperative Networked Systems (CNS), as part of the program "Robust Design of Cyber- Physical Systems" (CPS).

© Springer International Publishing Switzerland 2016
A. Remke and B.R. Haverkort (Eds.): MMB & DFT 2016, LNCS 9629, pp. 183–198, 2016.
DOI: 10.1007/978-3-319-31559-1_15

use little energy, these should be considered as a serious alternative. The main challenge of this paper is to fit Raspberry Pi 2's with ARM on-board in a data centre. Two major data centre applications elaborated in this paper are (i) big data; and (ii) video streaming. Big data solutions distribute data processing among various servers often with a high demand on storage devices. Big data's main task is to query large chunks of data to retrieve valuable information. On the other hand, demands with video streaming require more network capabilities, since the main task of video streaming is to seamlessly deliver data for the duration of the video. Many small tasks are processed in the case of video streaming, while big data applications perform rather large tasks.

This paper contributes by investigating the capabilities of Raspberry Pi's for micro data centres, thereby focussing on benchmarks and measurements of power, performance, temperature and hardware allocation of an experimental setup with a data centre ready Raspberry Pi cluster. These aspects allow us to analyse three main design criteria of a flexible future proof data centre [4, p. 6], namely: scalability, performance and manageability.

First, background information on cloud computing with big data and video streaming is elaborated in Sect. 2. A few cloud projects based on RPi hardware are described in Sect. 3. Then our own proposed RPi2 cluster will be discussed, and thoroughly tested with Hadoop and video streaming in order to investigate the possibilities of the RPi2 in a micro data centre.

2   Two Key Applications for Data Centres

In this section background is given for the two main applications big data and video streaming. Big data is about data too large and complex to be processed by normal data applications. In Sect. 2.1, a solution to big data is discussed that allows to distribute processing of these large chunks of data. Since the video streaming service Netflix is responsible for approximately 30 % of the downstream traffic in the US [2], this relevant application domain is elaborated in Sect. 2.2 by a short description of its operations and approach inspired by the existing video streaming service Netflix.

2.1   Big Data

Apache Hadoop [25] is an open source framework which offers necessary components for the distributed processing of large amounts of distributed data, using simple programming models like map/reduce. It has been designed to scale well from one to thousands of machines. Hadoop offers high-availability options for detecting and recovering from failures in both hard- and software. Hadoop is used for applications like risk modelling and recommendation engines which have petabytes of data to be analysed.

Map/reduce [9] as implemented in Hadoop is a programming model to allow for simple distributed processing of large data sets. A map/reduce program consists of two steps. The map step performs filtering and sorting. The reduce step can then do further computations on the output of the maps, which is usually a summarizing operation. Depending on the program the map and/or reduce tasks can be parallelised.

In Hadoop 2 *Yet Another Resource Negotiator* (YARN) was introduced as a new resource management layer. YARN handles workload management and monitoring, manages high availability features and allows for more programming models next to just map/reduce.

Big server manufacturers like Dell, HP and SuperMicro offer all kinds of servers for Hadoop applications. Hadoop usually runs on a multitude of 1U rack servers containing eight or more storage drives. 1U rack servers are relatively cheap, but bring a lot of space and energy overhead when you place a lot of servers compared to more expensive, but more efficient solutions like blade servers which are usually 10U [20]. Blade servers house vertically placed blades combined with a single power supply and network access for all blades combined, which makes them more space efficient [20] than traditional 1U servers. Hadoop setups can start with just a single server and be scaled to thousands of servers.

2.2   Video Streaming

Large video streaming providers often require various operations to deliver videos to their clients in an uninterrupted and fast manner. For this reason, the buffer time of a video is minimized, such that videos are accessible at any given time. These videos are then delivered by the server that has the best latency for the client. Large video streaming providers like Netflix require the following three operations for their services:

1. Content ingestion, which means that the studio master version of the films are received and uploaded to the cloud.
2. Content processing, which means that in the cloud many different formats are created for each video (e.g. AVI, MP4 and MKV format). These formats are uploaded to the content distribution network (CDN), which is a network of several data centres to spread the content to users. This means that all the formats been made are distributed over the CDN.

Netflix has its own CDN allowing better analysis of the network and improvements of load balancing and video streaming algorithms. In order to store all the video data, Netflix uses the file storage systems Amazon's AWS, simpleDB, S3 and Cassandra [2].

Video streaming heavily relies on data storage, most of the time spinning hard drives (HDD) are used. If a video is accessed frequently then a U1 SSD server is used to make faster streaming possible. This means there are two types of servers. The servers with HDD normally take 4U of server space and the SSD variant with servers consumes 1U server space [27].

3   Related Work

There have been several cluster projects with the Raspberry Pi Model B(+)(RPi).

The *Iridis-pi* cluster with 64 RPi's was built by Cox et al. [7]. A Message Passing Interface was used to communicate between the Raspberry Pi's. The research was done to investigate what the performance of a low-power high performance cluster was. It was designed as a portable and passively cooled cluster for educational purposes.

Tso et al. [26] built a data centre consisting of 56 RPi's that offers a cloud computing testbed including virtualisation management tools called the *Glasgow Raspberry Pi Cloud*. It was built for practical research on cloud computing without the limitations of simulation.

Kiepert [17] created a *Beowulf* cluster for a PhD assignment. It was built for collaboratively processing sensor data in a wireless sensor network. The Raspberry Pi cluster offers an alternative in case of the main cluster is unavailable.

The *Bolzano Raspberry Pi* cluster consists of 300 RPi's and was made as an affordable energy-efficient computer cluster by Abrahamsson et al. [1]. Applications such as a green research testbed and as a mobile data center are evaluated. Their main goal was to introduce a cluster of RPi's on a larger scale.

The RPi clusters described are for research, application performance and cluster mobility. The projects described above applied the first generation RPi which offers significantly lower performance than the newer second generation RPi. This research distinguishes itself from other RPi clusters by providing benchmarks of the temperature, power consumption and performance of the Hadoop and video streaming applications.

4   System Description

In the system description the software and experiment setup are elaborated. First short summary is given of the device used in the micro data centre, namely the RPi2 in Sect. 4.1. In the experimental setup our own micro data centre is elaborated for the Hadoop and video streaming variant in Sect. 4.2. The Hadoop software needed for distributed processing is discussed in Sect. 4.3. Then the video streaming software required for a large streaming service is elaborated in Sect. 4.4.

4.1   Raspberry Pi 2

The Raspberry Pi 2 Model B [24] is a small, cheap yet feature packed computer. It is based on the Broadcom BCM2836 system on a chip which offers a 900 MHz quad-core ARMv7 CPU combined with 1 GB of RAM and can currently be bought for about $35. Detailed specifications can be found in Table 1. 16 GB Adata Premier Pro UHS-I microSD cards are used as the storage solution (Fig. 1).

4.2   Experimental Setup

A total number of eight RPi2's is used in our experimental setup. A setup diagram for Hadoop and video streaming is displayed in Figs. 2 and 3, respectively.

Table 1. Raspberry Pi 2 Model B specifications [24]

System on Chip	Broadcom BCM2836
Ethernet	Onboard 10/100 Ethernet RJ45 jack
USB	Four USB 2.0
Video out	HDMI 1.4
Audio	2 x analog
CPU	900 MHz quad-core ARM Cortex-A7
GPU	Dual Core VideoCore IV Multimedia Co-Processor
Card slot	Micro SD

Fig. 1. Raspberry Pi 2 model B [24]

The numbers in the setup diagrams correspond to the physical setup shown in Fig. 4. The number (2) indicates a small router/switch that is connected to the power supply. The number (1) shows the eight RPi2's. In case of video streaming a load balancer and several video streamers are installed. For Hadoop there is one masternode and several slavenodes.

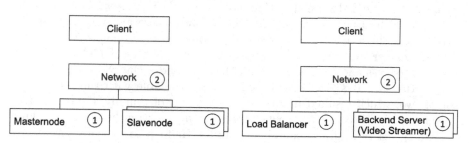

Fig. 2. Hadoop design   **Fig. 3.** Video streaming design

Dietpi [8] is used as the operating system for the individual nodes. It is a lightweight version of Raspbian which is the Linux distribution specifically tailored for the RPi2.

4.3 Hadoop Software

A basic Hadoop installation consists of three main parts: HDFS, YARN and the JobHistoryServer.

HDFS is the Hadoop distributed file system and consists of a couple of processes. The NameNode is the main process which keeps track of where all files are distributed and replicated. It is the main access point for all clients

Fig. 4. Project setup

and processes and runs on the master node. The SecondaryNameNode keeps a recent backup of the NameNode so the NameNode can be restored if it might go down. The DataNode processes run on the remaining slave nodes and handle data storage and retrieval.

YARN consists of a ResourceManager, which manages all jobs in the system, and on each slave node a NodeManager. The NodeManager process handles the execution of jobs allocated to a slave node.

Finally, the JobHistoryServer keeps track of all completed jobs and their logs.

A natively compiled version of Hadoop 2.6.0 with YARN was configured in conjunction with Oracle Java 7 ARM HF. Because there are only eight available RPi2's, a single master node runs the NameNode, Secondary NameNode, ResourceManager and the JobHistoryServer. The other (scalable) amount of nodes act as slaves and each runs a NodeManager and a DataNode.

The setup has 91 GB of distributed storage available with the replication factor of two, which resulted in an effective amount of roughly 45 GB. YARN has been configured so that two containers can run concurrently on a single slave node. This gives 14 available container slots for Hadoop to allocate tasks to in the test setup.

4.4   Video Streaming Software

This video streaming software consist of four software programs: nginx, FFmpeg, JW Player and Cassandra. For load balancing and streaming over HTTP, nginx [23] is used. nginx has an efficient algorithm for HTTP load balancing. The *Real Time Messaging Protocol* (RTMP) module from Arut for nginx is used to make a media streaming server over HTTP [5]. This has an efficient algorithm to transfer the HTTP with RTMP encapsulated data to the users. FFmpeg is a cross-platform solution to record, convert and stream audio and video [11]. Using this software makes adaptive streaming and streaming in different formats possible. JW Player is a HTML5/flash embedded media player [18]. JW Player makes load balancing possible dependable on the bit rate that is coming from the video. It supports dynamic streaming, that consists of multiple single streams with the same content, all in a different quality [18]. Cassandra is a database that helps replicating data across multiple data centres [6]. The data can automatically be replicated across the nodes for fault-tolerance. Therefore, the data is still available when a node crashes.

5   Cluster Benchmarking

This section elaborates benchmarks and measurements on power, temperature, storage, memory and network to test the cluster as if in a data centre environment.

5.1   Storage and Memory Performance

For basic system benchmarks, the SysBench suite [19] has been used. It serves as a tool to quickly determine system performance without setting up any complex software.

Table 2. SysBench storage & memory

Benchmark	Transfer speed
Random storage read	9.9718 MB/s
Random storage write	1.2604 MB/s
Random storage read/write	3.4046 MB/s
Sequential storage read	17.7400 MB/s
Sequential storage write	6.3972 MB/s
Sequential storage rewrite	13.0000 MB/s
Sequential memory read	207.5000 MB/s
Sequential memory write	177.0200 MB/s

The SD card storage was tested by running random and sequential storage tests. 4 GB of test data was prepared with SysBench. The benchmarks were run with a maximum execution time of 300 s. The memory test sequentially read and wrote 512 MB of data to memory.

Table 2 shows that the write performance of the SD cards is low. Read performance is below what was expected from the SD card, which promised 40 MB/s for sequential read operations but achieved barely half of that speed. The RPi2's memory is sequentially read at 207 MB/s while its write speed is 177 MB.

5.2   Energy Consumption

The energy consumption is measured with a simple setup. A prototyping PCB with two USB connectors and some jumper wires are used to allow for a multimeter (Elro M990) to connect for voltage and current measurements of a single RPi2. This way the actual power usage of the RPi2 is measured, because the

Table 3. Benchmarks to test energy consumption of Raspberry Pi 2 without power supply losses

	Current (A)	Voltage (V)	Power (W)
CPU 1 core	0.340	4.84	1.65
CPU 2 cores	0.365	4.79	1.75
CPU 3 cores	0.392	4.77	1.87
CPU 4 cores	0.415	4.78	1.99
Memory test	0.440	4.79	2.11
Storage read	0.442	4.77	2.11
Storage write	0.395	4.77	1.89
Idle	0.315	4.78	1.51

(in)efficiency of the power supply is not taken into account. When a measurement would be done at the wall outlet, power usage is expected to be higher.

The power consumption was measured under several workloads to find out what effect different kind of operations have on the power consumption of the RPi2. SysBench is used to consistently stress different parts of the board.

The RPi2 has a power consumption of at most 2.1 W in this test as shown in Table 3. A normal server needs about 500 W [21], so 238 RPi2's take as much power on one server.

5.3   Network Performance

Iperf3 [10] was used to find out whether the network, the storage or the memory is a bottleneck by reading/writing from/to the different mediums [10]. The RPi2 uses a 100 Mbit Ethernet connection which is connected via a combined USB 2.0/Ethernet chip [22]. This is important as Hadoop shuffles a large amount of data around the network, video streaming needs to transport a lot of data to the user and in between the servers. To find out if there is a bottleneck, 60 s iperf3 benchmarks with a congestion windows of 133 KB have been executed from memory to memory, memory to storage and from storage to memory.

Table 4. Ethernet throughput benchmark with RPi2 memory and SD card storage

Write direction	Avg. bandwidth (Mbit)
Memory → memory	93.4
Memory → storage	24.3
Storage → memory	94.2

For every throughput benchmarks the congestion window is 133 KB. From the results in Table 4 the write performance of the Raspberry Pi 2 and/or the SD card forms a bottleneck with only 3 MB/s. This number is in line with the results from the SysBench write tests which were between 1.26 MB/s and 6.4 MB/s for random and sequential writes respectively. USB 2.0/Ethernet causes some overhead, therefore it has a throughput of around 94 Mbit.

5.4   Temperatures

CPU temperature measurements were taken under SysBench CPU stressing with different numbers of threads. During this benchmark the temperature is measured by logging the operating systems data on temperatures with a shell script. The temperature is measured on the CPU. Results are shown in Fig. 5. The room temperature during this benchmark was around 23°C. The cooldown phase, that occurs after the benchmark has finished, is shown in Fig. 6. The room temperature during the cooldown phase was around 21°C and has been measured during a separate benchmark run. By default, the RPi2 is a passively cooled board without any heat sink or fan.

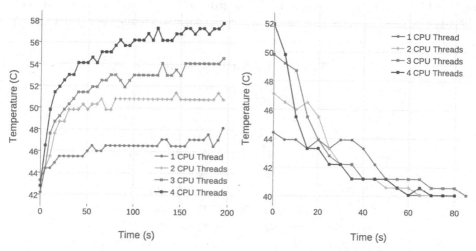

Fig. 5. Temperature benchmark   **Fig. 6.** Temperature cooldown

When running a four-thread CPU benchmark the maximum temperature is 60°C and the temperature is 42°C when idle, see Fig. 5. In Fig. 5, after a short period of time, temperatures converge to an upper bound. After benchmark completion, the CPU cools down quickly to idle temperature, as can be seen in Fig. 6. Data centres require a temperature of around 26°C and in order to do this, additional energy is required for cooling [12]. The most common workload for Hadoop and video streaming would be two CPU threads for which the temperature stays around 50°C. So, if multiple RPi2's are used, some cooling is required in order to keep them working at optimal performance temperature.

6   Application Benchmarking

In this section, several Hadoop and video streaming benchmarks are analysed to show that in a data centre environment the proposed setup has acceptable performance.

6.1   Hadoop Benchmarks

A selection of Hadoop benchmarks is made to cover the most important aspects of a Hadoop cluster. The benchmarks are part of the HiBench benchmark suite [13], the standard Hadoop test suite and cover CPU bound computation and generic computation on distributed big data. A comparison is made with the CTIT cluster of the University of Twente where Hadoop runs on 32 Dell R415 servers.

Terasort is a benchmark which measures sort speed on large distributed files. The benchmark consists of a map/reduce job which creates and sorts a multiple of 100 byte rows and validates the results. A replication factor of one for the output files was forced instead of the cluster default. This way the replication of data throughout the cluster does not affect actual map/reduce performance.

Table 5. TeraSort benchmark

	Raspberry Pi 2						CTIT		
Nodes	5	8	5	8	5	8	-	-	-
Slots	8	14	8	14	8	14	-	-	-
Maps	16	16	64	64	80	80	16	64	80
Reduces	8	8	8	8	8	8	8	8	8
Data (GB)	1	1	7	7	10	10	1	7	10
Total (s)	366	230	3584	1747	-	341	22	49	67
Avg. map (s)	70	72	144	141	-	261	7	10	11
Avg. shuffle (s)	70	88	-	698	-	830	4	19	24
Avg. reduce (s)	48	49	1741	406	-	550	2	15	21

The CTIT cluster has far more container slots and nodes than the RPi2 cluster. Enough slots were available to allocate all map/reduces at once in the CTIT cluster and thus available slots are not mentioned in Table 5.

An inherent problem to a smaller cluster showed up in the 7 GB run on five nodes and is caused by one of Hadoops optimizations for bigger clusters. When a map task finishes on a node, Hadoop starts a reduce task on that same node since the necessary data is already there. The nodes are configured to run two concurrent tasks. With seven nodes available, this gives a total of 14 container slots of which one is the Application Master. With more map tasks than the amount of available containers, part of the tasks will run sequentially. The problem is that as soon as the first batch of map tasks finishes, reduce tasks get started on the nodes, so only few containers are available for the relatively high amount of map tasks to be completed. The reduce tasks will have a lot of idle time, because input data from the map tasks becomes available at a low pace. Adding more nodes would solve this problem as enough slots should be available to allocate the map jobs. This would bring the total running time closer to the average map time.

Since the 7 GB run allocated 64 map tasks, it took a total of 1747 s to complete all jobs. The average reduce time is high, because the reducers were still waiting for new input data. The shuffle time is the time to get the required data as output by a map task to the correct reducer. As there are usually many more map tasks then there are reduce tasks, this is a vital number for fast Hadoop operations. The reducers were able to retrieve data from other nodes with a reported speed of about 11 MB/s. This means Hadoop is most of the time writing into memory, as iperf3 showed that the write speed to the SD card is much lower over the network.

The last problem showed up for the first time when TeraSort ran with 10GB of data on 5 nodes. If Hadoop assigns two reduce tasks to a single node, they have a lot of data to process, so the reduce tasks will use too much memory when writing their results to HDFS causing the DataNode process to crash and get kicked out of memory causing the reduce task to fail. Hadoop may then decide to start two copies of the same job to the cluster. This amplifies the problem with a small cluster, making the chance that two are running on a single node significantly higher. This problem can likely be solved by changing the YARN configuration so that only one reduce task may run on a single node.

Table 5 shows that the CTIT cluster's total running time is ten times lower when sorting 1 GB of data. The average map task also took roughly ten times longer on the RPi2 cluster. The runs with more data were a lot slower on the RPi2 cluster because not enough container slots were available in the cluster. The average map took 24 times longer on the RPi2 cluster when sorting 10 GB of data. This higher ratio could be the result of the low write speed to the SD card when more data has to be handled.

Table 6. Pi benchmark for computation of the number π

	Raspberry Pi 2			CTIT	
Containers	8	8	14	-	-
Maps	6	12	12	6	12
Total (s)	996	1975	996	40	40
Avg. map (s)	976	981	975	32	32
Avg. shuffle (s)	13	978	13	3	3
Avg. reduce (s)	2	2	2	0	0

The Pi benchmark was executed with a setup of five nodes with eight containers and a setup of eight nodes with 14 containers. The number π was computed in the benchmark with 10^9 samples per map. Increasing the maps or samples for the benchmark makes the estimation of π more accurate. From the Pi benchmarks in Table 6 it became clear that the average shuffle time depends on the availability of the data for the reducers. The Pi benchmark generates very small intermediate data which, if all maps can be allocated, takes only 13 s of shuffle time which is mostly overhead time from Hadoop due to hard coded polling intervals. The runs with 8 available containers show the impact of a setup with fewer available slots than there are maps to be run, compared with 6 maps and 12 maps with enough available nodes, the total duration depends on the speed with which individual maps are finished. The results in Table 6 show that the amount of maps does not influence running time for the Pi benchmark if enough container slots are available. Thus we can directly compare the results between the two systems. The CTIT cluster took 40 s to complete the benchmark with an average map time of 32 s. In comparison the RPi2 cluster took 996 s to complete with an average map time of 975 s. This means that for this CPU bound benchmark the processing cores in the CTIT cluster are roughly 30 times faster than the processing cores from the RPi2.

6.2   Video Stream Benchmarks

The first benchmark streams and tests a video over the RTMP. Apache JMeter is a benchmark tool that is executed on an external machine to measure the number of streams a RPi2 can handle [3]. Apache JMeter allows to measure HTTP capture. As a consequence, RTMP streams can be measured, since these are encapsulated in HTTP. After the RTMP video stream is started, the workload of the stream is analysed over HTTP by accessing a video via a web browser. The RTMP stream has a rate of about 800 kbit/s for a small 230 MB video. The following basic formula defines the theoretical maximum number of users:

$$\text{max users} = \frac{\text{bandwidth}}{\text{bit rate stream}}.$$

The theoretical maximum number of users with this formula is 118 with 100 Mbit bandwidth. The benchmark accessing videos through the web browser allows 25 simultaneously connected users for streaming MPEG-4 (MP4) files over HTTP. In the web browser less then the maximum users can connect, due to the buffer and video conversion time.

For *Synchronized Multimedia Integration Language* (SMIL) a special SMIL benchmark is used, that allows testing of different video streaming rates for a single file. It is possible to switch the quality depending on the amount of data that can get over the network, used in for example YouTube. Different video qualities have been created by FFmpeg in the H.264 codec from a 230 MB source video, namely: 720p, 480p, 240p and 120p. During the test with Apache JMeter 100 connections were simulated watching the video. There are two scenarios that use server-side JW Player: the first allows the user to select video quality, the second automatically switches to an appropriate quality based on the maximum achievable bitrate. In the first scenario the user chooses between the 120p, 240p or 480p version of the 230 MB video. When the 480p version is in use, freezing occurs; with the 120p and 240p versions no freezing is observed. As a consequence, freezing can occur when users are allowed to select their own quality; however when quality is automatically selected based on the maximum bitrate, no freezing occurs.

In order to test an automatic adjustable bit stream with quality constraints, a *Video on Demand* (VOD) benchmark is created. First, the converters FFmpeg and nginx need to be started to share a video over RTMP. The media player VLC is opened to indicate if there are any differences between VOD and a RTMP stream. VOD shows no signs of videos freezing. This is because, VOD is equipped to adjust the bit stream depending on the quality the stream and RTMP is not. RTMP only allows to watch the video that is played at that moment, which is similar to normal television.

7   Cluster in Server Racks

For the RPi2 to be useful in an enterprise environment, it must fit in standardised server racks. Hardware breaks all the time in data centres, so it should be easily accessible and replaceable to keep the data centre manageable. One disadvantage of current RPi2 is the placement of the power connector and Ethernet connector. The connectors are placed perpendicular to each other which makes it harder to place the boards in a confined space. To keep the manageability of the data centre two designs are proposed.

The rack must contain a power supply with sufficient ports and power to handle all RPi2. The casing must contain some fans to generate airflow.

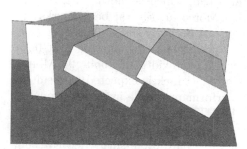

Fig. 7. Vertical and tilted RPi2 in a 1U server

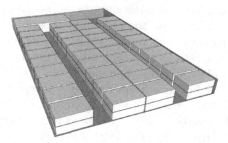

Fig. 8. Proposed RPi2 rack layout

Standard data centre racks contain often 42U of space. As defined by the EIA-310 standard a single U is 44.50 mm high [14]. A 1U rack's inside dimensions are defined to be 450 mm wide, 44.43 mm high and at most 739.775 mm deep [15]. The RPi2 is 85.60 mm wide, 56 mm deep and 21 mm high. It has four standard mounting holes for screws or spacers to fit through.

The most efficient way to place the RPi2 in a small contained space is with the power connector facing downwards. So it can be connected to power on the bottom of the rack, and to Ethernet on the side, which would allow the easiest access to a RPi2. Unfortunately, as can be seen in Fig. 7, a vertically placed RPi2 is a little higher than a standard U, so a bigger 1.5U rack should be used to make it fit. A variation can be tried by tilting the RPi2 boards so they fit in a 1U rack. The effect of this approach is shown in Fig. 7. Because of the low angle, practically no overlap between the RPi2's can exist. This removes the main advantage of this approach.

The most obvious way to place the boards is to stack them in pairs of two and fill up the rack. Stacks can easily be secured on the bottom of the rack server by using spacers. The downside to this approach is the accessibility of the RPi2, as either the top one or both RPi2 have to be removed. 12 RPi2 fit next to each other in the rack, this gives 24 boards for a single row. While keeping space for all cables and connectors, four rows fit in the width of a rack server. With the power supply the estimated amount is 72 RPi2 for a 1U rack, seen in Fig. 8.

In order to provide all boards with Ethernet a 2U switch will be needed as a 1U switch can house a maximum of 48 Ethernet ports.

8   Conclusion and Future Work

The contribution of this paper is a fully functional distributed Hadoop and video streaming setup with acceptable performance in the form of a micro data centre consisting of multiple Raspberry Pi 2 Model B (RPi2)'s. A high concurrency and low power setup that fits in a small 1U standardised form factor is proposed. This cheap setup is especially beneficial when lower performance is acceptable compared to expensive performance clusters. In the case of our two applications, acceptable performance is indeed attained, which is shown with the aid of several application specific benchmarks. Moreover, several benchmarks are performed on the cluster to ensure it functions properly inside data centre. A network benchmark confirms an acceptable performance by showing that both applications approach the maximum network bandwidth of about 94 Mbit/s under full load. An amount of 72 RPi2's in a 1U rack is expected to result in a highly concurrent rack with acceptable performance while using only roughly 160 W under full load. In comparison to the CTIT cluster that easily consumes kilowatts of power, programs with bigger map/reduce jobs like TeraSort ran only 24 times slower than this cluster. These numbers are promising when realising that the RPi2's have not yet an optimised architecture for support of a gigabit connection over USB and improved SD card reader performance. Before scaling this setup in a data centre environment, an appropriate solution to the large number of cables is still required for manageability purposes. Furthermore, the proposed setup could be used as a cheap micro version of a data centre to simulate existing applications before implementing the applications in an expensive cluster.

Acknowledgements. The authors would like to thank Marijn Jongerden and Boudewijn Haverkort (both from University of Twente) for their constructive feedback.

References

1. Abrahamsson, P., Helmer, S., Phaphoom, N., Nicolodi, L., Preda, N., Miori, L., Angriman, M., Rikkila, J., Wang, X., Hamily, K., Bugoloni, S.: Affordable and energy-efficient cloud computing clusters: the Bolzano Raspberry Pi cloud cluster experiment. In: Proceedings of 5th International Conference on Cloud Computing Technology and Science, vol. 2, pp. 170–175. IEEE (2013)
2. Adhikari, V., Guo, Y., Hao, F., Varvello, M., Hilt, V., Steiner, M., Zhang, Z.L.: Unreeling netflix: understanding and improvingmulti-CDN movie delivery. In: INFOCOM, 2012 Proceedings IEEE, pp. 1620–1628 (2012)
3. Apache Software Foundation: Apache JMeter (2015). http://jmeter.apache.org/
4. Arregoces, M., Portolani, M.: Data Center Fundamentals. Cisco Press, Indianapolis (2003)
5. Arutyunyan, R.: NGINX-based Media Streaming Server (2015). https://github.com/arut/nginx-rtmp-module
6. Cassandra: Welcome to Apache Cassandra (2015). http://cassandra.apache.org/
7. Cox, S.J., Cox, J.T., Boardman, R.P., Johnston, S.J., Scott, M., OBrien, N.S.: Iridis-pi: a low-cost, compact demonstration cluster. Cluster Comput. **17**(2), 349–358 (2013)
8. Knight, D.: DietPi for Raspberry Pi's (2014). http://fuzon.co.uk/phpbb/viewtopic.php?f=8&t=6
9. Dean, J., Ghemawat, S.: MapReduce: simplified data processing on large clusters. Commun. ACM **51**(1), 107 (2008)
10. ESnet: iperf/iperf3 (2015). http://fasterdata.es.net/performance-testing/network-troubleshooting-tools/iperf-and-iperf3/
11. FFmpeg: FFmpeg (2015). https://www.ffmpeg.org/
12. Google: Google Datacenters (2015). http://www.google.com/about/datacenters/efficiency/internal/#temperature
13. Huang, S., Huang, J., Liu, Y., Yi, L., Dai, J.: HiBench: a representative and comprehensive hadoop benchmark suite. In: Proceedings of 26th International Conference on Data Engineering Workshops (2010)
14. Innovation First, inc: 19-inch rack (EIA-310) (2007). https://www.server-racks.com/eia-310.html
15. Innovation First, inc: Rack Mounting Depth (2007). https://www.server-racks.com/rack-mount-depth.html
16. Clark, J.: Raising Data Center Power Density (2013). http://www.datacenterjournal.com/raising-data-center-power-density/
17. Kiepert, J.: Creating a Raspberry Pi-Based Beowulf Cluster, May 2013. http://coen.boisestate.edu/ece/files/2013/05/Creating.a.Raspberry.Pi-Based.Beowulf.Cluster_v2.pdf
18. JW Player: JW PLayer (2015). http://www.jwplayer.com/
19. Kopytov, A.: SysBench benchmark suite (2015). https://github.com/akopytov/sysbench
20. Leigh, K., Ranganathan, P., Subhlok, J.: General-purpose blade infrastructure for configurable system architectures. Distrib. Parallel Databases **21**(2–3), 115–144 (2007)

21. Meisner, D., Gold, B.T., Wenisch, T.F.: Powernap: eliminating server idle power. ACM SIGARCH Comput. Archit. News **37**(1), 205–216 (2009)
22. Microchip: LAN9514-JZX (2012). http://ww1.microchip.com/downloads/en/DeviceDoc/9514.pdf
23. Nginx: NGINX (2015). http://nginx.com/
24. Raspberry Pi Foundation: Raspberry Pi 2 Model B (2015). https://www.raspberrypi.org/products/raspberry-pi-2-model-b/
25. The Apache software foundation: Welcome to Apache Hadoop! (2015). https://hadoop.apache.org/
26. Tso, F.P., White, D.R., Jouet, S., Singer, J., Pezaros, D.P.: The Glasgow Raspberry Pi cloud: a scale model for cloud computing infrastructures. In: Proceedings of 33rd International Conference on Distributed Computing Systems Workshops, pp. 108–112. IEEE (2013)
27. Uptime Institute: Designing Netflixs Content Delivery Network.Uptime Institute Symposium (2014). https://journal.uptimeinstitute.com/designing-netflixs-content-delivery-network/

Ensemble-Based Uncertainty Quantification for Smart Grid Co-simulation

Cornelius Steinbrink[(✉)], Sebastian Lehnhoff, and Thole Klingenberg

OFFIS – Institute for Information Technology,
Escherweg 2, 26121 Oldenburg, Germany
cornelius.steinbrink@offis.de
http://www.offis.de

Abstract. Coupling of independent models in the form of a co-simulation is a rather new approach for design and analysis of Smart Grids. However, uncertainty of model parameters and outputs decreases the significance of simulation results. Therefore, this paper presents an ensemble-based uncertainty quantification system as an extension to the already existing co-simulation framework mosaik.

Keywords: Smart Grid · Co-simulation · Uncertainty quantification · Mosaik

1 Introduction

Smart Grid co-simulation is a relatively new approach for the development of future energy grids. It combines different pre-existing simulation models and thus decreases the modeling complexity of "systems of systems". The co-simulation framework *mosaik*[1] [1] has been developed to facilitate model coupling by providing an API for data exchange.

A crucial issue of simulation is the deviation between its results and observations made in the real world. This phenomenon is called uncertainty. It results from model simplifications and errors in the model input. Thus, the concept of *uncertainty quantification* (UQ) is used to compute the possible range of simulation results.

UQ is especially crucial in the context of co-simulation, as illustrated in [2], since the differently accurate component models make it hard for analysts to assess the bias of the combined dynamics. However, due to the relative novelty of Smart Grids and co-simulation, relevant UQ approaches are sparse and oftentimes fail to address important aspects of the problem.

This paper illustrates a flexible UQ approach for co-simulation that is implemented and tested within the mosaik framework.

---

[1] For up to date documentation and source code see: http://mosaik.offis.de.

© Springer International Publishing Switzerland 2016
A. Remke and B.R. Haverkort (Eds.): MMB & DFT 2016, LNCS 9629, pp. 199–202, 2016.
DOI: 10.1007/978-3-319-31559-1_16

2   Application: Smart Grid Co-simulation with Mosaik

The purpose and mechanics of mosaik may be best illustrated with the help of an exemplary use case. We assume a set of simple models of a power grid [3], a fridge (self-developed), and a PV panel [4], as well as a software module that provides weather data. All of these components are called simulators when implemented and integrated into the mosaik simulation environment. Since the modeling has typically been done by another party, the mosaik users can concentrate on the creation of a simulation scenario. Thus, every model is treated as a *black box* and is described solely via meta information specifying the type of the modeled system, the model's parameters, and the in- and output variables, called attributes, that are used to interconnect the models.

In the example scenario, an LV grid with four nodes is created. Each node experiences feed-in of active power P from one PV panel, and active power consumption by two fridges. The PV panels again receive irradiation input from the weather data file. This scenario may be used, e.g., to test an algorithm for the balancing of fluctuating producers and controllable consumers. However, due to model errors and uncertainty in the parametrization, the algorithm might not be exposed to all realisticly possible scenarios. A UQ system can help to calculate the full range of possible simulation outputs. The design of the UQ system is subject to a number of requirements, derived from the mosaik application use case:

- The user should not need to adjust the code of the black box models,
- uncertainty in parameters as well as attributes should be considered,
- probabilistic uncertainty should be considered where it can be assessed,
- simulation scenario creation should not be impeded by UQ.

3   UQ System Architecture

The presented UQ system (Fig. 1) is geared to the modular design of mosaik, i.e. a distinct UQ process is conducted for every utilized simulator. This process is often-times divided into two steps: assessment, i.e. the identification and modeling of initial uncertainties, and the propagation of these uncertainties through a model.

For the assessment, the UQ system provides a set of different uncertainty models so that users can represent their knowledge about uncertainty sources adequately. The most basic model for uncertainty is an interval while the most complete one is a probability distribution. Mixtures between these two are probability boxes and Dempster-Shafer structures that can easily be converted into each other and their marginal cases [5]. Uncertainty in respect to the parameter values or the output of a model can be specified by using one or more of these structures. This task is best conducted by the original modeler, and the uncertainty specification stored in a file.

The propagation is conducted by replacing each model instance in the scenario with an ensemble of model instances. Each ensemble consists of an input and an output module as well as a set of ensemble members (model instances).

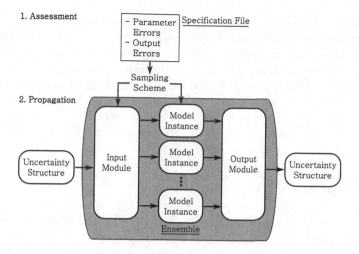

Fig. 1. Software architecture of the UQ system.

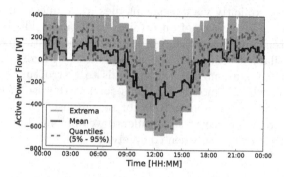

Fig. 2. UQ results for the flow of active power between two grid nodes over the course of one day.

Ensembles do not exchange single values like normal mosaik simulators. They exchange uncertainty structures that represent one of the uncertainty models discussed above. The input modules are responsible for splitting these structures into different input values for the ensemble members. The output modules combine the members' output values to a new uncertainty structure and add an output error if defined in the assessment file. Additionally, each member receives a different set of parameter values, also based on the assessment information. The partitioning of the uncertainty structures for parameters and attributes is based on a sampling scheme. For the standard cases, space-filling *latin hypercube sampling* (e.g. [6]) is sufficient. If probabilistic uncertainty models are employed, *kernel density estimators* are used to express the distributions numerically, and *copulas* to account for correlation between uncertainty sources.

The scenario described in Sect. 2 has been used to illustrate the operation of the UQ system. During the assessment phase, output uncertainty has been assumed for the weather data simulator due to given measurement error values. The uncertainty of the PV and fridge models are realized as variance in the parameter values since they may differ between varying real-world systems.

Figure 2 displays statistic measures for the flow of active power between two nodes of the power grid. The gray area depicts the range of possible values, the dashed dark gray lines the 5 %- and 95 %-quantiles, and the black line the mean value that lies within the same range as the original simulation results. It is obvious that averaged simulation results are not sufficient for, e.g., testing under extreme conditions.

4   Conclusion

The presented system provides ensemble-based UQ capabilities for Smart Grid co-simulation while satisfying the requirements set up in Sect. 2. It utilizes the mosaik interface to communicate with models so that users may still consider them black boxes. Uncertainty in the model output attributes and parameters may be considered explicitly via assessment files while uncertain model input is handled implicitly via exchange of uncertainty structures. These structures can incorporate different uncertainty models so that probabilistic knowledge can be considered (if available to the user) but is no necessity. Finally, the replacement of model instances by ensemble instances leads to a structure of UQ scenarios that is similar to standard mosaik scenarios so that the use of the UQ system should be rather simple and non-limiting for mosaik users.

The UQ system is currently still under development, but expected to be released as a mosaik extension when completed.

References

1. Schütte, S., Scherfke, S., Tröschel, M.: Mosaik: a framework for modular simulation of active components in smart grids. In: First International Workshop on Smart Grid Modeling and Simulation (SGMS), pp. 55–60. IEEE (2011)
2. Steinbrink, C., Lehnhoff, S.: Challenges and necessity of systematic uncertainty quantification in smart grid co-simulation. In: EUROCON 2015 - International Conference on Computer as a Tool (EUROCON). IEEE (2015)
3. Zimmerman, R.D., Murillo-Sánchez, C.E., Thomas, R.J.: MATPOWER: steady-state operations, planning, and analysis tools for power system research and education. IEEE Trans. Power Syst. **26**, 12–19 (2011)
4. Soto, D., Adkins, E., Basinger, M., Menon, R., Rodriguez-Sanchez, S., Owczarek, N., Willig, I., Modi, V.: A prepaid architecture for solar electricity delivery in rural areas. In: Proceedings of the Fifth International Conference on Information and Communication Technologies and Development, pp. 130–138. ACM (2012)
5. Ferson, S., Kreinovich, V., Ginzburg, L., Myers, D.S., Sentz, K.: Constructing Probability Boxes and Dempster-Shafer Structures. Technical report, Sandia National Laboratories (2003)
6. Janssen, H.: Monte-Carlo based uncertainty analysis: sampling efficiency and sampling convergence. Reliab. Eng. Syst. Saf. **109**, 123–132 (2013)

Author Index

Printed in the United States
By Bookmasters